T0316389

Freedom in Contention

Polycentricity: Studies in Institutional Diversity and Voluntary Governance

Series Editors: Lenore T. Ealy and Paul Dragos Aligica

This interdisciplinary series explores the varieties of social institutions, processes, and patterns of governance that emerge through individuals' coordination, cooperation, and competition in governance systems based on freedom of choice, freedom of exchange, and freedom of association. Under conditions of relative freedom of association, human diversity leads to institutional diversity and polycentric structures. In contrast to monocentric, unitary, and hierarchical command and control systems, polycentric social systems comprise many decision centers interacting freely under an overarching set of common rules. First introduced by Michael Polanyi as a descriptive and normative feature of free societies and further elaborated by Nobel Prize in Economics recipient Elinor Ostrom and public choice political economy cofounder Vincent Ostrom, the notion of polycentricity has proven itself able to offer a powerful analytical framework for expanding our understanding of the operation of governance regimes, constitutional federalism, law, public administration, private ordering, civics and citizenship, subsidiarity, nonprofit organization, cultural pluralism, civil society and entrepreneurship. Studies in this series will refine the conceptual framework of polycentricity and its governance theory implications, while expanding their application in the study of what Alexis de Tocqueville called the art and science of association. These studies should be of interest to scholars, policymakers, executives, social entrepreneurs, and citizens working to devise ways of living together harmoniously in civil societies.

Recent Titles in the Series

Freedom in Contention

Social Movements and Liberal Political Economy

Mikayla Novak

LEXINGTON BOOKS
Lanham • Boulder • New York • London

Published by Lexington Books
An imprint of The Rowman & Littlefield Publishing Group, Inc.
4501 Forbes Boulevard, Suite 200, Lanham, Maryland 20706
www.rowman.com

6 Tinworth Street, London SE11 5AL, United Kingdom

British Library Cataloguing in Publication Information Available

Library of Congress Cataloging-in-Publication Data

Names: Novak, Mikayla, author.
Title: Freedom in contention : social movements and liberal political
    economy / Mikayla Novak.
Description: Lanham : Lexington Books, [2021] | Series: Polycentricity : studies
    in institutional diversity and voluntary governance | Includes bibliographical
    references and index.
Identifiers: LCCN 2021018570 (print) | LCCN 2021018571 (ebook) |
    ISBN 9781793627667 (cloth) | ISBN 9781793627674 (epub)
Subjects: LCSH: Social movements. | Liberalism.
Classification: LCC HM881 .N68 2021 (print) | LCC HM881 (ebook) |
    DDC 303.48/4—dc23
LC record available at https://lccn.loc.gov/2021018570
LC ebook record available at https://lccn.loc.gov/2021018571

Contents

List of Figures and Tables

FIGURE

TABLE

Acknowledgments

Production and distribution of this book has been made possible through the efforts of many people, whose support has been greatly appreciated. I wish to sincerely thank the Lexington Books team for publishing this book under its important *Polycentricity: Studies in Institutional Diversity and Voluntary Governance* series. In particular, I thank Lenore Ealy and Paul Dragos Aligica (series editors), and the Lexington Books publishing team for their firm encouragement and assistance. Your professionalism and support, throughout the process of furnishing this book, was invaluable.

I also wish to thank the Cato Institute ("Cato Unbound" discussion series, August 2020) and the Institute for Humane Studies (seminar presentation, October 2020) for enabling me to convey, and to test, some of this book's key ideas. Along similar lines, I thank the organizers of the Arizona State University Center for the Study of Economic Liberty's "Voluntary Governance Conference" (November 2020) for allowing me to present key facets of my work.

I would like to thank Prof. Fabio Rojas (Indiana University, Bloomington, U.S.), and Dr. Jayme Lemke (Mercatus Center, George Mason University, U.S), for providing feedback on a draft copy of this book. I thank an anonymous reviewer for their constructive suggestions in response to a draft. I also express my thanks to Joshua Ammons (George Mason University), Akiva Malamet (Queen's University, Canada), Nathan Goodman (George Mason University), and Cory Massimino (independent scholar) for discussing relevant issues, and referring me to relevant literature. Their insightful and constructive feedback is deeply appreciated and, of course, they bear no responsibility for any errors of omission, or commission, appearing in this book.

Over the past few years, I have been guided by a growing sense of curiosity in investigating social dimensions of liberal philosophy. Along this journey I have been inspired by a number of astute "socially aware" liberals—some of whom I've met, but others not. They include, in no certain order, Virgil Storr, Emily Chamlee-Wright, Peter Boettke, Fabio Rojas, Joshua McCabe, Jacob Levy, Erwin Dekker, Stefan Kolev, Deirdre McCloskey, Jayme Lemke, Stefanie Haeffele, Matt Zwolinski, Steven Horwitz, Lenore Ealy, Nick Cowen, Nathan Goodman, Cory Massimino, and Akiva Malamet. There are, assuredly, many more people I could add to this list, and I also thank them for their insight and inspiration.

This book—imagined, planned, and written during the period from November 2019 to February 2021—would not have been completed without the support and encouragement of friends and family. In particular, I thank my spouse, Dee Trainham, for her most inspiring encouragement and support, and not to mention her next-to-infinite patience, as I precariously juggled varied commitments. This book is dedicated to you.

Chapter 1

Social Movements

Setting the Scene

INTRODUCTION

This book, to put it concisely, is about social movements. Popular conceptions of social movements see them as collective arrangements of protest, strikes, and other kinds of contentious action, organized by highly motivated activists seeking societal change. Raising their voices in the public square, and thrusting their bodies toward the barricades, social movement participants are commonly perceived as a highly disruptive force in society, challenging hegemonic authority and the institutions underpinning them. The picture painted here may impart a conception of social movements as a regressive phenomenon. However, as this book will illustrate, social movements also have the capacity to engender constructive, even positive changes that most people reasonably agree and find to be beneficial. Movement-induced changes may be evident in the domain of laws, rights, and legal entitlements (in other words, formal institutions), as well as cultural-social norms and practices (informal institutions). All in all, social movements are phenomena of significant social, economic, and political consequence, in both developed and developing countries.

For as long as human beings have banded together for a common cause, doing so beyond the "micro-cosmic" confines of family and tribe (Hayek 1988), social movements have been observable. Researchers have identified traces of social movements in the ancient world, from Greece and Rome and stretching throughout the Middle East, East Asia, and beyond (e.g., Blasi 1988; Clement 2016). Even today, we see social movements calling for change on issues as diverse as respecting and empowering disabled people, members of lesbian, gay, bisexual, and transgender (LGBT) communities, and immigrants, as well as redressing inequality, tackling climate change, and so on. As

1

Lawrence Cox (2018) recently described, social movements are woven deep into our fabric of humanity, posing as catalysts for social and other changes.

As an intellectual enterprise, the study of social movements goes back centuries. There remains uncertainty as to when the term "social movement" was first coined. Some researchers attribute it to German economic sociologist Lorenz von Stein (Udehn 1996), whereas others refer to French socialist Henri de Saint-Simon (Jo. Scott 2014). To be clear, collectively organized phenomena—such as protests and rebellions—were of interest to philosophers and other keen observers of society, even if no moniker of "social movement" were attached to them. John Locke, for example, wrote of the ethically appropriate circumstances under which a ruler may be overthrown, whereas Edmund Burke and Mary Wollstonecraft debated the consequences of the French Revolution (D. O'Neill 2007).

The study of social movements gained impetus from the late-nineteenth century. The fission of social science into specialized subdisciplines generated new studies of behavior in crowds and similar public gatherings. Investigating crowds served as a ready-made research topic among key participants within the emergent subdiscipline of sociology, including Emilé Durkheim, Georg Simmel, and Gabriel Tarde (Tiratelli 2018). Social movement studies represented a mainstay of sociological scholarship and, if anything, has grown even further over the past fifty years. In addition, economics, cultural studies, political science, history, and law have shaped a richer account of social movement organization and activity, by incorporating strategy, identity, and emotion (Peoples 2019). Contemporary theory also entails additional insights regarding the congruence between social movement goals and societal outcomes.

This chapter introduces the social movement concept. We not only seek to define a social movement, but aim to situate social movement studies within the framework of modern liberal political economy. There has long been an intellectual presence for political economy within social movement studies—for example, Marxist theory is well represented, with its representations of social frictions between owners of labor and capital production inputs. Alternative approaches have emerged in recent years, such as the mesocentric "field theory" approach of Fligstein and McAdam (2019). The book pointedly seeks room for a liberal perspective of political economy to become part of social movement theorization and analysis. We end this chapter with a general outline of the structure for this book.

DESCRIBING SOCIAL MOVEMENTS

Generations of scholarly investigation into social movements has, quite naturally, led to the development of a voluminous theoretical literature.

Consensus about how to study social movements is lacking, although explanations for this situation seem relatively straightforward. Social movements vary enormously in terms of their objectives, strategies, and tactics. It has also been said that "a 'movement' does not have the clear boundaries of a party or group, and 'social' covers all aspects of behavior from the public and collective to the private and personal" (Byrne 1997, 10). Another issue is that types and activities of social movements are influenced by historical, political, economic, and other exigencies prevalent during the time in which they exist. Most certainly, as suggested by Diani and McAdam (2003), it would be intellectually injudicious to reduce social movements to a single event, organization, or individual.

The development of a diverse body of social movement academic literature is also shaped, and fundamentally so, by the conduct of social scientific inquiry. Social movement theory is marked by interpretation through varied sub-strands of thought. Non-unification of social movement studies partly results from the emergence of new public issues, and novel modes of protest, and how those issues facilitate new forms of scholarship. The effect of open-ended scientific processes upon the production of research aids in the growth of knowledge, but may not be necessarily conducive to conceptual clarity. To be certain, patterns of explanatory complexification are observed for virtually every other topical field within social science.

The study of social movements is riven with complication, but all is not lost. It is possible to identify some shared attributes, or "family resemblances," surrounding social movements (Crossley 2002). There have also been fruitful research efforts tracing commonalities, or at least complementarities, between various modes of conduct by social movement participants. For example, Cohen (1985), Foweraker (1995), and Opp (2009) argue that materialistic and nonmaterialistic bases of collective action by movements may complement one another. Even contrasting theories potentially fit together, within reason, to help build a generalist picture of social movements.

In this book, we adopt a generic description of a social movement: *sustained collective engagement by multiple participants, typically involving counter-hegemonic or extra-institutional activities, aiming to effect change within society.* Embedded within this definition are an interrelated range of considerations, which we shall now seek to justify as appropriate elements of social movement conceptualization.

Sustained Collective Engagement

An elementary feature of all social movements is that they involve shared efforts by a group of people, to fulfil a common end. As discussed later, it is widely agreed among scholars that a common end typically sought by social movement participants is "to establish a new order of life" (Blumer [1951] 1995, 60) or, simply, societal change.

Social movement theories from the early twentieth century, until roughly the 1970s, were predominated by the "collective behavior" school. Social movement activity was adjudged as "irrational," and "disorderly," insofar that such phenomena emerged rather spontaneously as well as outside institutionalized conventions, or typical norms of public intercourse. As behaviorally problematic as movements were seen to be, they were not viewed as entirely purposeless. Collective behavior theorists generally identified social movements as expressions of grievance against felt injustices or structural strains, such as endemic poverty and other deprivations of opportunity (Morris 2019; Smelser 1962). An intriguing contribution by Butler Shaffer (1975, 760) suggests "'order,' imposed by the state, may have created a general milieu in which people perceive a frustration of their personal, economic and social expectations, a frustration which may lead to acts of violence and other forms of disorder." There remain theoretical traces which are receptive toward collective behavior notions (e.g., Muukkonen 2008; Marx 2012).

Collective behavior treatments of social movements were superseded by alternative propositions. Rational choice theories in economics, political science, and sociology, emerging during the 1970s, contributed to a renovation of social movement theory. Contrasting the vision of movements as irrational phenomena instigated by discontented masses, rational choice emphasizes individuals' agency and choice when deciding to strategically pursue goals through collective actions. Perhaps the most prominent application of rational choice scholarship to social movements has come in the form of "resource mobilization theory" (McCarthy and Zald 1977). Subsequent theoretical extensions pointed to social movement activity being contingent upon institutional and related factors (e.g., Tilly 1978; McAdam et al. 2001).

Other theoretical edifices have been developed in recent decades to describe social movements. "New social movements" perspectives, originally developed by European sociologists during the 1980s (e.g., Touraine 1985; Melucci 1985), as well as "framing" scholarship (e.g., D. Snow and Benford 1988), stress that individuals commit to movements through shared senses of culture, ideology, and identity. The resulting sense of "we-ness" (Hartley and Potts 2014) among heterogeneous individuals helps coordinate and galvanize commitment by disincentivizing abstention from, or shirking contentious, social movement activities.

The style of collective engagement assumed by social movements is observationally case-dependent and contextualized. Whichever way one looks at the basis for collective engagement through social movements, what is important to bear in mind that a social movement tends to be a *sustained* exercise, agitating for change within society. While there remains scholarly interest in temporally punctual events, such as short-lived revolutions (Markoff 2015), a social movement tends to persist over time and carries out multiple strategic and tactical operations. This assessment is not to suggest that social movements are immune to failure (in the form of relative decline, or extinguishment altogether), but that *time* is necessary to allow the influence of social movements to potentially diffuse throughout a population (Koopmans 2004b; Francisco 2010). Recognition of time as the corollary of collective engagement facilitates the analysis of nonlinear, discontinuous tactical "waves" or "cycles," as well as interactions between social movement participants and other actors (e.g., legislators, law enforcement agents) in response to repressive (or liberalizing) sociopolitical conditions.

Multiple Participants

Social movements usually comprise multiple kinds of participants, each being embroiled with differing levels of resourcing, organizational, and participatory commitments. Movements need not maintain formalized, and tightly disciplined, organizations to ensure participation. Indeed, many individuals and groups may not be considered as part of "core" social movement activity; nonetheless, they fruitfully engage in "discussing ideas, exchanging information, pooling resources, sharing emotions, engaging together in acts of defiance and social criticism" (Saunders 2007, 239). A good way of describing this is that movements embody multilevel interdependencies between people (Bereni and Revillard 2012).

Conceptualizing the participatory pluralism and interactivity of social movements brings to the fore social-networking perspectives (e.g., Diani and McAdam 2003; Crossley and Krinsky 2015). The ties developed between movement participants enable the interpersonal sharing of resources, as well as the dissemination of meanings about "who we are" as a movement and "what we do" to foment desired changes (Diani 1992). Scholarship also highlights the capacity of movement networks to build "social capital," or trustful relationships, which may, in turn, promote consensus about purpose and embolden commitments to act collectively (Tindall et al. 2012). Social movement theorists have built upon the insights of Burt (1992) to also acknowledge the contribution of individual agents, and group alliances, in bridging otherwise disparate social movements together.

Underpinning the network relationships are communications between participants. This aspect of the social movement has been raised by Christian Fuchs's complexity approach. Specifically, social movements are seen as "dynamic communication systems that permanently react to political and societal events with self-organized protest practices and protest communications that result in the emergence and differentiation (production and reproduction) of protest structures (events, oppositional topics, alternative values, regularized patterns of interaction and organization)" (Fuchs 2006, 117).

None of the preceding discussion implies that networks operate to perfectly unify social movement participants. Social movements are rarely unified actors but, rather, seen as complex conglomerates whose components, and degree of unity, vary across issues and time (Rucht 2010). Additionally, there may be significant inequalities with respect to social movement effort and influence—for example, social movement "leaders" receive disproportionate recognition, fame, and esteem for the successful campaigns largely waged by movement "followers." In any event, the network perspective features the dynamic, and relational, character of social movements, including the distributed and complex nature of multi-person participation, coordination, and commitments.

Counter-Hegemonic or Extra-Institutional Activities

Social movements possess a capacity to help invoke changes affecting broader society. What commonly distinguishes social movements from most other kinds of collective engagement is their preparedness to use alternative, nontraditional, and often unconventional means to fulfil their objectives. Some of the other tactics available to social movement may include rallies, protests, and demonstrations, strikes, boycotts, sit-ins, flash mobs, and so on. A very important matter, to be discussed in subsequent chapters, is to what extent does a social movement engage its targets using violent tactical means. As will be seen, in addition to empirical research, aiming to identify the relative successes of nonviolent versus violent social movement actions, the potential for social movement violence is the subject of an extensive literature in ethics and philosophy.

When appreciating the tactical prowess of social movements, we should be mindful that activists do not limit themselves to political questions. As demonstrated by the history of social movement activity, people can group together to pose challenges to religious, corporate, educational, or cultural institutions, as well as their practices. Indeed, social movements need not restrict themselves to insider political petitioning, say, but may also be found "operating most characteristically at the level of everyday life and relationships" (Sawer and Maddison 2018).

Social movements are most clearly identifiable in their adoption of tactics and strategies outside established institutions and widely recognized conventions. However, the reality is that there is porousness between what is conventional and unconventional movement action, going beyond the disposition of certain social movements to work "outside the system" at all costs. To be noted later in this chapter, social movements occasionally experience formalization, culminating in their transformation into political parties, interest groups, and other mainstreamed entities. Consequently, the original movements risk losing their counter-hegemonic vitality, not to mention credibility among potential supporters who prefer radical approaches when engaging with their opposition.

Societal Change

Finally, a distinguishing feature of social movements is that they seek change in society. What does this mean? The central difficulty in defining societal change is that the concept and its boundaries are, much like movements themselves, subject to considerable ambiguity and disputation (Boudon 1986; Sztompka 1993). There remain questions as to whether societal change most appropriately applies at marginal or substantial scales, in the short- or long-term, whether quickly or gradually, or any variation upon those dimensions. This book is not the place to attempt a gargantuan effort to resolve the varying, and oftentimes conflicting, perspectives constituting societal change theory. Our interest is to identify those events and contexts which would enable us to see that social movements are operating to invoke changes in the world which surround their participants, allies, and opponents, alike.

We seek to invoke something of a pragmatic approach to comprehend societal change. This approach concedes the "entangled fact" that adjustments are always being carried out, and at varying scales, which, in turn, affect interactions and relationships between individuals and groups (Leicht 2020; L. Smith et al. 2019). Societal change is also interpreted broadly. It is registered within and across multiple domains of human activity—including cultural, economic, political, and scientific institutions, organizations, and practices—and assumes materialistic and nonmaterialistic dimensions.

The following chapters will aim to show that social movements have long been active with respect to pursuing societal change. Social movements engage in a struggle to amend and reform structures and flows pertaining to human behaviors, interests, organizations, practices, and values. Although actions by movement participants bear the marks of intentionality, the effectiveness of any given social movement in promulgating change in society is by no means a certainty. The contingent effects of social movement activity partly reflect the reality that a given movement confronts multiple opponents and rivals—not only governments, but alternative social movements and groups (e.g., religious orders, lifestyle groups, cultural and ethnic cleavages), and dissenting individuals, all of whom seek to frustrate the movement's success in reaching its objectives. Generically speaking, different groups vie for the limited attention, labor, resources, and time of their social compatriots

(Hilgartner and Bosk 1988; Almudi et al. 2017), and social movements are an active part of this broader contestation.

Another key to comprehend societal change, from our perspective, is that there is no smooth, lineal process between the origination of a proposition for social change and its eventual habituation, or institutionalization. Social evolution tends to be discordant and discontinuous, with setbacks on the idealistically constructed "path of progress" empirically discernible. Liberal theorists have leveled sharp criticisms against preconceived, totalizing schemes (drawn up by social movement participants, and by others) aiming at wholesale change *to* society. Expressing the dangers surrounding the imposition of socialist schemes, Mises ([1920] 1988, 73) writes of "the peace of the graveyard . . . not the peace of pacifists but of pacifiers, of men of violence who seek to create peace by subjection." Our interest is firmly in the contribution of social movements toward changes unfolding in free and open societies, as well as the movement struggles of oppressed peoples to upend the horrors of totalizing collectivism .

DISTINGUISHING SOCIAL MOVEMENTS
FROM OTHER COLLECTIVE PHENOMENA

Having outlined the major attributes of social movements, it is necessary to now consider the distinction between them and a host of alternative entities operating within (and across) economic, political, and social domains. At the outset, consider political parties. A political party is an organization dedicated to recruit and elect like-minded political candidates for office, primarily through general elections. The conception of "like-mindedness" here refers to the sharing of common beliefs, ideologies, and principles concerning the use of political power, management of public governance arrangements, and the formulation of public policies. Consisting of executive office-bearers and a broader rank-and-file membership, political parties are typically hierarchical bodies seeking to raise funds, organizing the selection of political candidates, and presenting policies which electorally attract sufficient numbers of voters. Public choice scholars often present parties as a central focus of political activity within liberal democracies, considering how such organizations attempt to optimize their share of electoral votes through advocacy, and similar appeals, to material interests, as well as beliefs and values.

An interest group is another form of organization, which tend toward intensive involvement within the political domain. Typically managed and operated by paid staffers in hierarchical fashion, and usually with a paid membership base, the purpose of an interest group is to advocate for, and influence, governmental policies favoring those constituencies or interests they purport to represent. The basis for representation is diverse, and may reflect commercial or industry imperatives, but also cultural or social priorities, moral positions, and so on. Interest group activities are trained upon direct political lobbying and negotiations with legislators and bureaucrats, but it is recognized that interest groups may also attempt to influence general public opinion by producing media campaigns, publishing position papers or research, and related outputs.

Another collective which is well represented in contemporary organizational ecology are non-government organizations (NGOs). NGOs vary in terms of their organizational structure, ranging from relatively centralized bodies with paid executive (with, or without, professional support) staff, through to a loose association of unpaid volunteers, performing various tasks to pursue certain causes. The kinds of operations maintained by NGOs vary. Some bodies primarily exist to advocate on cultural, ecological, humanitarian, social, and related grounds. Other NGOs perform charitable redistribution and service delivery, often to the aid of disadvantaged and marginalized social groups. These bodies mainly operate on a not-for-profit basis, and seek finances from a variety of sources—including donations (which may be treated as tax-exempt under certain legislative provisions), paid memberships or subscriptions for supporters to access certain services, and, occasionally, grants from private and public entities.

Notwithstanding that social movements together with the alternative entities, described here, are all engaging in collective action, it is possible to draw distinctions along various aspects of structure, conduct, and performance. The first issue is that social movements, and perhaps many of the participants constituting them, are, at best, loosely connected with formal, institutionalized political institutions, mechanisms, and opportunities. In contrast, political parties and interest groups, together with their members, appear far more tightly connected within the political systems they aspire to influence.

Consistent with a lack of ready access to formal politics, social movements tend to rely more heavily upon protests and similar forms of contentious action (Císař 2013). Interest groups and, to a lesser extent, NGOs are seen to access formal communication channels to discuss concerns and issues with political actors. Structural distinctions have also been made between social movements and other collectives. It may be possible to identify a small set of organizational entities, and under some circumstances even a single entity, such as a political party, interest group, or NGO, but it is usually not possible to attribute a single outfit as being an entire social movement. According to Johnston (2014, 24), "[s]ocial movements are structurally diverse, made up of *numerous, networked groups, organizations, and individual adherents.* " Finally, social movements generally rely on unpaid volunteer activists and supporters for effort, time, and logistical support. Political parties, interest groups, and NGOs, by contrast, tend to rely upon the finances, and labor, of paid memberships and remunerated staff.

Attempts to draw clean, nonfuzzy distinctions between social movements and other collectives may, to some degree, reflect differing conceptual and analytical priorities among social scientists (Beyers et al. 2008). Prioritization upon organizational formalization may, in itself, be reflective of historical and macro-institutional approaches to social theory (e.g., Tilly 1979, 1981). For the critics of such drives to formalism, presenting purist, if not enduring, typologies of collective actors' strain plausibility, given the growing cross-sectoral and cross-domain emulation of practices and strategies. Under the theoretical threads of "dynamics of contention" (McAdam et al. 2001) and "social movement society" (Meyer and Tarrow 1998), macro-level hypotheses present the case that economic, political, and social actors are increasingly pursuing the unconventional pressure tactics commonly associated with social movements. This noted tendency may be couched as part of progressively intensive struggles for public acknowledgment, recognition, and representation.

In terms of the meso-level of human action, it is widely acknowledged that social movement participants might seek (formal and informal) alliances with interest groups, and other non-movement bodies, to realize shared objectives. This acknowledgment has carried over into studies alluding to blurriness of organizational differences between social movements and other collectives. In one interesting case, Hasenfeld and Gidron (2005) refer to "multi-purpose hybrid voluntary organizations" combining features of social movement activity, nonprofit services, and volunteer-run associations. These authors refer to the evolution of these hybrids "having multiple purposes, combining to various degrees goals of value change, service provision and mutual aid . . . and a deliberate mix of organizational forms borrowed from volunteer-run associations, social movements and non-profit service organizations" (ibid., 98). Another paper, by Ahrne and Brunsson (2011), offers a synthetic account of collective engagements structured along varying degrees of "partial" organization, as opposed to formal (and hierarchical) organization at each and every turn. In practice, social movements may be situated in any place along this spectrum in accordance with their norms and practices governing membership, hierarchy, egalitarianism, rules, monitoring, and sanctions.

Difficulty in neatly pinning down distinctions between social movements and other collectives actually affirms a noteworthy insight. It is that "social movements can only be understood in their context, especially with regard to their structural location, and their relations and interactions with major reference groups. Among these are, or can be, political institutions and control agencies, bystander publics, mass media, informal and formal brokers and arbiters, and counter movements" (Rucht 2010, 1443). In addition to the inherently entangled nature of social movement activities, one must appreciate that contextualization cannot be formulated statically. What this means is that movement network structures—as well as strategies and tactical dispositions developed by participants within such structures—are recognized as shifting over time.

Under some circumstances, social movements (or some elements thereof) may institutionally transform into organizations such as interest groups and political parties (Cohen and Arato 1992). For example, labor unions have evolved (or, more precisely, have splintered some of their political activities) into laborist political parties in countries such as the United Kingdom, Australia, and New Zealand. Another example is the evolution of the highly formalized Greenpeace NGO from its antinuclear social movement origins (Zelko 2017). In other cases, certain movements may decentralize, or even fragment and splinter. Other movements might redirect themselves from formal political petitioning, and toward actions against nonpolitical targets. The combination, and recombination, of structural, ideational, and performative attributes of social movements (Johnston 2014), and what these entail for the achievement of a freer, liberalizing society, is seen to warrant further investigation.

LIBERAL POLITICAL ECONOMY: AN APPROACH TO STUDYING SOCIAL MOVEMENTS

This book is not solely motivated by the need to comprehend social movements and their myriad activities. One of the novel attributes of this book is its attempt to interpret the meaning and value(s) of social movements through the prism of liberal political economy. Although there is no set definition for "political economy," the term is often used to describe a strand of intellectual inquiry focused upon the complex relationships between economy and polity, with cultural-social considerations having a major bearing upon economic-political configurations and involvements (Boettke 2012; Boettke and Storr 2002). When reference is made to "liberal political economy," as is the case throughout this book, we simply mean political economy with liberal characteristics.

It should be stressed that liberalism is not a fixed notion, and nor is it immune to intellectual contestability. These statements imply there are alternative conceptions of liberalism. An epistemic consequence of this is that the domain of liberalism exhibits a certain "stretchiness," highlighted by the likes of Merquior (1991), Fawcett (2014), Gaus (2018b), and Kolev (2019a). Liberalism appears best conceived as a constellation of ideas, sometimes loosely, or tensely, related with one another. Even so, there seems reasonably widespread agreement about its normative commitments. Generally speaking, these include the advancement of: market-based economic arrangements exemplified by competition, entrepreneurship, and innovation; a civil society exhibiting openness through freedom of association, and institutions of free inquiry and expression; and a democratic political order characterized by limited government in accordance with the rule of law.

As mentioned earlier, explanations of social movement characteristics and activities are very well represented in alternative ideological and philosophical traditions. These include Marxism (Barker et al. 2013), post-modernism (Handler 1992), and critical studies (Habermas 1981; Cini et al. 2017). We submit that intellectual inquiry remains, or should remain, sufficiently open to enable liberalism to meaningfully join the diverse cast of social movement scholarship. Clearly, there is a range of liberal scholarship addressing themes of potential interest to social movement researchers, such as class (e.g., Lemke 2015; Hart et al. 2018) and collective behavior (e.g., Gasset 1932; Rüstow 1980). It is equally considered that liberals can learn much from non-liberal treatments of social movement phenomena, without any loss of deeply held commitments on the part of the former. From this standpoint, offering an explicit liberalism of social movements aims at presenting fresh opportunities for cross-ideological discussion, debate, and learning.

Why are we interested in *liberalism* as a lens through which to study social movements? Conventional methods in liberal political economy, chiefly drawn from the Austrian (with Hayek as figurehead), Bloomington (Ostroms) and Virginia (Buchanan) traditions, are posited to provide useful insights with respect to why and how social movements are organized, and conduct themselves, in the ways they do. We go a step further in concurring with Peter Boettke and Nicholas Snow's (2014) judgment concerning the efficacy of a blended approach to liberal political economy, using Austrian, Bloomington, and Virginia school insights. The fusion proposed by Boettke and Snow, and applied to the social movement case, allows for a dynamic conceptualization of societal change. This change is facilitated by citizens choosing to associate in an effort to challenge the purveyors of concentrated power structures, discover tactics of raising public issues and persuading compatriots, and to learn the arts of democratic coordination and governance.

We now turn to a brief description of each of the three main schools of liberal political economy, starting with the Austrian school of economics. With its analysis grounded in methodological individualism, Austrians emphasize the benefits of market processes in distributing knowledge about value-added means of production and exchange. Under conditions of considerable (if not radical) uncertainty, creative decisions inherent in entrepreneurial activities are pivotal in discovering profitable ways to better serving consumers, and in correcting economic errors over time. The Austrian school is noted for its normative emphasis upon liberty and freedom, and aversion to extensive public-sector policies which could compromise entrepreneurial opportunities. This has led to a distinctive conceptual and historical literature concerning the properties of emergent self-governance (Leeson 2014; Stringham 2015).

Led by scholars such as Don Lavoie and Peter Boettke, an extensive body of work over the past three decades interprets social and cultural phenomena through the lens of Austrian economics. Recognizing the ubiquity of entrepreneurship, liberal thinkers examine the non-economic bases of entrepreneurial action within civil societal spaces (Frank and Shockley 2016; Haeffele and Storr 2019b; A. Martin and Petersen 2019). Further applications of this work include the entrepreneurial interpretability of cultural symbols and social cues (Lavoie 1994; Chamlee-Wright 1997; Storr 2013) and the applicability of social capital in distilling knowledge (Chamlee-Wright and Myers 2008; Ikeda 2008; Meadowcroft and Pennington 2008).

Contemporary Austrian scholars also compare the efficacy of social entrepreneurship in directing support and care services for vulnerable individuals and groups, accounting for variations in incentives and feedback mechanisms between economic and non-economic institutional environments. An important, and closely related, literature focuses upon community resilience (e.g., Storr et al. 2015), including the influence of decision-making structures upon recovery from natural disasters and other cataclysmic events. All of these considerations provide a basis to study social movements in a fresh light.

Another important strand of liberal political economy is the so-called Bloomington school, originally associated with the works on diverse public governance by Elinor Ostrom and her husband Vincent Ostrom. Arguably the chief contribution of the Bloomington school is its understanding of the maintenance and resilience of non-state forms of collective engagement. In particular, this strand of thought highlights the contribution of individual actors, and their groups, interacting within distributed sites of decision-making and power. In so doing, it is often found that people can discover and implement their own solutions to social dilemmas and other collective-action problems (E. Ostrom 1990, 2000, 2005; V. Ostrom 1997; also, Aligica and Tarko 2012; Tarko 2017).

The Bloomington school's location within liberal political economy is attested by a recent description of it, placing "a premium on competition, pluralism, open societies, and constitutional alternative modes of collective action that maximize personal liberties" (Richard J. Stillman, quoted in Aligica 2015, 117). With the Ostroms (also Lavoie 1993; Goodman 2019) arguing that liberal democracies are better characterized as self-governing societies—and with their robustness informed by the integrity of emergent, non-state orderings therein—there appears ample scope to accommodate social movements into a broader framework of liberal social order. The Bloomington inspiration for "civic studies" of methods and techniques affirming democratic competence and experience, likewise, provides potential to better understand social movements and their activities (Pe. Levine 2019; Pe. Levine and Soltan 2014).

Public choice theory, a novel integration of economics and political science, represents the third leg of the tripod that is modern liberal political economy. The rational-actor element of public choice, in particular, considers the role of instrumental self-interest in political behavior, in turn justifying constitutional, legislative, and electoral rules channeling collective action to conform with generalized interests. The unmitigated pursuit of particular, or self, interests in politics are seen to be reflected by such interrelated maladies as rent-seeking (Tullock 1967), discriminatory policies (Buchanan and Congleton [1998] 2003; Boettke and Thompson 2019), and a lack of fiscal, monetary, and regulatory policy control (e.g., Buchanan and R. Wagner [1977] 2000). The public choice assumption that the potential exercise of self-interest, politically, might cause serious harms to members of the community—in the form of, say, political repression, extirpation of individual freedoms, and discriminatory legal and policy advantages—often align with the concerns that motivate social movement activity.

There are other ways in which the lessons of the Virginia school are relevant to social movement theory and analysis. Public choice theory draws attention to questions about the feasibility of large-scale collective action (Olson 1965). Olson's predictions continue to raise debates in social movement literature but, even so, there are now several variations of public choice theorization accommodating non-instrumental motivations and patterns of behavior. Of particular interest are public choice studies of emotions and affect (van Winden 1993, 2007), as well as expressive political behavior more generally (Brennan and Lomasky 1993).

Table 1.1 illustrates the envisaged nature of correspondence between aspects of social movement theory and liberal political economy. Throughout this book, case examples will be nominated to further shed light upon social movements, and the ways in which their activities may be interpreted using liberal theoretical approaches.

To be sure, our interest extends beyond a liberal political economy lensing of social movement theory. Social movements are significant both in historical and contemporary contexts. In addition, it is considered that movements are an intriguing case to help interpret certain tensions in liberal thought. In this context, liberalism not only tells us something about social movements; social movements illuminate certain, perhaps underappreciated, intuitions about liberalism itself.

This book largely aims at a positive political economy account of social movements. However, a range of normative considerations are never far from the foreground. After all, the general impression gleaned from academic and

Table 1.1 Key Concepts and Themes Outlined in Book

Conceptual Orientation	Fundamental Postulates	Social Movement Attributes
Austrian School (Friedrich Hayek)	• Methodological individualism • Subjectivism • Entrepreneurship • Spontaneous and emergent orders	• Moral and norm entrepreneurship by key activists • Self-organizational ability, including in repressive environments • Contributions toward societal transformations
Bloomington School (Elinor and Vincent Ostrom)	• Nonmarket and non-state decision making • Polycentricity	• Building democratic competencies among participants • Concessional arbitrage among polycentrically situated decision makers
Virginia School (James Buchanan)	• Behavioral consistency • Collective action theory • Rules of political organization and conduct	• Movement participants challenging oppressive political institutions and repressive policies • Expressive political motives and epistemic choices

Source: Author's illustration.

popular writings is that twentieth-century liberals (of the "classical" Smithian-Hayekian variety, as well as libertarians, anarcho-capitalists, and fellow travelers) largely harbored, at best, indifferent, or, at worst, negative, sentiments toward social movements and activism. Social movements have often been seen as a front for rent-seeking within existing liberal-democratic systems, or as a vehicle to propound affective rhetoric risking productive enterprise in the name of redistribution. Such antipathy toward social movements has, at times, discounted the functional existence of liberal commitments by movement participants, toward freedom of assembly, expression, and speech, as well as the desire to protect minorities from socio-political domination by majorities. Other proponents of liberal ideas have simply overlooked or dismissed social movements outright. In this sense, it is intriguing that certain scholars and advocates have identified a similar neglect of other social phenomena—for example, philanthropy, NGOs, and civil society—within liberal scholarship (Cornuelle 1992; Ealy 2018; Garnett 2011).

We share liberal sensibilities against rent-seeking and political favoritism, and we strongly disfavor violent tactical ploys by social movement participants harming and destroying life and property. It is also our view that not all social movements should be tarred with the same brush of negativity, or dismissal. There have been certain periods wherein people have collectively organized to facilitate an environment enabling, say, marginalized groups to participate more freely and effectively in economic, political, and social decision-making (Novak 2016, 2018c). A liberal theorization interpreting social justice—and, most recently, the concerns of "identity politics"—as efforts seeking redress from ill-treatment by government, and other powerful actors, may also explain mobilization and action by social movements. However, not all social movements are pro-liberty in orientation or effect, so it is important to critically undertake a case-by-case examination of social movements, and their strategies, and to check for the due contributions they make to a freer world.

ORGANIZATION OF THE BOOK

The central aim of this book is to add to scholarly literature by providing a better understanding of the features, operations, and activities of social movements. We attempt to achieve this aim by situating social movement studies within a broader framework of liberal political economy. Contrary to any preconceived notion that this strategy may be intellectually infeasible, we refer to the Austrian-sounding opening of a relatively recent work referring to social movements as "collective efforts orientated towards social change that point to circumstances in which *creative human action* actually shapes and alters social structures, rather than being shaped by them" (G. Edwards 2013, 1–2; emphasis added). Interpreting social movement characteristics, and functions, from a liberal standpoint also unveils insight about the manner in which societal change and progress, more generally, is achieved.

In chapter 2, we explore the manner in which collective engagements are elicited by social movement participants. We refer to how social movement developments are motivated not only by pecuniary motives or economic incentives but, perhaps more importantly, by powerful socio-cultural forces. Chapter 3 outlines the strategies and techniques employed by social movements to raise awareness of their causes among the broader community, persuade decision-makers about the merits of their narratives and claims, and to signal strength of commitment to others. Chapter 4 describes the effectiveness of social movement challenges within their economic, political, and social institutional contexts, specifically considering the manner in which movements engage with organizations and groups elsewhere within society.

This book also provides a historical treatment of social movements toward certain liberalizing changes in modern societies, as well as raising issues resulting from contemporary social movement activity. In chapter 5, we present selective case studies about social movement contributions toward liberalization along economic, political, and social dimensions. Chapter 6 outlines key matters raised by contemporary social movement activities—such as economic freedom, repression of protest, and engagement with digital technologies—which are reshaping our world.

The final chapters of this book provide an effective "stocktaking" of the contributions and value of social movements. In chapter 7, we consider the implications of social movement activities for the validity of several core commitments commonly attributed to liberalism. Chapter 8 presents a summary of the key arguments of the book.

The social movement literature is vast, and subject to evolution as researchers actively investigate dynamic methods of contention against governmental, and other, actors. This book does not aspire to provide an exhaustive survey, or comprehensive overview, of social movement theory. In laying out the general aims, and schema, of this book, we seek to provide an invitation to liberal theorists to more closely consider how social movements work, and in which ways movement activities acts as a driver of societal change. Admittedly, such an invitation may be regarded as contentious in its own right, given that movement activities could be predominantly seen as being illiberal in character. Being mindful of that such perceptions do exist, in the following chapters we shall conceptually, and analytically, explore how social movements have the potential to inspire and catalyze changes extending the domain of freedom in its economic, political, and social guises.

Chapter 2

Commitment without Coercion

Social Movements and Collective Engagement

INTRODUCTION

The social movement is premised upon the basic idea that changes usually cannot be achieved by a single individual. Social movements consist of multiple participants taking action collectively, and working to sustain such collective action, to realize an aspiration to effect societal change. It also stands to reason that movement goals, should they be realized, will be enjoyed not only by those who directly participated in movement activities but also by members of the society more generally. Social movements may be pivotal in eliciting and maintaining struggles against domination and injustice, but the non-excludable nature of achieving movement goals suggests a potentially serious lack of participatory effort to ensure movement success.

A critical question is: Why would anybody engage in social movement activity? To collaborate within social movements is costly and risky, and there is no assurance that movement participants could appropriate the gains of successful initiatives for societal change for themselves. How are social movements sustainable under such circumstances? Certainly, collective behavior theorists regarded tactical movement operations, such as protests, as both irrational and unsustainable. However, subsequent scholarship points to the persistence of many campaigns, and refer to how movements are sustained by the efforts of people from many walks of life (and not exclusively by aggrieved social fringes). Social movements, it is argued, present a good case for how people can resolve collective action problems and generic social dilemmas in interaction with, but also *beyond*, the boundaries of market and state.

This chapter describes the processes underpinning the formation and propagation of social movement collective engagements. As a starting point, we outline an economic theory of collective action which relies upon the work of Mancur Olson. We then discuss the potential for nonmaterial considerations to encourage commitment to social movement causes and actions—including the roles of emotions, frames, narratives, and stories in motivating sustained social movement activity. This chapter also assesses how social movement organizations (SMOs) and network configurations may be used to facilitate coordination, with consideration also given to entrepreneurship and leadership qualities in inspiring collective action. We conclude this chapter with brief reflections.

MANCUR OLSON, COLLECTIVE ACTION, AND SOCIAL MOVEMENTS

One of the hallmarks of modern social movement theory has been the substantial research effort devoted to resolving the so-called "collective action problem." This problem relates to situations wherein multiple numbers of people are unprepared to cooperate in the production of a joint good, or to work together to achieve a common objective in some other respect. Widely attributed to Mancur Olson and his seminal work *The Logic of Collective Action* (1965), descriptions of the collective action problem corresponded with the growing tendency to utilize fundamental economic precepts when describing and diagnosing social problems. In this regard, Olson adjudged that rational behavioral constructs—and the commensurate weighing, by individuals, of the costs and benefits associated with alternative actions— readily extends to interest groups and certain other entities. Applying economic logic to agency in its social contexts, Olson saw much potential for shirking and reneging in undertaking collective engagements.

To some extent, Olson's efforts were not original. Economists previously described how individuals are likely to abstain from voluntarily contributing finances that support provision of "public goods." Public goods are those with characteristics such that it is not possible to exclude somebody from consuming the good without paying for doing so ("non-excludability condition"), nor does the consumption of such goods prevent others from simultaneously being able to consume ("non-rivalrous condition"). Consequent to such characteristics it is generally agreed that it is unprofitable for commercial enterprises to attempt to provide public goods, which, then, leads to arguments about how to use political institutions to enforce participation in their financing and to determine allocation.

The scholarly innovation introduced by Olson was to extend the logic of the collective action problem beyond public goods, to a broader gamut of social dilemmas. Olson expressed the central problem as follows: "unless the number of individuals in a group is quite small, or unless there is coercion or some other special device to make individuals act in their common interest, *rational, self-interested individuals will not act to achieve their common or group interests.* In other words, even if all of the individuals in a large group are rational and self-interested, and would gain if, as a group, they acted to achieve their common interest or objective, they will still not voluntarily act to achieve that common or group interest" (Olson 1965, 2). The starkness and originality of Olson's formulation led sociologist Pamela Oliver (1993) to exclaim that collective action became so problematized in academic imagination that collective *in*action became viewed as the natural state of affairs.

Olson's work rests firmly in rational choice scholarship. Individuals are conceived as rational actors, taking it upon themselves to decide if they should engage in collective action, or not. The rational actor is a calculative, though fallible, who weighs up the benefits and costs associated with alternative courses of action and, then, acts upon their preferred choice. Again, the collective action problem encapsulates the potential that individuals rationally abstain, or shirk, from contributing to the cost of a public good or, more broadly, a collective activity. There is no evading the fact that most social movement activities are aimed toward objectives with publicness attributes— for example, attainment of equal gender rights not only benefits movement participants who engaged in activism, but also benefits non-participants. It is conceivable that sizeable numbers of people would engage in so-called non-participatory, "free riding" conduct, consistent with an expectation that others will decide to bear the cost burden. To put this in another way, the "distance" between individual action and the non-realization of collective interest is manifested in free-riding tendencies.

A relevant cornerstone of Olson's analysis is the connection between the collective action problem and group size. People are assessed as more likely to fail in their collective efforts to coordinate in a larger-group setting compared with a small group. Pivotal to this idea is the so-called "noticeability problem," or the "1/n problem" (Hodgson 2019), in that the capacity of an individual to make a perceptible difference toward public good contributions diminishes as the number of contributors increase. As described by Oliver (2015, 247), "each individual's share of a collective good—and thus her payoff—goes down with the number who share the good, while the cost of providing the good goes up with the number who share in it. People will not contribute to large-group goods because individual contributions have to be divided up among too many free-riding recipients." To apply a simple example, the noticeability of a given individual's contribution toward the social movement will be greater if only 100 participants were involved, as opposed to 100,000 participants.

The noticeability problem implies demotivation in participating in collective action episodes, compounding the aforementioned free-rider issues. As a group grows in size, individual participants tend to become anonymous (or at least less well-known to others), and it becomes difficult to monitor, and punish, noncontributing members. To be sure, altruism, or a similar kind of other-regarding behavioral impulse, is not ruled out, but Olson makes the empirical claim that most people would not rationally act to realize collective action—unless coerced or otherwise incentivized to align individual and group prerogatives.

The implications of the collective action problem for movement organization and activity should be clear by this stage. If social movement goals possess public good attributes then potential participants will be incentivized to engage in free-riding behavior. The benefits of achieving movement aims are *distributed*. In contrast, the costs of engaging in the collective actions necessary to fulfill the aims—such as staging public protests, or conducting other risky tactics, that publicize opposition to *status quo* arrangements—are *concentrated*.

The collective action problem raises an additional set of questions. Can the collective action problem be resolved? If so, how? Mancur Olson suggests that an inducement of some kind could help suppress collective abstention and free riding. Specifically, a "selective incentive"—or "individually appropriable inducement" as coined by Stigler (1974)—provides a good, or reward, as a condition of persistent movement involvement. As Olson states:

> group action can be obtained only through an incentive that operates, not indiscriminately, like the collective good, upon the group as a whole, but rather *selectively* toward the individuals in the group. The incentive must be "selective" so that those who do not join the organization working for the group's interest, or in other ways contribute to the attainment of the group's interest, can be treated differently from those who do. (Olson 1965, 51)

In exchange for committing to the movement, a given participant receives, for instance, exclusive information or literature, or enhanced access to key organizers and activists. The material reward provides the beneficiary participant with certain benefits or advantages over those who are less committed. In the case of information provision and intelligence sharing, selective incentives could contribute to a group-based epistemology and "insider" knowledge, which might turn out to be advantageous when social movements wish to mobilize against their targets.

The economic explanation for selective incentives is fairly straightforward. Their provision is anticipated to re-weigh the costs and benefits of becoming involved with the movement, in favor of strengthening the (subjectively perceived) net benefits. Selective incentives may be "positive" in that they encourage collective action, but social movements could also dispense "negative" selective incentives, attempting to punish those who do not contribute, or contribute insufficient shares (Olson 1965; Salmon 1987). Negative selective incentives may be complemented by the invocation of fairness norms and similar values, to further deter free riding in group contexts (e.g., Fehr and Schmidt 1999; E. Ostrom 2000).

It is eminently possible to extend the conception of selective benefits beyond those small-scale, or tangible, private goods attached to the provision of the public good. In an important review of Olson's book, Richard Wagner (1966) observed that privileged policy access may become an important by-product of successful collective action by interest groups (and, presumably, certain social movements with good access to legislators, bureaucrats, and other key political actors). Groups enjoying such access are likely to presumably command greater levels of engagement and support from people, than would otherwise be the case. Other scholars have adapted Olson's selective incentives proposition. Tullock (1971) suggested that a potential inducement for political revolution is the expectation that political offices may be provided to those involved in such actions (also M. Silver 1974; Muller and Opp 1986; Lichbach 1995). Similar theories have been used to explain why terrorist groups provide incentives for supporters to participate in violent actions (Caplan 2006; Francisco 2010).

To what extent are collective actions encouraged by selective incentives? Among the earliest criticisms has been that selective benefits, of a materialistic nature, are probably insufficient to induce commitment and continuing involvement in group activity, such as those undertaken by social movements. For example, Robert Salisbury (1969) refers to nonmaterial "solidary incentives" as a more compelling mechanism to galvanize people into offering support. Tuck (2008) contends that disinclination to contribute toward collective action, due to a lack of noticeability, may be overcome by building esteem for contributors. In a strident critique of rational-actor sociology in a social movement context, Fireman and Gamson (1979) ask: Why are (material) selective incentives even necessary when key movement organizers and activists can instigate moralistic calls to collective action?

Additional criticisms have been directed toward Olson's depiction of collective action. Some raise the point that Olson insufficiently explained the empirical reality that collective action is abundant, with friends and strangers, alike, participating in common projects (Barnes 1990; Hilhorst 1997; Klandermans and van Stekelenburg 2013). Mark Pennington (2011) indicates that for cause-oriented groups—especially those with an expressive commitment toward a given ideology, religion, or social identity—the free-riding problem is minimized because participation is a desired outcome in its own right.

To what extent is there a strong correspondence between group size and incentives to contribute? Marwell and Oliver (1993) contend there may well be a *positive* correlation between group size and participation, with larger groups able to facilitate collective action by virtue of their command over a relatively greater set of resources (such as finance, participant competencies and skills, etc.). Marwell and Oliver refer to the American Civil Rights and feminist movements as case examples of large, and effective, constituencies for change that built capability as their supporter bases grew. Others challenge the Olsonian conception that large-number groups necessarily break down. For example, Uhlaner (1989) describes "relational goods"—including those supplied by social movements—whose realization actually depends upon active co-contributions by members of the general public.

Although social movement research has profited from studying collective action problems, it should be noted Olson himself largely refrained from the detailed study of social movement–style entities. In the final chapter of *The Logic of Collective Action*, it is stated the specification of collective action problems are "not very useful for the analysis of groups that are characterized by a low degree of rationality" (Olson 1965, 161). This includes so-called "mass movements" of utopian nature, whose membership base feel alienated from broader society. Even if strong rationality precepts may not apply to such cases, we recall the earlier point that Olson said that coercion *or some other means* could be used to galvanize commitment. It is in this regard that solidary incentives may arouse sustained multi-person commitment. Olson also did not rule out that a self-selecting "privileged group" with a high degree of commitment may emerge to provide the public good, or activity, itself, even if the overall outcome remains macroeconomically suboptimal (also G. Brennan 2015).

The collective action problem raises many questions, and has motivated numerous scholarly refinements. However, there is little doubt regarding the significance of this issue. While Olson has been charged with applying a simplistic model of rational action to complex social questions, a fair-minded reading of *The Logic of Collective Action* suggests that rationality was primarily used for heuristic or theoretical purposes, rather than as an explanatory *dictum* (Udehn 1993). Discussions by Olson himself about non-instrumental bases of individual motivation and collective engagement suggest a careful treatment of relevant methodological issues at the "dawn" of rational-choice social movement scholarship. Multiple values inspire social movement activity, as we shall see, but it is a testament to the utility of Olson's model that it is so frequently cited and applied by social movement theorists.

IDENTITY, FRAMES, CULTURE, EMOTIONS:
NON-MATERIAL REQUISITES OF COLLECTIVE ACTION

Mancur Olson's work motivated the production of an immense literature concerning the relative benefits and costs of participating in contentious, and often extra-institutional, social movement activity. As important as Olson's theories are to the understanding of collective action, they have not been immune to intellectual challenge from sociological and other perspectives. Arguably commencing with the European "New Social Movement" theorists of the 1980s, academics increasingly emphasize non-instrumentalist foundations of movement commitment and participation. Broadly speaking, this scholarship identifies four interrelated features—the use of *identity*, *frames*, *culture*, and *emotions*—in sustaining movement activities.

Identity

Identity is manifested at multiple levels of personal and social existence, and has assumed immense political significance as individuals both establish alliances and seek recognition for their shared ascriptive or non-ascriptive characteristics. It is difficult to arrive at an all-encompassing definition of identity but, for some researchers, the concept is subsumed in the expectations, meanings, representations, and understandings about who a person is, and how they relate to others (Fearon 1999). According to Burke and Stets (2009, 3), "[a]n identity is the set of meanings that define who on is when one is an occupant of a particular role in society, a member of a particular group, or claims particular characteristics that identity him or her as a unique person." Identity may be grounded in some localized, grounded, or, perhaps, traditionalist, notion of perceived reality, rooted in time and place, or it may be shaped by broad-ranging, even abstract, conceptions—for example, the cosmopolitan view of a shared identity of humanity.

Contrary to popular notions that identities are, somehow, fixed, a key point we make is that identities *evolve*. As individuals familiarize themselves with mechanisms through which they author their own lives, and exert changes (even if at the margins) upon the world about them, it becomes increasingly feasible for identities to change. Added to the complexity of studying identity is the potential for intersectional "modularity" in identity, wherein multiple identity affiliations are maintained through the epistemic and moral frameworks held by individuals and groups (Novak 2018b,c). Hartley and Potts (2014) similarly explain that identity is inextricably tied to the "demic narratives" (or stories) people frame about themselves, and each other, with such narratives being subject to change.

Social movements often seek to engender a coherent sense of identity among their supporters. This construction of identity may be construed as part of a broader movement agenda to make, and give, meaning to collective actions. Polletta and Jasper (2001) outline four broad ways in which social movements use identity: (i) to create collective claims; (ii) to encourage recruitment into the movement; (iii) to facilitate strategic and tactical decisions; and (iv) help ensure the realization of preferred movement outcomes. In addition to promulgating shared narratives, social movements may create and reinforce identity through techniques of cultural symbology—such as assigning meaning to names, signs, verbal styles, rituals, clothing, and so on.

Academic literature suggests that social movements help connect a participant's "self-sense" of identity with collective and social identities, providing motivational pathways through which collective action is facilitated. Furthermore, identity can be seen as a catalyst for developing communities of interest, entailing strengthened interpersonal links, and building networks and alliances, with like-minded people. Movement alliances help diffuse understandings about problems, and the nature of struggles against authority. Historical experiences of anti-hegemonic struggle may, in turn, craft shared identities. Drawing upon experiences, social movement participants may reflexively build a better understanding of "who we are" (Polletta and Jasper 2001). Of course, exogenous events such as "moral shocks," economic and political disturbances, and similar events may galvanize a population to identify, and develop sympathies, with social movements (Jasper 2011, 2014), coalescing previously disconnected people together into a "movement identity" (Smithey 2009; della Porta and Diani 2020).

Identity appears to be an inherently relational construct, inviting interpersonal comparisons of inclusion ("we-ness") or exclusion ("otherness"). Inasmuch as social movements attempt to maintain a strong group-identity, instilling a sense of identity among participants may also include finely-grained senses of whom one's opponents are. Indeed, social movements are among many groups implicated in the manufacture of the "we" in-group and "they" out-group distinction. Social movement research is replete with descriptions concerning the agonistic and oppositional nature of social movement activities, typically directed against political and other targets (including counter-movement entities). Adherents of *status quo* societal arrangements also exploit identity to denigrate and stigmatize social movement participants—in these cases, the movement "other" allegedly advances degenerative or disorderly societal potentials, or, even worse, those involved in movements are presented in a dehumanizing manner (Harris and Fiske 2006; Haslam 2006).

Considering identity as a dynamic, non-binary concept complicates the narrowcast "we-versus-they" prism through which movement activity is usually discussed in popular circles. Arguably the basis for social movement success does not rest in the ability to segment supporters and non-supporters, and friends and enemies, but to grow the *aggregate number of supporters*. It seems an important component of this challenge is for movement participants to promote societal change through *persuasive efforts*. This encompasses turning those who identified as "enemies," and "adversaries," into "friends." As discussed later in this book, this may be construed as a form of Hayekian catallaxy. Another matter is that liberatory social movements have exerted pressure to ease, if not abolish, discriminatory treatments in accordance to some aspect of identity (Novak 2018c). Successful efforts by such "pro-liberty" identity movements may work to the benefit of core activists as well as passive supporters, and, under certain circumstances, even their opponents.

Consider the contribution of identity to the formation of the disability movement, one of the great liberalizing forces of the modern age. While there has been a long history of care and support for people with disabilities—particularly by families, together with local peer and friendship networks—this community has unconscionably also been subjected to systemic abuse, neglect, violence, and other instances of dehumanization. As indicated by Lennard Davis (2006, xv), "[p]eople with disabilities have been isolated, incarcerated, observed, written about, operated on, instructed, implanted, regulated, treated, institutionalized, and controlled to a degree probably unequal to that experienced by any other minority group." One aspect of historical experience for people with disabilities has been the prosecution of venal biopolitics by governments—in the guise of such illiberal measures as incarceration, segregation, and sterilization (e.g., Reilly 1991; Geloso and March 2020). Other impediments to autonomy and respect are also evident, such as lack of access to public buildings, as well as a lack of consultation with people with disabilities in policy formulation.

It is understandable that people with disabilities would engage in social movement struggles to overcome the abuse, discrimination, mistreatment, and prejudice leveled toward them. A few decades ago, the "independent living" movement emerged in the United States, and elsewhere, to challenge traditional, yet largely unaccountable, service models of dependency. This movement suggested new ways of affording people with disabilities greater autonomy, and choice, regarding their needs and how they want to live (DeJong 1979; Fleischer and Zames 2001). There are many other elements within the broader disability social movement seeking to build a shared identity. One of these is the disability pride movement, encouraging people with disabilities to affirm their self-worth, and to challenge ableism and its problematization of bodies (e.g., Ni. Martin 2012).

The work of disability movements is focused upon equipping people with disabilities the means to flourish in a world that has, all too frequently, operated in a manner inimical to their interests. While acknowledging the practicality of goals and objectives of this movement, we also note their ideas often connect with key philosophical commitments. Independent living, and subsequent models interweave with the proposition that all individuals should enjoy the capability to live, work, play, and function in the world more effectively, including in comparison with others in society (Nussbaum 2006). The identity work conducted by various disability advocacy and support groups also seeks to invert self and public perceptions, and stereotypes, of powerlessness and lack of agency.

Frames

It would be misleading to think that identities exclusively succeed in forging social movements and sustaining their collective action. Social movement scholars have long noted that additional efforts are undertaken to design, and diffuse, resonating "frames" with the aim of emboldening activity (D. Snow et al. 1986; Benford and D. Snow 2000). Frames are described as "specific metaphors, symbolic representations, and cognitive cues used to render or cast behavior and events in an evaluative mode and to suggest alternative modes of action" (Zald 1996, 262). These insights were inspired by Erving Goffman's (1974) seminal work, explaining a process whereby people interpret and communicate their representations of reality, often through reference to images, symbols, narratives, performances, and stereotypes. Framing devices become important in a movement context because "social movements are dynamic collective actors able to engage in the production of meanings and interpretations to be shared with and contrasted by constituents, antagonists, bystanders and outsiders" (Vicari 2010, 506).

David Snow and Robert Benford (1988) disaggregate the framing concept into three components. These are *diagnostic frames* (identification of a problem or set of problems, and establishing which individuals or groups are implicated in perpetuating the problem), *prognostic frames* (description of potential solutions to the problem/s, including strategic and tactical responses as well as the need for collective action), and *motivational frames* (elicitation of "calls to action" for existing and new supporters, mobilizing and engaging people with regard to the movement objectives). Meyer and Kretschmer (2007) follow up on these fundamental concepts to suggest framing encourages collective action if they convey a sense of *urgency*, suggest *feasible* alternatives, and invest activists and supporters with a sense of *agency*. In sum, framing motivates by publicly describing problems that need resolution, outlining potential solutions, and inspiring the necessary (if contentious) actions collectively deemed necessary to resolve the problem.

It is obvious that social movements would seek to construct frames for their specific cause. Movements can also draw upon preexisting meanings and understandings about the world—so-called "master frames" (D. Snow and Benford 1992)—which are ubiquitous yet sufficiently elastic for use in multiple contexts. A good example is the reference to injustice (Gamson 1992), advancing an understanding that adverse economic, political, and social situations are, *inter alia*, the product of unjust treatments at the hands of others. Experiences of racism and sexism, for instance, may be attached to an injustice-oriented master frame. Whereas master frames often portray the existence of structural phenomena as the source of problems experienced by oppressed peoples, such frames need to be complemented by depictions of agency. Persuasive framing along those generic lines is likely to encourage social movement participants to believe that it is both necessary and possible to change conditions for the better (Gamson 2013).

The concept of "freedom" has, itself, long served as a highly effective frame to engender societal change. Social movements have been observed to apply freedom frames in a "negative" sense (Is. Berlin 1969), a "positive" sense (C. Taylor [1979] (1985)), or in a "triadic" or "relational" sense (McCallum 1967; Pettit 2001). Arguments for freedom have often been used in conjunction with (master or specific-issue) frames asserting the need for expanded rights and choices (Benford and D. Snow 2000), as well as the remedy of injustices. A hallmark of modern societal evolution extending liberties and rights to previous out-groups (Singer 2011; Welzel 2013; Novak 2018b, c) arises from, to some extent, efforts of social movements and other collectives to compellingly deploy freedom argumentation as a framing device.

The mobilization of social movements is also connected with the ability of framers to connect issues with recognizable attitudes, mores, and understandings. The economic psychology of Brendan Markey-Towler (2019a) alludes to those conditions underpinning the successful cognitive incorporation of frames by movement participants. Frames are more likely to "stick," mentally, when they connect with preexisting ideas and notions held by individuals, and are more noticeable and resonant in affective character. Of course, the success of any given movement's frames, from a cognitive standpoint, is a qualified one. As noted by Whittier (2002), oppositional movements produce their own countering frames, potentially diluting the persuasive efficacies of alternative frames. This "framing contestation" could sow confusion and uncertainty about the reasonableness and viability of certain social movement activities, and, along various margins, could disincentivize collective action possibilities.

Communications and cultural researchers have pointed out that frames are typically woven into stories, songs, and similar forms of communication, referred to as "collective narratives" (Fine 1995; Polletta 1998; Mayer 2014).

As the term suggests, collective narratives are honed by, and spread among, multiple persons to assist with meaning-making, promote shared senses of identity, develop shared expectations, and, ultimately, motivate individuals to engage in group actions. Social movements are noted for their efforts in crafting collective narratives, which "foreground resistance to the dominant norms and institutions of society. They raise questions about the possibility of alternative world-views and alternative dispensations, and in so doing they challenge participants and observers to re-think meanings that are too often taken for granted" (Kurzman 2008, 6).

As with framing, persuasive collective narratives have the capacity to persuade people to get involved with collective actions. Narratives posited to resonate are those which credibly enable people to imagine themselves immersed within, or otherwise connected to, the plots encapsulated within the narrative being told, as well as presenting a potent rationale for action (Somers 1994). As we shall describe later in this book, social movement participants attempt to encourage others to engage in risky counter-hegemonic activities, by portraying their contemporary situation as part of a morally noble, and often historicized, struggle. However, it is important to stress that the production of collective narratives may be differentially received by the public; some narrations will be seen as more credible, applicable, and valuable than others. Furthermore, social movement figures are likely to vary in their capability to present a compelling narrative justifying action (Polletta and Chen 2012).

Culture

Although culture has been defined in numerous ways, for convenience we may regard it as the cognitive and symbolic assemblages of shared meanings and values held by multiple people. Culture is inclusive of beliefs, norms, and values expressed in either small or large groups, publicly and privately, and through a range of techniques such as storytelling (Hartley and Potts 2014), dance and song (D. Klein et al. 2015), and other ritual performances (R. Collins 2004). Over the past few decades, scholars have appreciated the involvement of social movements in the production of cultural precepts. Social movements are seen as actively generating cultural changes within society as a whole, in addition to attaining concessions on specific matters.

Our primary interest in culture rests in its capacity to energize collective action on the part of social movement participants, often in the face of resistance by proponents of traditional cultural authority and prestige. In this context, "culture is a tool through which a group cements members to itself, legitimating requests for commitment and practical assistance. Moral and social discourse helps groups counteract the free-rider problem. Culture becomes a central means by which the movement itself becomes valued to members, separate and apart from any material rewards that might be provided, mitigating economic or psychological costs" (Fine 1995, 131).

A crucial aspect of cultural development within social movements is the use of language and discourse by organizers, activists, and other participants. Drawing from the moral insights of Adam Smith ([1759] 2002), language serves as a platform for exchanges of approbation between individuals and, in so doing, helping build mutual support and friendship (also Badhwar 2008). Narrative development and propagation contribute to shaping movement boundaries, and promote discipline among activists, through a communicative reinforcement of shared repertoires and practices. The significance of discussion within social movements is aptly underscored by Gary Fine's (1995, 142) remark that "a movement in which . . . talk is absent, is impossible. Movement actors are awash in talk."

Elinor and Vincent Ostrom also noted the coordinating capacity of language, together with its ability to generate public attention. The epistemic efficacies of language were noted by Vincent Ostrom (1980, 310): "[b]y the use of language, human beings have radically amplified their capabilities for learning and sharing their learning with one another. The aggregate pool of knowledge, the potential repertoire of adaptive behavior, and the resulting harvest of effects assume extraordinary proportions." Social movements are associational networks engaging in a critical function of using language to structure debates, discourses, and ideas. These efforts provide an aid for members of society to identity and clarify sources of contestation, recognize and clarify legitimate interests, and discover appropriate strategies to transform society (Boyte et al. 2014).

The range of topics potentially communicated by movement participants is vast. They may include: the specification of problems, and describing aspirations and goals; debating tactics and strategies; discussing how to mobilize supporters to engage in collective action; negotiating activities and the use of resources; memorializing success and lamenting (and learning from) failure; and gossiping about friends, adversaries, and enemies (Mische 2003). Movement discourses may be regarded as part of that generalized human proclivity in exchanging sympathies among group participants. Nathaneal Snow (2020) invokes Smithian philosophy in suggesting that movement participants cooperate by internalizing the responses of others (including signaled expressions of approbation and disapprobation) to their own behavior.

The synchronization of images, languages, symbols, and practices—and the replication of such repertoires over time—helps formulate a movement culture that, in turn, reduces the relative costs of collective action. However, as the Ostroms also discussed, language can also confound or deceive people. Linguistic innovation by social movements—say, in the field of human rights or identity-recognition—may also have the effect of provoking criticism by traditionalists, and other proponents of *status quo* arrangements. Opponents of linguistic innovations may apply counter-frames back at the "linguistic entrepreneurs" of social movements, perhaps sowing further confusion, if not fostering enmity, toward the original movements.

The ability of social movements to craft narratives, initiate rituals, and strike agreements about ways of being, doing, and knowing, suggests that culture is an object of choice. This defies structuralist notions of culture as socially pre-determined, or otherwise given to individuals and groups. As noted by Jasper (2004, 6), "[e]ven the most culturally saturated group or individual makes choices, carries out strategies, anticipates the reactions of others, and has some sense of what it would mean to "win." All of their intentions, understandings, and actions are filtered through cultural and psychological lenses."

Emotions

Over the past two decades there has been something of a renaissance in emotions research applicable to social movement activity. Jasper (2011) offers a rough separation between emotional impulses as *urges* (strong bodily impulses of a largely physical nature, and which are difficult to control), *reflex emotions* (reactions to socio-physical environments, evidenced by facial expressions and bodily reactions, which rapidly appear and subside), and *moods* (a state of mind or feeling, which may or may not be influenced by reflex emotions, of a more persistent nature). Accompanying these are *affective attachments* or *aversions*, expressed in feelings of liking, loving, respecting, trusting, and admiration (and their negative counterparts). Finally, Jasper identifies *moral emotions* which consist of feelings of approval or disapproval based on moral intuitions and principles.

Social movements play active roles in arousing and manipulating emotions. Emotions may be deployed to help galvanize social movement participation, sustain longer-term mobilization by building emotional rapport and trust, and, finally, to undergird elements of movement strategic action and choice with an affective base (Almeida 2019; Jasper 2004). For example, social movement figures may arouse anger, outrage, or compassion, and exploit deep-seated fears and anxieties, all in ways that build momentum for collective actions. Researchers suggest that movement participants may undertake an additional amount of "emotion work," so that intense feelings do not escalate or manifest themselves in undesirable actions, such as violence against tactical targets (Goodwin et al. 2004).

Scholars such as Randall Collins (2001) and John Scott (2018) argue that people derive emotional energy from the contentious, risky, extra-institutional activities organized by social movements. They also see an accompanying build-up of solidarity, also propelling individuals to engage collectively. Inglehart (2018, 21) observes emotions help individuals "to make lasting commitments to stand by one's friends or one's tribe through thick and thin, in situations where a purely rational person would defect if it were profitable," and emotions also provide short-cut heuristics when making complicated decisions. Emotional prompts to promote recruitment—even if they come in the form of peer pressure acts, such as cajoling, or questioning the sincerity of a supporter's commitment to their identity or their inclination to fight oppression—was described by Chong (1991) with respect to Civil Rights campaigns in the American South.

There is a school of thought within classical liberalism suggesting that emotional displays and expressions could be detrimental for collective action, and for social coordination more generally (Wolf 2018). On a related matter, Hayek (1988) indicated that social justice narratives evoked primal emotions of envy and unfairness (also Schoeck [1966] 1987). More recently, liberals have mentioned the dangers of extremism in aggravating public fears, giving impetus to political measures that erode civil liberties in the name of security (Buchanan 2005a). These views appear, at least on the surface, to be consistent with longstanding fears about social movement irrationalism from the collective behavior theoretical perspective.

For the critics, the "emotional turn" in academic literature merely reinforces the evaluative caution that ought to be applied to social movement study. We affirm the fundamental liberal premise that violence is morally inadmissible, and agree that liberals are well within their rights to critique social movement projects aiming to restrain liberties. But is the wariness toward emotions justified in each and every circumstance? Certain movements have affectively rallied supporters toward pro-liberty causes; in other words, social movements energized participant emotions to assist with agendas which broaden freedom (Wolf 2018). In a similar vein, most social movement activists aim to instill senses of other-regarding virtue among peers and allies, in a manner described by Deirdre McCloskey (2006). It is also noted that social movements have frequently encountered logistical and *affective* resistance (including tactics designed to instill fear) from the state, counter-movements, and other proponents of the *status quo*.

ORGANIZING AND NETWORKING
THE SOCIAL MOVEMENT

Organizations

The key insight of this chapter is that collective engagements are neither self-generating nor automatically sustaining phenomena. Intentional human involvement, entailing a great measure of foresight and intelligence, is needed to ensure societal change objectives are being met. Thus, another factor influencing the capacity for meaningful social movement action is the existence of some form of supportive *organization*. The tendency toward sustained social movement campaigns from the 1950s and 1960s—on issues as diverse as racial equality, women's rights, environmental amenity, and decolonization—facilitated a revision of social movement scholarship in several ways. One of these was a transition away from collective behavior notions of movements as temporary, fitful episodes of public grievance, and toward enduring, organizationally sensitive approaches.

Scholars such as John McCarthy, Mayer Zald, and Andrew Oberschall were involved in the development of what is known as "resource mobilization theory" (RMT). The key insight of RMT is that the collective struggle for power and influence by social movements is waged through organizational activity. The organization, from this standpoint, provides a focal point for attention and a vehicle to amass resources for collective action. The central hypothesis of RMT is arguably that "[g]roup organization is . . . the major determinant of mobilization potential and patterns" (Jenkins 1983, 527). From the RMT viewpoint, sustained collective action on the part of a social movement requires a semblance of control, if not ownership, over certain resources over a period of time. However, exactly what those kinds of resources are to be, or how much are needed by social movements, remains a bone of theoretical contention.

Social movements naturally require a sufficiently large number of people to organize significant movement activities. A heterogeneous body of social movement participants provide diverse and enriching experiences, educational backgrounds, and other forms of knowledge—all regarded as "human capital" (Becker 1964)—to potentially contribute toward attaining effective movement outcomes. In addition to knowledge creation and sharing assumed to arise from participant comingling, movements may gain social and political credence by signaling their numerical strength (whereas opponents attempt to discredit the movement by deflating estimates of the aggregate number of people involved).

There has also been growing recognition within social science as to additional, albeit largely intangible, resources to support social movement activities. These include "cultural capital" in the form of skills, talents, credentials, manners, and other socio-cultural cues (Bourdieu 1977, 1986). Elements of cultural capital, in turn, could be used by a social movement to gain advantages—such as peer and public recognition, distinction, fame, and prestige—over their competitors and rivals. This is followed by the concept of "social capital," or those benefits emanating from personal connections and relationships, such as intersubjectively shared meanings, mutually recognized norms, and stronger trust bonds (Coleman 1988; Putnam 2000).

For RMT proponents the inclusion of such intangible capital concepts enhances the integrity of their theories, by eschewing a strictly materialistic focus upon resourcing advantages potentially accessible to a social movement (B. Edwards et al. 2019).

In addition to people and the human, cultural, and social capitals in their possession, access to finance seems necessary to aid movement activities. The ability of a social movement to raise funds, and acquire other sources of revenue, may depend upon the interaction of legal, taxation, and related systems (Coglianese 2001; Cummings 2017). In addition to finance, movement participants may perceive the need to control, if not own outright, some forms of physical capital, and noncapital goods and services. Another important resource seen as indispensable to all social movements is time itself—which is necessary to develop deep and meaningful interactions between movement participants, to sustain protests, and to extend meso-level societal influence (McAdam et al. 2001; Haydu 2020).

Physical resources, finances, people, and time are seen as advantageous in waging tactics, and in providing movement infrastructures that garner public support. In the words of McCarthy and Zald (1977, 1213), RMT "emphasizes both societal support and constraint of social movement phenomena. It examines the variety of resources that must be mobilized, the linkages of social movements to other groups, the dependence of movements upon external support for success, and the tactics used by authorities to control or incorporate movements." However, under conditions of uncertainty it may be difficult to establish what resources, and how much of them, are necessary to effect societal change. Some studies focus on the perceived usefulness of particular resources for movement organization; however "[t]he problem with schemes based on uses . . . is that most resources have multiple uses. Any scheme that ignores the intrinsic features of resources is therefore of limited value" (Jenkins 1983, 533). As will be noted in this book, entrepreneurship and competition may be crucial in enabling social movements to discover more efficient and efficacious uses of the resources they obtain.

From the RMT perspective the SMO serves as a vehicle through which resources are amassed, as well as an embodiment of what the movement aims to present to supporters and to wider society. It is important to recognize that not all SMOs are created equal. One example of an SMO is a highly formalized body, reflective of the Weberian modernist vision of organizational bureaucracy and highly rationalized internal procedures. This type of SMO would presumably maintain a professional staffing body, and perhaps even charge for the provision of certain services (such as campaign literature, clothing, equipment used in protests and other public events, and so on). For such a SMO user-charging might prove somewhat advantageous in respect of assuring a revenue base, as well as easily identifying motivated supporters. However, following our previous discussions, some may argue that classifying this entity as part of a social movement is questionable, given such an SMO bears strong similarities with an interest group or political lobby, or even an economic firm (Jo. Scott 2018).

The place of organization within social movement theory is contentious. The creation of an SMO—and the instigation of categorical distinctions (and, perhaps, interactional estrangements) between SMO leaders and social movement supporters—could run the risk of "crowding out" the intrinsic motivational basis for widespread participation (Frey and Jegen 2001). In a well-known criticism of the RMT framework, Piven and Cloward (1979) suggested that organizational bureaucratization risks deterring movement participation as a whole. Another issue is that an organizational presence presents opportunities for funders to strategically influence, if not manipulate, movement agendas. For example, Francis (2019) claims that funding pressures swayed the National Association for the Advancement of Colored People (NAACP) to transition from raising awareness about racial violence toward an agenda of educational desegregation. Other criticisms directed toward SMO analysis, and RMT more generally, include its apparent disregard for culture (Turner 1981; Hilhorst 1997), individual agency (Gould 1991; Jasper 2004), and ideational factors (Gamson et al. 1982).

There still remain defenders of SMO analysis. Almeida (2019) indicates that materially deprived individuals can capture scale economies for their movements by organizationally *pooling* resources. The experience of labor unions appears a good example of working-class constituencies using organizational methods to accumulate resources, and to launch campaigns against employers and governments. From Jasper's (2004) perspective, a potential benefit of building strong SMOs, especially those with coherent identities, lies in their ability to forgo costs arising from accommodating outsiders who might undermine the movement. In other words, a strong organizational focus may work to avert any dilemmas associated with an expansive membership with conflicting perspectives.

We should also remind ourselves that the RMT approach to social movement theorization also emerged as an explicit response to Mancur Olson's depiction of collective action problems. Individuals on their own accord are seen as unlikely to want to bear the costs of undertaking contentious, oppositional action for the sake of change within society. Designing and maintaining organizations, that can accumulate and manage the resources necessary for social movement action, are seen by RMT scholars as a pivotal strategic move to incentivize mobilization and foster greater participation.

Another way in which SMOs benefit a movement is by acting as a medium between two groups: "potential beneficiaries" and "conscience constituents" (McCarthy and Zald 1977). Beneficiaries may be construed as egoistic individuals, expediently involved with a given movement on the expectation they will benefit from the successes enjoyed by that movement (Udehn 1996). Constituents provide aid, and similar resources, but not in the expectation, or hope, that they directly benefit. They do so on account of the values they feel they share, and a sense of solidarity they identify with the social movement as a whole. Udehn (1996) and Klandermans et al. (2015) suggest that modeling altruistic conscience constituents enable RMT scholars to import nonrationality considerations into their framework. In a recent contribution, Nathaneal Snow (2020) adds to these suggestions in arguing that social movements are able to bind together through sympathetic exchanges among participants.

A remaining issue concerns how SMOs, which do not ostensibly conduct economic calculations, coordinate their resources and engage in social learning. Recent developments in Austrian economics provide some useful guidance (Chamlee-Wright and Myers 2008; Boettke and Coyne 2009). Specifically, esteem, reputation, and status act as *implicit* guides as to where, and when, to allocate resources. Those SMOs perceived as credible and effective in conducting persuasive campaigns, and in winning concessions from policymakers and other targets, are more likely to attract resources. It could also be argued that the flow of resources among competing social movements *per se* can provide a public signal as to where resources should go. Similarly, Sandell and Stern (1998) indicated that the size of an SMO supporter base is likely to influence the ability of movements to win additional resources. The likes of esteem and prestige are unlikely to be as tight a feedback mechanism as relative price movements (A. Martin 2010) but, nonetheless, they could be meaningful in an environment wherein social movements strive to obtain resources.

For all its strengths and limitations, RMT has been critical for our understanding as to how social movements organize collective engagements. However, it would be imprudent to consider the institutional and operational spaces in which movements exist as being solely represented by highly formalized, bureaucratic SMOs with strong internal disciplines. As indicated earlier, it is possible to identify a variety of organizational forms associated with social movements. Let us, briefly, consider the organizational capacities of anarchist social movements.

Anarchist social movements are the subject of growing academic focus, particularly in the wake of self-declared anarchist activism in response to a host of economic, political, and social issues. Within this, sociologists have particularly devoted attention to the ways in which anarchist social movements organize, and devise their own rules of conduct and decision-making. Recent analysis of such movements, by the likes of Shantz (2020) and Williams (2017, 2019), emphasize a tendency toward non-hierarchical (or so-called "horizontalist") organizational structures. A number of anarchist movements have also been identified to promote deliberative, or highly participatory, decision-making involving large numbers of participants, and eschewing executive decisions by an internal movement elite. Underpinning the selection of such organizational patterns and governance rules is a "prefigurative" desire on the part of anarchist movement participants to pre-emptively model the behavioral standards and governance styles that they, themselves, prefer to see throughout society (e.g., Leach and Haunss 2009; Polletta 2002).

The suggestion that self-avowed anarchists would construct rules may, at first glance, appear paradoxical, given the commonly held association between anarchism and a lack of rules, or, perhaps, disorganization. Although not all anarchists profess a subscription to liberal ideologies or world-views their social movements appear deserving of further study by liberals, given the perceptible affinities between the anti-statist orientation of many anarchist movements and analytical scholarly interest by liberals in the generic terms of endogenous (non-statist) rule formation and self-governance (Boettke and Candela 2021; Leeson 2014; Stringham 2015). For our immediate purposes, this discussion about movement anarchism is intended to reinforce the insight that the capacity for endogenous rule formation, and self-governance capacities associated with that, is not restricted to such highly formalized SMOs as originally valorized in RMT literature. Indeed, Shantz (2020) supposes that resources are a necessary, but not sufficient, condition to support enduring "infrastructures of dissent," which can help maintain an effective, working unity among diverse *networks* of movement organizers, activists, and supporters. The significance of networks to movement conduct and persistence is a subject to which we now turn.

Networks

In the introduction to this book, we emphasized an interpretation of social movements through the lens of network theory. Without denying organizational presence in social ontology, the network conceptualization of social movements best illuminates the idea that heterogeneous agents (and their entities) interact, and not necessarily in uniform or harmonized ways, to fulfill objectives. A useful description of social movements in this regard is as follows: they are "networks of informal interaction between a plurality of individuals, groups and/or organizations, engaged in a political and/or cultural conflict, on the basis of a shared collective identity" (Diani 1992, 3). The key ideas contained in this quotation are those of the *pluralism* of actors (individuals and groups) who associate on the basis of *shared* values (such as identity, but also conscience, interests, norms, and values), but who are, themselves, engaged in *conflict* with others.

Social movement networks facilitate collective action by enabling multiple people to combine their material and nonmaterial resources for subsequent campaigns. Indeed, it is unlikely that sufficiently scalable, and noticeable, collective actions would take place without networks. In addition, networks provide an "insurance" function in that responsibility for managing social movement resources can be spread among multiple people. This, in turn, minimizes the probability that governments, counter-movements, or other potentially hostile actors can attack a single, or dominant, movement figurehead. The coordinative counterpart to resource pooling is the ability of social movement network participants to *access* resources when the opportunity arises to instigate collective action. In that regard, however, one should be mindful of the potential ability of resources, embedded within networks, to be "hoarded by insiders and denied to outsiders, which often intensifies pre-existing inequalities among groups in their ability to access and utilize crucial resources of other kinds" (B. Edwards et al. 2019, 81).

A recent example of the resource-generation capacities of social movement networks has been the flood of financial donations, and in-kind provisions, provided to the Black Lives Matter (BLM) movement. These include GoFundMe and other crowdsource funding websites for the families of victims of police brutality. In numerous U.S. jurisdictions so-called "cash bail" systems are in place, wherein money is payable for pre-trial release of defendants from detention and is only refunded upon their appearance at trial (Surprenant and Brennan 2020). Numerous bail funds—for example, the Minnesota Freedom Fund, and Missouri Black Protestor Relief Fund, also supported by national initiatives such as the National Bail Fund Network and The Bail Project—work to financially bail out arrested BLM protestors. The provision of in-kind support—such as food, water, and medical supplies—to protestors by a range of donors (including established retailers, and impromptu makeshift and home-grown suppliers) have also sustained social movement activities. Other examples of networked supports include anti-racism educational campaigns, pressure to induce policy changes to policing practices, as well as general donations to Civil Rights and related groupings.

Although estimates vary in relation to the aggregate amount of funding dedicated to BLM, they are, nevertheless, substantial. One report indicated that, during the second half of 2020, donations to BLM-related causes were in excess of U.S. $10 billion (Economist 2020). Financial estimates such as these do not take account of the time and emotional energy expended by protestors, and by those who volunteered to help BLM participants on the streets. Even so, it is evident that the generation of support was attributable to the networking activities of an entangled assortment of individuals and groups. The latter have included nonprofit organizations and charitable bodies, and even private-sector corporations—all seeking to identify with, and to publicize their support for, a cause dedicated to anti-racism and the cessation of police brutality.

Social capital is a valuable resource propagated by, and leveraged through, social networks. Strong and trusting relationships between people within a network help detect and sanction free riders who frustrate collective action, and facilitate identity and cultural works ensuring that participants feel a sense of belonging and camaraderie. Overall, network-level social capital is seen to reduce various costs of human interaction. The implications of social capital have become a focus for the Austrian school of economics, as mentioned earlier (e.g., Chamlee-Wright 2008; Chamlee-Wright and Storr 2015). Networks with relatively dense levels of social capital are likely to transmit information and resources among participants more quickly than would otherwise be the case, which can advantageously elicit collective action. Austrians also acknowledge the contribution of "brokerage" agents, who enable communication and resource flows between otherwise disconnected networks of social movement participants (Burt 1992).

Mancur Olson, and certain social movement scholars, saw that additional incentives may be needed to entice potential participants to become collectively engaged. Material and nonmaterial incentives may be more readily forthcoming in environments in which people know each other. In turn, this is more likely to be the case within networks exemplified by homophilous relationships—wherein social ties are developed with people of similar backgrounds, interests, and other characteristics. In other words, "when people know or like each other, rewards for participation will be more likely than in groups consisting of isolated individuals" (Opp 2009, 71). According to Karl-Dieter Opp (1998) the late-1980s protests engulfing former East Germany, and other European communist states, were the result of moral suasion by family members, friends, work colleagues, and other people known to each other, to participate. Protest participation also grew in size as the police and military abstained from violent repression of the protests. Attached to participation was a "moral" incentive, as well as reward, in the form of social recognition and esteem, for joining the movement against totalitarianism.

Obviously, the organization, and prosecution, of social movement activities require people. Indeed, one might suggest that people are the "ultimate resource" for a social movement. Therefore, one of the more readily identifiable advantages of networks is that they serve as a mechanism for recruitment. In a study of religious and political movements, D. Snow et al. (1980) found that the probability of being recruited into a particular movement was informed by links to one, or more, movement members through an interpersonal tie. Across different case studies, an average of at least 60 percent of respondents said that social networks were their primary avenue for recruitment. The recruiters, and the recruited, invariably form friendships which, then, reinforces adherence to the social movement, as well as discouraging exit (della Porta and Diani 2020). Critically, people are more likely to join a movement, even if this potentially entails being involved in high-risk collective activities, if they know somebody who has prior experience of activism. This finding was a key feature of Doug McAdam's (1986, 1988) studies of the American Civil Rights "Freedom Summer" campaign of June 1964, which aimed to increase the registration of African American voters in Mississippi.

Thus far, we have considered the manner in which social movement network serve to encourage collective action. Now, we briefly consider how network configurations additionally work to discourage shirking. The sense of familiarity with which people acquire of each other, when they interact within a networked setting, is conducive to the setting not only of formal rules, but of informal codes, mores, and values. The mutual influence of each actor upon one another is said to help galvanize social movement cooperation and loyalty, and to induce norms of fairness and reciprocity with respect to involvement in collective action (Oliver 2015). Bonding within the network could, similarly, help reduce the costs of sanctioning noncooperative behavior (Opp 2009).

Consider, in further detail, the relational efforts undertaken within, and even between, social movements for improving coordination. Social movement networks may be perceived as arenas of cultural production and maintenance. Communication among networked participants provide a solid basis for generating and disseminating a "movement culture," pivotal to motivating collective opportunities down the track. For Mische (2003, 263), "[i]t is through these conversations that what we commonly describe as "network ties"—e.g., friendship, assistance, exchange of ideas, resources, or support—are co-constructed and take on meaning and weight within the practical operations as well as the legitimizing lore of social movements." Similar sentiments concerning the cultural importance of movement networks are found in the works of Melucci (1989) and McAdam (2003).

Just as has been the case with resource mobilization models, the network approach endures its share of detractors. The dynamism of many social movement networks has been interpreted, to some extent, by critics as evidence of their instability (e.g., Staggenborg 2002; M. Gurri 2018). Whereas networks are generally praised for their ability to solicit valuable information and resources from a wide range of sources, and to create vast webs of human relationality, one is also aware of Weber's ([1922] 1978) "network closure" proposition, raising the specter of actor exclusion and opportunity hoarding. While one should be alive to prospects for network dysfunctionality, it seems a great normative value of networks, generally speaking, is that they typically embody fundamental precepts of voluntarism and polycentrically ordered partnership (Chaumont-Chancelier 2003; Lomasky 2002).

We posit that the networking dimension of social movements dovetails quite neatly with Vincent Ostrom's (1980, 1997) precondition of a democratic "artisanship." The artisanship proposition incorporates the ability of individuals to converse, understand, negotiate, and to agree with each other, as a foundation, if not the precondition, of effective democratic governance for society as a whole. Negotiations and planning among movement activists, supporters, and allies, even if aimed at confrontation with purveyors of societal *status quo*, appear to serve the function of internally investing in citizenship competences (Pe. Levine 2011, 2019) or, as Zeynep Tufecki (2017) would describe it, "building the muscles" of democratic capability (also Polletta 2002). The strength of these arguments may be qualified by the limitations of deliberative democracy, including the biased nature in which negotiation and decision-making might take place (Pennington 2003; Gaus 2008; Gastil 2018). Such biases may be ameliorated, along some margins at least, by the argumentative jostling and contestable negotiability convened within, and especially between, movement network participants, in addition to discursive contestations between movements, counter-movements, and broader target groups.

LEADERSHIP AND ENTREPRENEURSHIP WITHIN SOCIAL MOVEMENTS

Leadership

In this section, we do not immediately ask *how* social movements achieve collective action. We ask the following: *who*, if anyone in particular, is responsible for those innovations easing the burdens of acting collectively through movements? Instinctual responses would probably raise leadership as a factor in redressing collective action problems. Putting it simply, a single individual is, or a small (and strongly connected) subgroup of individuals are, tasked with originating and/or implementing movement activities. To take from a recent contribution to social movement scholarship theory, leaders are seen as "strategic decision-makers who inspire and organize others to participate in social movements" (Morris and Staggenborg 2004, 171).

The stress upon leadership is not only reflected in biographical accounts of social movements, but appears suffused throughout the social sciences. Consider, for instance, the "Great Man" leadership conceptions of history, sociology, and of other disciplines. There also exist residues of "trait" theories, situating leadership within some genetic or psychological frame of explanation (Sutherland et al. 2014). Leadership in these guises implicitly entails a notion of nonconsultative exertion of decisions, enacted by an elite over greater numbers of people. However, even in social movements organized on dehierarchical, democratic-participatory principles, there is usually some implicit recognition that certain people occupy leadership roles—if not by setting agendas and making important decisions, but by setting inspirational examples for others (den Hond et al. 2015; Jasper et al. 2015).

When considering the social significance of leadership, one might be forgiven for saying: "it all begins with Weber." Max Weber is undoubtedly famed for his treatment of economic, political, and social affairs, particularly exemplified by his theories of organizational bureaucratization and its broader impact upon ordering community arrangements and practices. For our purposes, we note Weber's ([1947] 1964) modernization narrative, which partly focuses upon the nature of authority and how it evolves. We recognize the Weberian description of *charismatic authority* (or leadership) as a temporal and intermittent, but, nevertheless, effective, force for social change. In this, Weber explicates an elitist view of the distribution of charismatic leadership. To quote him at length:

> The term "charisma" will be applied to a certain quality of an individual personality by virtue of which he is set apart from ordinary men and treated as endowed with supernatural, superhuman, or at least specifically exceptional powers or qualities. These are such as are not accessible to the ordinary person, but are regarded as of divine origin or as exemplary, and on the basis of them the individual concerned is treated as a leader. (Weber [1947] 1964, 358–359)

Through their ability to rally people to a cause, charismatic leaders have the potential to inspire collective action (Rubinson 2009). Part of the drawcard of charisma is that certain figures are seen as embodying superlative qualities. These may include public recognition as having undertaken heroic feats, being perceived as possessing significant cultural-social credence, or otherwise credibly connected with deep-seated cultural, social, or political stories (Willner 1984). Charismatic social movement leaders may be seen to possess rhetorical gifts, and exercise authority through force of personality, or will. They discursively manufacture grievances and diagnostically frame social problems, publicize new belief systems, negotiate the accumulation and organization of resources, as well as craft emotional bonds with movement participants. The function of charisma here is to reconcile individual anxieties (i.e., perceived senses of strain and grievance) with the resolution of such anxieties, through collective actions by the social movement (Andreas 2013).

Social movement leaders can also be seen as adding to the affective and cultural capabilities of movements. To encourage risk-averse members of the public to get involved, leaders are seen as needed to describe compelling rationales for participation. Rubinson (2009) explains the role of leadership in reframing the prior beliefs of followers, convincingly attaching emotional appeals with logical reasons for participation, and possible action. However, leadership styles can vary, thus enabling scholarship to move on from the charismatic leader stereotype. Aminzade et al. (2001) refers to "task-centered" (pragmatic) and "people-centered" (charismatic) leadership orientations. The implication of this distinction is that a given individual does not necessarily possess the knowledge and skills necessary to carry a movement on their own. Instead, successful leadership is viewed as requiring participation and, thus, cooperative interaction, among a number of people.

It is often forgotten that Max Weber had a major influence upon, and was influenced by, other key thinkers straddling economics and sociology during the early twentieth century. Consider the figures of Friedrich von Wieser and Joseph Alois Schumpeter whom, in combination with Weber, form a "triumvirate"—to use the expression of Stefan Kolev (2019b)—of scholarship about leadership. Each scholar profiles a "super-hero" leader with the socio-psychological ability to induce structural change, at least in the economy, if not elsewhere within society. In urging the masses to validate their innovations, including by replicating them across meso-social spaces, leaders are adjudged to be less responsive to the dictates of traditional, bureaucratic, and other rule-bound obligations. Schumpeter, Weber, and Wieser made clear distinctions between "leaders" and "followers" on classist grounds, with the former imbued with the qualities of virtuosos (Tilly 1978).

We now turn to consider "followership" attributes. To put it simply, followers are people in non-leadership positions within SMOs and networks. In response to charismatic leadership, followers produce expressions and deeds of devotion to their leaders. Bilaterally, this devotion is considered as an "input" translating into the senses of esteem, fame, and prestige felt by members of the leadership (Cowen and Sutter 1997). However, it is important to understand that social movement non-leading participants and supporters retain agency. What we mean by this is that followers can exit a movement, and express disapproving voice, in response to perceptions of movement underperformance (Hirschman 1970). Of course, disassociation does not necessarily signal the sum total of followers' displeasure—it may be possible that the followers come to passively disbelieve the "preaching" of the leadership (Gaus 2018a), or subtly undermine the leader's authority, without exiting the movement.

On a related issue, according to Wieser, actions undertaken by the following masses should not be presumed to be a direct replicant of leaders' preferences. Indeed, "masses tend to create a final rule 'far beyond [leaders'] expectations'" (Arena 2010, 119), suggesting social movement operations could be marked by an element of unanticipated consequences (Merton 1936). Potential deviation of follower activities from social movement leadership preferences reinforces the inherently complicated relationality of the leader–follower interaction. In keeping with themes of complication, it should also be understood that social movement leaders are not necessarily self-selecting individuals. As noted by Peter Levine (2016), it is often the case that: "[s]ocial movements identify individuals who have potential to lead. They offer them opportunities to develop leadership skills and expand their reputations. Often, movement members must cajole the prospective leader into playing that role. They then deliberately construct a reputation for their leader, for the consumption of outsiders."

It is possible to perceive leadership through the aegis of contemporary social movement theories. For example, a rational-choice perspective suggests a movement with strong leadership possesses the capacity to attract resources and followers to a greater extent than its competitors (Oberschall 1973; Morris 1984). The SMO serves as a key site for the accumulation of resources, with leaders essential to fulfill the needs of organizational survival and growth. While the organization may be exploited as a platform by leaders to disseminate their messages, and gain societal influence (Kretschmer and Meyer 2007), a leader needs to be sufficiently other-regarding to maintain organizational credibility. They need to provide selective incentives to mobilize participation, as well as make promises not to shirk on their obligations to followers (Chong 1991). In effect, the leader needs to develop a reputation for promoting social movement objectives, whilst accommodating the interests and values of their follower base, in similar fashion to impulses applicable to the political domain (Wittman 1995, 20–22).

Leadership of social movements seems to be more of an art than a science. Ensuring an alignment of leaders' preferences and followers' actions requires a delicate balance, on the part of leaders (and, in some respects, also followers), between: (a) providing necessary direction to social movement activity to concretely achieve objectives and; (b) providing inclusive settings to facilitate information, knowledge, and resources sharing, and to form common expectations to act and engage in certain ways. Of course, there are other matters affecting the quality of leader–follower interaction (and movement success), such as the reactions of counter-movements, political organizations, and other actors external (but entangled with) the movement. These matters will be discussed later.

Returning to an issue already mentioned, certain movements explicitly aim to reduce an emphasis upon leadership. Significance is placed upon the need for participant consensus in the selection of tactics, and other relevant activities. Consensus ideally reflects an effort to take into account, among other things, diversities in belief, opinion, and perspectives, as well as the interest of (minoritarian) movement "sub-communities." Maeckelburgh (2014) and Williams (2017) suggest that decision-making processes in this guise are synonymous with open-ended discussions among a crowd of activists, which may or may not be moderated by a facilitator.

As was noted in the case of the Occupy Wall Street (OWS) anti-capitalist movement—active during the early 2010s, and with various branches aspiring to operationalize anarchist principles—deliberations were typically coupled with "super-majority" voting decision-rules. The motivation for these decision-making techniques was to avoid domination by any given individual, or given sets of individuals, within the network. Motivation is one thing, but there were practical drawbacks. Consistent with public choice precepts surrounding veto rights (Buchanan and Tullock [1962] 1999), decision processes in some branches of the movement tended to be protracted. Many proposals which could garner majority support among participants nonetheless failed to be ratified by the movement, because they did not meet super-majority voting thresholds. These difficulties were seen to occasionally inflame tensions within OWS, and to challenge movement cohesion when addressing key organizational and tactical matters (Kinna et al. 2019).

Entrepreneurship

Finally, we consider the concept of entrepreneurship, and how entrepreneurs facilitate collective action as an aspect of social movement activity. Characterizations of entrepreneurship certainly vary from author to author, but the treatments generally describe individuals who undertake initiatives of a creative or novel character, in often risky, if not uncertain, environments. Entrepreneurship is often viewed as synonymous with leadership, as seemed to be the case with Schumpeter's ([1928] 2003; [1934] 1961) early conceptions as heroic "entrepreneur-as-leader." However, as we shall soon discuss, entrepreneurialism may also serve a broader view of human agency, which then feed into collective action episodes by social movements.

Entrepreneurship is commonly understood economically, but what is significant is that it need not be understood strictly within economic bounds. It is, in fact, an aspect of generalized human conduct present in all societies across time and space. Entrepreneurial prescience is aptly noted in the following statement: "[e]ntrepreneurship is an aspect of all human action. Entrepreneurship is a human universal" (Koppl 2006, 1–2). As also emphasized by Boettke and Coyne (2009), entrepreneurship is now considered to be exercised among numerous domains of activity—such as economic, institutional, political, and social entrepreneurship. David Pozen (2008) identifies the exercise of entrepreneurialism in additional areas (e.g., policy, norms, and moral beliefs) and highlights the implications of this outgrowth of entrepreneurial comprehension from the standpoint of strategic behavior, societal change, and the blurring of organizational–institutional boundaries.

The universality of entrepreneurship is actually encapsulated in later research efforts by Schumpeter. In this vein, Becker and Knudsen (2002, 2003) and Campagnolo and Vivel (2012) detected an intellectual pivot by Schumpeter which, to some extent, "depersonalizes" entrepreneurship. Schumpeter's leadership emphasis was gradually displaced by a generic entrepreneurial function, "which could be achieved by others, even as part of semi-automatic and bureaucratic procedures" (Campagnolo and Vivel 2012, 914). Intriguingly, the suggestion is that Schumpeter undertook this pivot to entrepreneurship theory to account for the expanding role of rationalized, rather than dynamic, procedures in economic life.

We have no reason to doubt this research interpretation concerning Schumpeter's change of position. Our primary purpose, instead, is to reinterpret the nature of entrepreneurial function, in light of contemporary observations about its universalizing character. Our suggestion is that the entrepreneurial function—not being limited to any kind of person in particular—connotes the *radically egalitarian* proposition that, potentially, anybody can act entrepreneurially. Furthermore, anyone can engage with the entrepreneurial function in any conceivable domain of society, or strand of activity therein. Entrepreneurship should be seen as improvised action by people sufficiently mentally alert, and socially adept, to opportunities potentially enhancing their position, and that of others, in typically novel ways (Koppl 2006). This proposition is consistent with "analytical egalitarian" insights (Peart and D. Levy 2005); all human beings possess similar capability to generate novelties, with actual variations borne of history, incentives, and luck.

Extending entrepreneurship to social movement activity means we are able to identify the functions and roles of so-called "movement entrepreneurs" (e.g., King and Soule 2007; Staggenborg 2013). Functionally not dissimilar to leaders, a movement entrepreneur seeks to generate awareness within the population about a certain issue, help create a sense of identity for those aggrieved about the issue raised, and frame narrative and deeper cultural meanings to entice contentious collective actions. Rao and Giorgi (2006) examine how movement entrepreneurs aim for mobilization by creating "insider-outsider" group boundaries, and encourage movement participants to embrace various contentious tactics, including subversion or appropriation. Entrepreneurs developing SMOs, and drawing in material resources, are other possibilities.

The entrepreneurial function not only implies contestability in the selection of entrepreneurs but, profoundly, a capacity to induce structural change within social movement network ecology. To the extent that social movements exhibit features of openness and inclusivity, people with novel, "value-added" ideas and suggestions have every chance to supplant existing forms of organization and practice. Incumbent leaders can be replaced by the up-and-coming and the new, and by potentially anyone with an enhanced ability to "read" the environment of contention. Not only are well-established SMOs incentivized to compete in this environment for certain resources, such as members and supporters (Stern 1999). Entire social movement networks are propelled toward improvement through the constant exercise of entrepreneurship, and the social discoveries created by virtue of continuous, multi-person entanglements.

A salient feature of entrepreneurship from the movement perspective is that entrepreneurial action invariably involves an act of *dissensus*, or resistance and opposition against prevailing economic, political, and social arrangements (Boettke and Coyne 2008). This accords with liberal principles, as suggested by Peter Boettke (2017): "[l]iberalism is in theory and in practice about emancipating individuals from the bonds of oppression. In doing so, it gives individuals the right to say NO." By opposing unsatisfactory institutions and situations, people such as William Lloyd Garrison, Emmeline Pankhurst, Mohandas Gandhi, Martin Luther King Jr., Lech Walesa, and Nelson Mandela extended the effective domain of freedom, even if they, themselves, were not necessarily classical liberals by orientation. Indeed, resistance to coercion and oppression has been pivotal to many of the seismic changes that have enhanced the scope wherein human liberties are exercised.

CONCLUSION

Social movement theorization has been greatly influenced by debates over the opportunities and challenges of engaging in collective action. Public choice theorist Mancur Olson produced an intricate, and surprisingly nuanced, account of the dilemmas faced by social movements when trying to gather support. Campaigning for significant societal change is associated with risk on several fronts—such as earning the opprobrium of one's fellows in "polite society," as well as running afoul of the law. The rationalist posture of Olson brings to sharp relief the issue of individual behavior by those who may be, in principle, attracted to the social movement.

To some extent, the shadow of Mancur Olson still looms over the scholarly pursuit of comprehension about social movement characteristics and activities. Even so, scholarship has moved on to consider how it is that movements come together, let alone sustain themselves in the face of adversities. Some people may be encouraged to participate by the offering, or at least the promise, of materialistic rewards, conditional upon joining and contributing. Other key mechanisms for commitment, *without coercion*, include the promulgation of persuasive solidarity rhetoric by movement entrepreneurs—often necessitating pervasive "framing effects" solidifying emotional attachment, and senses of shared identity, among social movement activists and supporters.

As Elinor Ostrom (2000) powerfully stated, the Olsonian prediction of "zero contributions" toward collective action is observationally refutable. People *do* work to resolve collective action problems, and related social dilemmas, on a regular basis. In addition, social movements are an important prism through which people figure out how to *strive together* for what they believe would be a better world. Social movements practically invite projects which signal commitment, empathy, as well as sympathy, toward causes subjectively perceived in favor of human betterment. From the normative liberal position, emphasizing the desirability of voluntary consent (Aligica et al. 2019), strategies to encourage or incentivize involvement with movements imply that no one be physically or psychologically coerced into implicating themselves with such engagements.

We should stress that the potential ability to rely upon instrumental and non-instrumental responses to counter free riding, and other lapses of commitment in social movement contexts, are not foolproof. Most participants might agree upon goals and objectives at an abstract level, or perhaps consent on the detail, but potential for conflict and contestability cannot be realistically removed from the scene. The perceived mission of a movement could change. So, too, could key personnel within the movement. Additional factors may motivate social movements but, then again, those same additional factors may demotivate movements under different settings. Borrowing turns of phrase from Roger Koppl (2002), efforts to overcome lack of participation may influence some—and they may, indeed, be subjectively perceived as constraining to others—but, in the end, they are neither commands or marching orders.

The institutional and organizational capacities of opponents (such as repressive governments) can also be difficult for a given movement to overcome. Problems for movement cohesion may remain, even if incentives, and efforts, to build shared cultures, emotional feelings, and identities have sufficiently unified a set of movement participants. Oppressive economic, political, and social conditions may quell the most unified movement, and the most motivated participants. As the next chapter will indicate, activists could sincerely disagree about the appropriateness of counter-hegemonic tactics. These factors suggest that social movements remain susceptible to breakdown, even if they have stumbled upon potential resolutions to collective action problems.

Chapter 3

Varieties of Voice and Exit

Social Movement Tactics

INTRODUCTION

Academic and popular accounts describe social movement activities as being directed toward some aspect of societal change. As previously discussed, social movements engage in struggles to amend and reform structures and modes of interaction underpinning human behaviors, interests, practices, and values. The ability of any movement to realize its objectives is contingent upon a host of factors, such as institutional forms, socio-political opportunities, oppositional presence, resource endowments, and so on. An ability by social movement participants to enact societal change also depends upon the effectiveness of their tactics.

In this chapter, we look at the tactical strategies and techniques deployed by social movement organizers, activists, and their supporters. Tactics are deployed for several reasons, including to raise awareness about their causes throughout the community, and to pressure decision-makers to help implement the changes that movement participants prefer. As indicated by Morris (1984) in regard to the American Civil Rights movement, tactical exertion of pressure may present itself through mass participation events, such as boycotts and protests. Complementing this view is Charley Tilley's (1994, 2006) insight that social movements deploy tactics to publicly display, or otherwise signal, the strength of commitment by their proponents.

Applying tactics to fulfill social movement causes are often socially, if not economically and politically, disruptive. The selection of violent versus nonviolent tactical postures is a major source of controversy, and has led to the development of a substantial literature in philosophy and ethics. Many social movements strive to engage others in an exclusively nonviolent or violent manner, but it is also the case that movements may choose to alternate between violence and nonviolence. To complicate matters, different participants within a movement may tactically apply violence and nonviolence at much the same time, and only occasionally toward different targets. It is sometimes true that the eruption of violence is an unanticipated consequence of encounters between movements and their opponents, and even between competing social movements. The application of tactics in a nonviolent or violent manner has significant implications for the long-term effectiveness of social movement activity, and is a key point for discussion in this chapter.

This chapter, focused upon tactical strategies and choices by social movements, is structured in the following manner. In the next section we will describe tactical strategies adopted by social movements, and consider some factors influencing choice of tactic. We then discuss the selection of nonviolent or violent tactics by movement participants. This discussion includes an assessment of the relative effectiveness of violence in inducing socio-political changes, as well as its ethical implications. A brief set of remarks will conclude this chapter.

SOCIAL MOVEMENT TACTICS: AN OVERVIEW

Tactical Typologies

The study of social movements has laid, as its foundation, a premise that they exist to challenge and contest habits, institutions, practices, structures, and values within society, which are seen as unsatisfactory or, otherwise, deeply inadequate. In other words, the desire to effect societal change, and taking the option of using dramatic means to fulfill that desire, is seen to be at the heart of contemporary social movement theorizing. It follows that an appreciation of the tactical maneuvers, and the underlying strategic basis for the tactics employed, is crucial to understanding social movement activity.

As mentioned earlier in this book, conceptual understanding of social movement involvement in collective action has changed over the decades. As explained by Soule and Roggeband (2018, 236–237), "recent scholarship has worried less about the contagion of maladaptive impulses and aggression among individuals, and instead examines the diffusion of innovative tactics, frames, and organizing structures between social movements, and articulates the mechanisms by which this happens." Modern scholarship generally illustrates that for movements to contend effectively there needs to be semblance of organization, or at least some strategic forethought, on the part of key social movement participants.

Even if social movements embody elements of tactical planning, at least in some respects, they are still largely considered as unconventional or "nonroutinized ways of affecting political, social, and cultural processes" (della Porta and Diani 2020, 164). Social movements are said to regularly apply novel, if not conspicuous, tactical ploys to draw attention to the need for societal change, to gain additional participants, funds, and other resources, and, ultimately, to solicit political and other actors to agree to proposed changes. The dramatization of movement tactics does not suggest that social movements, or their allies, avoid conventional means of political expression—say, through letter-writing, petitioning legislators and bureaucrats, or tendering submissions to official inquiries. Nonetheless, social movement participants are known for using financial resources, as well as symbols, identities, practices, discourses, and even their bodies, for a wide array of tactical purposes (ibid.).

What kinds of tactics do social movements utilize? It is not possible to provide an all-inclusive account of social movement tactics and, in any case, tactics are perennially the subject of refinement. In his seminal works on nonviolence, Gene Sharp (1973, 2010) catalogued close to 200 methods of tactical action undertaken by social movements, and other groups. This point, alone, illustrates the sheer number of tactical options available to those involved in movements. Specific tactics were categorized as sitting within spectral categories of "protest and persuasion" (symbolically peaceful opposition to, or attempted persuasion with, movement target groups), "non-cooperation" (suspension of cooperation with, or assistance to, targets) and "intervention" (intentional disruption against targets). To be clear, and as Sharp himself caveated, these are loosely and nonrigidly depicted categories.

Sharp's tripartite distinction between broad tactical categories may be further reduced to create a binary distinction. Doug McAdam et al. (2001) classified specific tactics as examples of either "constrained contention," which are routine and widely known to others (in addition to movement participants themselves), or "transgressive contention," tending to be novel and previously little-known, or unknown, to others. In his discussion about activist influence upon African American studies in university curriculum offerings, Rojas (2006) points to tactics being recognized as either "disruptive" or "non-disruptive" by nature. Examples of movement tactics of a disruptive nature include riots, sit-ins, vandalism, and violence, which aim (or at least have the effect) to disrupt the routines of targeted individuals and groups. Nondisruptive tactics include peaceful demonstrations, marches, rallies, and forms of publicity. The purpose, or effect, of tactics of a non-disruptive caliber is to attract public attention toward certain issues and problems, in the hope that those targeted will provide concessions facilitating their resolution.

Other scholars conceive social movement tactics as belonging to either end of a "moderate" ("consensual") or "radical" ("conflict") spectrum. The moderate–radical tactical distinction appears largely synonymous with the disruptive versus nondisruptive classification outlined in the previous paragraph, although the use of moderate and radical terminology is associated with literature concerning so-called "radical flank effects." Formally attributed to the work of Haines (1984, 1988), the radical flank effect alludes to the manner in which tactical radicalism by certain elements, or factions, of a social movement amplifies support for moderate elements of the same movement. It is considered that radical tactical ploys, especially of a violent nature, could, similarly, generate backlash from political authorities and members of the general public, consequently reducing overall support for the movement.

Many tactics employed by social movements have the dual purpose of signaling to others a certain discontent with the *status quo*, together with the desire for change. Accordingly, and as recognized by Albert Hirschman (1970), movement tactics also belong to the broader category of the "voice" corrective mechanism. We recognize "exit" mechanisms as yet another method of expressing dissatisfaction with existing political arrangements, as well as revealing deep-seated unease with societal and economic habits, institutions, and practices. In later work, Hirschman (1993) identified the many years of East German emigration to the West—a phenomenon reflecting disaffection with living under a communist regime—as a contributing factor behind the 1980s pro-democracy protests, and the momentous fall of the Berlin Wall. Other examples of jurisdictional exit, used as a tactical method undermining oppressive legal systems and policies, are identifiable. For example, American nineteenth-century abolitionists, their sympathizers, and even slaves themselves, helped establish an "Underground Railroad" of secretive routes, shelters, and social networks to enable people to escape enslavement (Gara 1961; Presley 2016).

The relevance of the exit tactic extends beyond the complementarity between political emigration, on the one hand, and the reactive accumulation of "within-border" grievances by those left behind, on the other. Social movements can, sometimes, find their expression in a desire to present variations in lifestyle choice vis-à-vis the "conformist" world-at-large. These arrangements, representing an "internal secession" from conventional socio-political affairs of sorts (Buchanan and Faith 1987; MacDonald 2019), are commonly referred to as "communes." For example, certain feminist and lesbian separatist movements of the late-twentieth century established their own communes (e.g., Valentine 1997). Researchers suggest that the creation of communes effectively integrate a *critique of society* (Wallmeier 2017) with a potential model for *reconstructing society* (Price et al. 2008).

Academic attention has also been directed to the manner in which communes attempt to sustain involvement on the part of their members. For example, Iannaccone (1992) refers to the partaking of rituals, acts of self-sacrifice, and other unconventional behavioral standards by commune members, all of which effectively raise the costs of their involvement with noncommunal activities. However, it remains an open question as to whether such techniques to galvanize commitment are effective. Indeed, a number of scholars have insisted that communes are, by and large, susceptible to failure (e.g., Shey 1977; Clay 2017). Issues such as intra-group diversity and organizational scale diseconomies are often seen as contributing to commune non-robustness. The ability of other, and potentially rival, groups, such as social movements, to achieve preferred outcomes through more conventional means—for example, actual legislative and cultural gains—may be another determining factor behind the lack of widespread traction for commune developments.

The point of this discussion is not to provide an exhaustive appraisal of tactical classifications, but to highlight the impressive range of tactical possibilities available to, and exploited by, social movements. The diversity of tactics at the disposal of social movements also implies the existence of tactical innovation (McAdam 1983; Polletta 2002; Isaac 2019). A good contemporary example of movement tactical innovation is the development of online activism in social media platforms, and on the Internet generally. Indeed, the inherent fluidity of social movements, not to mention their contribution toward societal change, rests in their preparedness to engage with such innovation, rather than necessarily lean on tactics that worked previously under different conditions.

In raising the possibility of social movement tactical innovation, we foreground the micro- and meso-social aspects of experimentation, improvisation, artisanship, and even playfulness (Markey-Towler 2019b), in the realm of socio-political contention. This perspective recognizes not every tactic pursued by a movement will be considered as effective in realizing societal change, no matter how much collaboration and planning was performed, *ex-ante*. Tactical innovations are certainly not created equal—for example, Galli (2016) examines the perceived failings of "glitter bombing" tactics by LGBT and other movements. Other tactics, still, will be viewed as innovative, if not effective, within their institutional contexts. Consider, for example, the use of humor by the Serbian *Otpor!* ("Resistance!") movement to denigrate, mock, and undermine the political authority of the autocratic Slobodan Milošević (Popovic and Miller 2015). The critical point here is that trial-and-error learnings about tactical effectiveness provide opportunities for social movement organizers and participants—and, for that matter, the remainder of society—to accumulate valuable knowledge about what tactics succeed under which conditions.

Influences upon Tactical Choice

Social movement researchers have also attempted to establish the determinants of tactical selection. This literature has grown significantly over the past three decades, partly due to scholarship theoretically situating specific tactical maneuvers within a broader set of collective strategies, the latter referred to as "repertoires of contention" (Tilly 1978, 1994, 2006). The availability of an expanding array of tactical moves within a repertoire are, according to Tilly, shaped by institutional developments in economic, political, and social contexts, all of which unfold over historical time.

Consider, for the time being, the political dimension of movement tactical choices. A central idea is that tactical choices are affected by "windows of political opportunity" in which a movement's interests may be advanced. Tilly (1978) advanced a general macro-historical scheme of political opportunity informed by interrelated factors, such as shifts in power configurations, the costs imposed upon collective action arising from repression, and adjustments in perceived opportunities and threats regarding political vulnerability to social movement claims. Some key considerations in accordance with this approach include:

- *Repression or toleration of political challenges*: Social movements typically express the need for societal change, which could threaten disturbance to political offices. Autocratic political systems, which limit electoral contests, speech expressions, as well as public protest and other contentious public displays of disaffection and grievances, tend to be associated with limited opportunities for social movement influence. Democratic systems grounded in free speech, and freedom of association and of assembly (including the right to protest in public spaces), seem far more likely to provide generous opportunities for social movements to advance their causes. Within any given political system there may be practical variations in policy and legal enforcement stringency across areas of government, providing niche opportunities for social movement activity.
- *Openness or closure of access to political elites*: The effectiveness of social movement collective actions will also be affected by the extent to which political actors become receptive to concerns expressed by nonpolitical actors. Relatively open political networks—evidenced by the likes of multiple political parties, regular electoral contests, changeability of political leadership, policy consultation opportunities, and public access to legislative sittings and procedures—are more likely to equip social movements with opportunities to influence the political agenda. The existence of a closed political network is presumed, in contrast, to have the effect of constraining social movement political opportunities.
- *Extent of political elite factionalism*: The number of political parties, the existence and strength of alliances between the parties, and the degree of intra-party differences (on policy, ideological, or even personality grounds)

may shape opportunities for social movements to undertake collective action. A higher degree of factionalism among political actors may also influence the way in which movement participants articulate their problems and concerns.

• *Degree of political centralization or decentralization*: A greater degree of public-sector centralization, at a given level of government, is likely to reduce the opportunity for a diverse array of groups (such as social movements) to have their concerns registered politically. Greater decentralization of governmental organization appears likely, all else being equal, to present greater opportunities for movement activism and engagement. The existence of multiple levels of government—say, within a federation or confederation—is more likely to increase the receptivity of the political system to social movement demands.

Drawing upon this approach, it becomes evident that democratizing political tendencies are likely to open up the set of available tactical choices—insofar as movements, and other collectives, can organize as well as express opposition to disagreeable arrangements, and can push for desired transformations. The connection between democratization and expanding movement tactical repertoires not only results from limitations upon repressive governmental impulses, as mentioned earlier, but becomes apparent as political actors increasingly seek to engage activists for democratic electoral advantage (Tilly and Tarrow 2006). Democratization may induce additional changes—for example, movement participants may become incentivized to establish SMOs with professional practices and standards to manage political, and related, relationships in a systematic fashion.

The emergence of formal political organizations, practices, and institutions are not only implicated in the development of the modern, democratic, and secular, nation-state. Speculatively, it might be possible to identify Adolph Wagner's (1890) "law of increasing state activity" as resting upon the political fulfillment of democratic demands for additional public goods, as articulated by individuals, as well as by social movements and other groups. Urbanization, listed as a key influence underpinning "Wagner's Law," has itself been associated with a tendency for movement participants to reorient their campaigns from "petty" localist toward "big-picture" national concerns. The concentration of people in urban spaces also allows movements to organize mass-participatory tactics, such as protest marches and strikes, in strategic locations such as capital cities (Buechler 2011; Tilly and Wood 2013).

Another conditioning factor shaping the available set of movement tactics is technology (V. Taylor and Van Dyke 2008). Although the participatory potentials of digital technology may appear to destabilize social movement disciplines (Tufecki 2017), these developments are also suggested to have extended the range of tactics movement participants can draw upon.

According to Cisař (2015, 60), "[a]s a result of the recent digital media revolution, political participation now includes novel repertoires, including episodic flash mobs, personalized connective action, clicktivism, and trolling." A specific example is the use of mobile phone applications by asylum seeker and refugee social movements in southern Europe. Mobile phone apps, such as *Alarm Phone* and *WatchTheMed*, are being used to track the safe transit of migrants across the Mediterranean Sea (Stierl 2016; Heller and Pezzani 2019). In this instance, we see not only the use of technology in challenging restrictive formal border and immigration policies. Refugee movement campaigners use technology as a form of "reverse," or "humanitarian," counter-surveillance of state actors (Topak 2019), if not a "disobedient gaze" to pressurize the state to ease barriers to freedom of movement (Heller et al. 2017).

The repertoires of contention framework dictate that the tactics available to social movements are shaped by path-dependent experiences, such as those arising from political and other opportunities. It is also apparent that, once familiarization with social movement tactics takes hold within society, it is possible for a given tactical ploy to be emulated by others. In other words, "tactical modularity" becomes a reality in that different groups and causes copy movement tactics. There appears a relatively high degree of consensus within social movement research literature that the tactical successes of the American Civil Rights movement inspired subsequent anti-war, environmental, feminist, and other movements, in turn reflecting a form of learning concerning the prosecution of contention within modern societies.

The efficacy of social movement tactics are influenced by the degree of commitment demonstrated by individual participants toward implementing and maintaining their chosen tactic. Recall the discussion in the previous chapter about the desire of movements to galvanize shared senses of solidarity against potentially disunited, even weak, adversaries (Opp 2009; Walsh-Russo 2014). Consider movement rituals such as publicly reciting oaths and undertaking pledges, and singing songs together, which are performed at protests, and other tactical events, to energize feelings of group encompassment (D. Klein et al. 2015) and accompaniment (Lynd 2013). These binding efforts are related to strategic imperatives to recruit new participants (including those with potentially valuable resources) into movement activities. Recruitment may involve a certain degree of encouragement, or perhaps cajoling, of others to participate, as part of the broader project to publicly reveal non-complicity with the objectives, practices, and strategies of oppressive institutions and regimes.

The propositions expressed here relate to scholarship outlining the importance of publicly displaying and projecting senses of *worthiness*, *unity*, *numbers*, and *commitment*. This is what Charles Tilly abbreviates as "WUNC"

(Tilly and Tarrow 2006; Tilly and Wood 2013). Whatever the purpose, affirming the WUNCness of a social movement *qua* collective in a credible manner is no small feat. Individuals may elect to deviate from performing the tactic (including through free riding), and they even choose to splinter away from the main social movement by engaging in alternative tactical choices (M. Gurri 2018; N. Snow 2020). Indeed, the history of social movement activity is replete with instances of participants rejecting moderate, or peaceful, tactics and breaking away from moderate movement factions to undertake disruptive actions, such as street rioting. These considerations are aside from any prevailing disincentives to participate, due to credible threats from, or the implementation of effective counter-tactics by, opponents.

Considerations of Time and Space

We referred briefly in the previous chapter to time as one of many potential resources available to social movements, necessary to facilitate within-movement interaction and effective planning for future collective engagement. Time is a critical factor in determining the most appropriate moment to mobilize against governments, corporations, and other targeted groups of actors. The length of tactical duration may help underpin the credible signaling of WUNCness. Consistent with factors such as degree of political responsiveness, and broader institutional openness, lengthier tactical application by a social movement may be pivotal to gaining concessions over reform matters (Francisco 2010).

In addition to a movement's extra-institutional activities unfolding in time, they are also conducted over space (Nicholls 2007; Fine 2010; Francisco 2010). For example, protest actions conventionally take place within a geographical area enabling large numbers of people to congregate, and express their voice. The spatial configurations within which any given tactic proceeds can influence crowd numbers, as well as have significant implications for the ability of law enforcement to control and limit participant numbers.

Spatial considerations are of greater consequence for social movements than is generally recognized. Indeed, the creative, if not entrepreneurial, ability of activists to exploit their geo-spatial environments is crucial to the sustainability, indeed the success, of their campaigns for societal change. This is not only apparent with respect to the selection of political jurisdiction to best fulfill their objectives (Tarrow 2012), or to the challenges and opportunities that different geographical scales present to social movement operations (Nicholls 2007). Drawing upon Ikeda's (2012) conceptualization of an "action space"—wherein economic entrepreneurs profitably advantage from their geo-spatial environment when creating value-added products for consumers—we contend it is possible to explore the implications of space for *social movement* tactical efficacy and innovation. In this respect, we provide additional meaning to Hayek's (1945, 521; emphasis added) appreciation of action undertaken by people endowed with "knowledge of the particular circumstances of time *and place*."

A reasonable hypothesis is that choice of location to solicit a protest, or some other tactic, would be made to amplify the benefits, and minimize the costs, of mass participation. One consideration is to find a location familiar to members of the general public for the purposes of publicly displaying strength of numbers for the movement (and to minimize the search costs for potential attendees in finding the protest site). Importantly, a location should be reasonably accessible to media reporters, and crews, to publicize the protest, though it is conceivable that accessible public spaces are also available to the movement's opponents. For example, a protest venue may presumably be located close to a public transport hub for easy, cost-effective access and, preferably, is also readily accessible by private transport on a similar basis.

Symbolism also matters when selecting locations for social movement activity. Movements focused upon expressive collectivist concerns, or those whose goals are highly attuned to political reform, are likely to select public sites which resonate with symbolic political authority. These sites might be, say, landmarks replete with flags and statutes, or official buildings such as legislatures and government agency headquarters (Huemer 2012). However, decisions to undertake tactics in close proximity to politically significant sites would need to take into account the potential for governmental repression. The modern state has acquired for itself, using Weberian logic, a status as monopolistic applicant of force over geographic space within its relevant jurisdiction. Governments have a habit of using law-enforcement personnel to quell publicly displayed movement tactics in the name of public order and stability, and it also applies its cadastral intelligence, and ever-growing surveillance capabilities, to frustrate social movement tactical campaigns.

At first glance it would seem that social movements would prefer to publicly conduct tactics in prominent, yet open and accessible, public spaces within major population centers. In doing so opportunities for protestors to interact and network, providing not only the means to unify, but to discover new alliances and access contentious repertoires, are likely to become apparent. To conduct a protest in relatively confined or concealed spaces, such as alleyways, may achieve other purposes, such as frustrating detection by authorities or minimizing disruptive counter-protests. However, such an alternative might prove infeasible if the objective is to spatially engage in large-scale WUNC displays. As mentioned, governmental authorities may also prefer protests to be conducted within the archetypal urban square, facilitating identification of social movement organizers, activists, and supporters. Although the right to protest is putatively held as a human right, in practice most countries require permits and similar official permissions to conduct protests. There is ample anecdotal evidence, however, that regulatory restrictions on peaceful assembly have been tightening around the world, leading to an effective criminalization of protest (e.g., INCLO 2013; Freedom House 2015).

Flexibility in locational choice presented to social movement activists can yield some surprising developments. Hong Kong has one of the heaviest population densities in the world. The 2019–2020 mass protests in this jurisdiction, waged against proposed extradition arrangements to mainland China, were initially concentrated outside the territory's Legislative Council building in the Central district, Hong Kong Island. With the desire to minimize punitive resistance from law-enforcement officers, the protestors developed a "Be Like Water" tactical innovation. Based on a movie quote from famed actor and martial artist Bruce Lee, the strategy dictated that protest participants disperse quickly in response to police harassment, and reappear at a different protest site, in the Hong Kong area (Purbrick 2019; Ting 2020). This strategy has been noted in social movement scholarship, and by activists struggling to advance other causes worldwide, for its innovativeness.

The key point we wish to make here is that the selection of sites for tactical usage is one of many decisions made by social movement participants. Such decisions are made under conditions of uncertainty, often arising from anticipated opposition by counter-movement forces and by repressive governmental authorities, yet they invariably entail improvisational choices and the exercise of human creativity. In other words, locational choices in the deployment of tactics represent movement entrepreneurship within "Ikedian action space." Spatial selection for movement activities has significant long-term implications with respect to their sustainability, especially if congregation in readily accessible spaces brings creative and influential network participants together.

NONVIOLENT AND VIOLENT TACTICAL DISPOSITIONS

An ongoing source of controversy attached to social movements is their choice between the nonviolent and violent application of tactics. As we shall note shortly, the subjective qualities attached to both nonviolence and violence—either on the part of parties exerting such application, and by those experiencing them—can frustrate definitional simplicity. At the risk of over-simplification, nonviolence represents the disavowal by social movement organizers, activists, and their supporters to apply force against other people, in the pursuit of their objectives. Violence, in contrast, involves force, which may cause injury or the killing of people, or the sabotage or destruction of property. The domain in which nonviolence or violence is exercised by social movement participants may be broad-ranging, and may include physical, psychological, and symbolic actions (Bosi and Malthaner 2015).

Irrespective of how a social movement pursues their tactics, the intent of such actions is likely to be similar. Nonviolent and violent tactical applications invariably aim at persuading their targets to (willingly, or otherwise) agree to societal change, or encouraging the target groups to interact with movement participants in a manner that is preferred by the movement. The type of tactic selected, and the intensity or severity with which the tactic is applied, could have broader implications for the social movement's success. Game-theoretic perspectives aptly illustrate that movement success is likely to be conditioned by expected responses to nonviolence or violence. The nature of those responses, alone, may weigh heavily upon public opinion about the appropriateness and credibility of the movement itself (Pierskalla 2010; Stockemer 2012). Nonviolence or violence may enable a social movement fulfill their objectives, depending upon the circumstances, but a successful outcome is far from guaranteed in every given tactical instance. A moderate, nonviolent movement may be ignored by public authorities, counter-movements, and by members of the general public, whereas radical, violent movements may risk backlash and repression from societal counter-parties.

Practically speaking, it is a misnomer to believe that nonviolence and violence are strictly separable or cleanly delineated choices rendered by social movements. The history of many social movements is complicated, if not vexed, by the mixture of nonviolent and violent tactical application by different participants. This intermingling of nonviolence and violence may be conducted at roughly the same time—and with or without the approval of social movement organizers and key figureheads. Alternatively, a movement may toggle between nonviolence and violence over time in response to changing circumstances, and as a reflection of tactical choice.

It is often difficult for movements, or, perhaps more accurately, key players within movement networks, to control violent outbreaks. The informality of movement activity, perhaps typified by the lack of organizational discipline, potentially limits the degree to which nonviolence is maintained by all those involved. Indeed, movement narratives are colored by images of renegades and dissidents on the fringes of social movement networks who chose violent strategies against targets. Such narratives may refer to persons who act violently in the name of the "true meaning" of a movement's cause, albeit without the endorsement of the leadership or core participant elements. Even movement leaders, or key activist figures, may toggle between nonviolence and violence in their approach to the hegemonic purveyors of power, running the risk of disapprobation by peers and opponents alike. Finally, we observe that opponents often seek to frame the tactics of a social movement in a poor light—for example, by construing nonviolent acts as violent, even if such descriptions are debatable or misleading.

Nonviolent Tactical Measures

Normative ideas tied to nonviolence in dealing with others, such as pacifism, are ancient themes embedded in commercial, diplomatic, religious, and other customs throughout the world. Liberals have consistently proffered arguments in favor of domestic peace, as well as peaceful international relations. Avoidance of destructive conflict between individuals, groups, and even nation-states, are said to contribute to immense material and nonmaterial gains, due to the realization of economic, political, and social cooperation and exchange (Passy [1909] 1972; Buchanan [1975] 2000). Through a social movement lens, however, the position of nonviolence does not usually prescribe an avoidance of resistance against oppressive forces and structures. Indeed, in contemporary thought nonviolence is often equated with a concerted, deliberate kind of resistance to authority known as "civil disobedience" (but, to complicate this story, some movements may promulgate violence, and try to label it as an act in the name of civil disobedience).

There are many figures populating the genealogy of civil disobedience, including David Henry Thoreau and Gene Sharp. In his tract "Resistance to Civil Government," Thoreau ([1849] 2014) laid the case for resisting what individuals conscientiously perceived as unjust laws and regulations, even if disobedience risks the pains of financial penalties and even imprisonment, together with a loss of esteem in the eyes of other community members. An abolitionist, tax resistor, and opponent of war, Thoreau gave practical guidance to anti-statist civil disobedience which inspire to this day. Gene Sharp, a figure whose name was invoked earlier in this chapter, devoted his intellectual career to comprehending the features and effects of civil disobedience. These efforts earned him the respectful titles as the "Machiavelli of nonviolence" or the "Clausewitz of nonviolent warfare" (Ammons and Coyne 2018). Indicating that nonviolent tactics may substitute for the weapons of violence, Sharp also said that successful application of nonviolence requires "purposive coordination, training, and knowledge of the weapons of resistance" (Ammons and Coyne 2020, 35).

Sharp and, perhaps to a lesser extent, Thoreau, understood the sociopsychological basis of adherence to political authority. This understanding traces back to Etienne de la Boetie's sixteenth-century insight that a state of political domination is, ultimately, contingent upon the tacit consent (even if begrudgingly so) by subjects. From this standpoint, civil disobedience signals the withdrawal of such consent and, by implication, reveals a growing sense of public displeasure and unease toward state depredations. Nonetheless, Sharp (1980, 181–182) understood that "[t]he basic problem of all radical politics is *how* to act with political relevance to improve the social, economic, and political life of the people." The challenge for social movements assuming nonviolent tactical postures, therefore, is to (a) to convince others of the need for change, (b) counteract the political and nonpolitical powers of those seeking to maintain the *status quo* situation, and (c) to implement the desired change (Sciabarra 2000, 310).

Nonviolent tactics have been advanced in a number of celebrated cases during the twentieth century. The example of Indian lawyer and politician Mohandas K. Gandhi appears particularly instructive. India was controlled by British interests from the 1850s until Indian independence in 1947, a period exemplified by economic hardships and political subjections under the British Raj (Sen 1981; Tharoor 2017). The legitimacy of this British rule was gradually undermined by persistent nonviolent civil disobedience campaigns, conducted by supporters inspired by Gandhi's practices and teachings.

Gandhi took great care to encourage mobilization by developing campaigns of nonviolent resistance. These campaigns were, in turn, based upon principles of moral truth-seeking and justice, as well as stoicism and self-discipline in the face of hegemonic counter-resistance. These principles were labeled *Satyagraha*. In effect, Gandhi sought to promote a nonviolence virtue ethic which intersected the strategic objective of developing a supporter base, the latter working to build economic, political, and social pressure upon the British colonizers and their supporters (Carter 2010). More fundamentally, some consider that Gandhi opted for nonviolence as a robust political strategy in a world wherein both individuals deeply disagree about political *ends*, and where behavioral asymmetries exist (Mantena 2012; Pe. Levine 2018).

Nonviolent tactical waves were deployed from the First World War until Indian independence by Gandhi and his supporters. This included economic boycotts, nonpayment of agricultural and other taxes, calls for disengagement with colonial public administration and regulatory procedures, hunger strikes, protests, vigils, efforts of international outreach, and other techniques to air grievances against perceived injustices imposed by the colonists. The selection of tactics was improvisational, if not experimental, in some respects, and some setbacks occurred as supporters and opponents (including law-enforcement personnel) responded violently. Nonetheless, there appears widespread agreement that Gandhi's nonviolent tactical dispositions, with a conscientiously noncooperative face, contributed to the eventual abandonment of British colonization of India.

Tactical dispositions tend to diffuse to other movements, whether locally, nationally, or globally, through combinations of inspiration and example. The venerated American Civil Rights campaigner Martin Luther King (1929–1968) cited the influence of Gandhi's philosophies upon the development of his own civil disobedience approaches (M. L. King 1960). Combining the Gandhian approach with inspiring rhetoric drawn from Christian theology (Selby 2008), King played a key role in building nonviolent resistance by African Americans, and their allies, against several focal points of racial inequality. These included the maladies of racial segregation—including obstructed access to private and public goods under the Southern "Jim Crow" laws—as well as a lack of voting rights, and general discrimination on the basis of race. Some of the adaptive tactics used by those involved in the Civil Rights movement included protests and marches, boycotts of racially segregated services, and "sit-ins" at lunch counters, and similar food-service providers, dividing customers along racial lines (Isaac 2019). As noted by Jim Powell (2000) the tactical repertoire deployed by activists was diverse but, nonetheless, was aimed toward a common objective of disrupting racialized economic and social systems, and to expose underlying racial injustices.

The strain of nonviolent civil disobedience persists among many social movements into the early decades of the twenty-first century, including in so-called "techno-libertarian" circles. Essentially, techno-libertarianism refers to the use of digital technologies and innovation to realize libertarian commitments, such as free markets and limited (or no) government interference. In this spirit, some liberals have suggested the Internet, and similar digital technologies, empower individuals and groups to withdraw from offline environments increasingly subject to governmental control and influence. The founder of the British Institute of Economic Affairs think-tank, Arthur Seldon, for instance, described the Internet, among a range of facilities and methods (including electronic money), as a potential mechanism to escape perceived over-government (Seldon 1998).

A notable recent addition to the techno-libertarian literature is presented by Adam Thierer. Specifically, we refer to his discussions about "evasive entrepreneurship" in response to overly restrictive public policies. The basic hypothesis is that evasive entrepreneurship—a form of entrepreneurship confounding prevailing legal or social norms—can be facilitated by technological developments that enable individuals to avoid (or otherwise work around) irritating, outmoded, or restrictive governmental regulations and rules. Thierer couches these acts within the broader tradition of civil disobedience, "best viewed as useful correctives when laws and the regulatory system become untethered from new realities and begin to lose their sense of legitimacy with the public" (Thierer 2020, 114).

The use of the likes of 3D printers, blockchains, drones, and sharing economy digital platforms may be regarded as mechanisms for "technological civil disobedience." Engaging with such technologies, in a "micro-rebellious" fashion, "can act as checks and balances that encourage a realignment of laws and regulations that have failed to keep pace with the times or have grown burdensome, unwieldy, inefficient, or even unjust" (ibid., 115). As will also be discussed later, certain technologies (such as smartphone devices) have already been used to directly mobilize protest crowds and relatedly contentious forms of connective action (Bennett and Segerberg 2013). The technological potential to constrain public-sector predation is not restricted to conscious acts of anti-statist resistance. Using technologies to pursue conveniences and efficiencies—including in the guise of "user innovation," as raised by von Hippel (1986, 2005)—may have a disciplinary effect upon authority, similar to that of explicitly technological civil disobedience.

Violent Tactical Measures

A controversial aspect of social movements is their capability of using violence to advance their strategic objectives and goals. As described by Bosi and Malthaner (2015, 439), violence "is used by actors across the political spectrum and includes actions such as attacks on property, bodily assaults, the planting of explosive devices, shooting attacks, kidnappings, hostage taking and the seizure of aircraft or ships, high profile assassinations, public self-immolation," and so on. For collective behavior theorists of the early to mid-twentieth century, violence was seen as rooted in the psychological aberrance of frustrated individuals and, similarly, groups who are agitated into a state of frenzy against their societal targets. In not-dissimilar fashion, Gamson (1989) refers to the exuberant unruliness of some individuals, whose actions magnify the risk of violence in the name of certain causes.

Recent scholarly contributions have emphasized the processual nature of violence, and how violence is the product of relationships embodying ever-escalating tensions over claims (Bosi et al. 2014; Bosi and Malthaner 2015). The deployment of violent tactics is seen to be part of, and resulting from, temporal sequences of events, and causal dynamics between a social movement and its target(s), which evolve in often unexpected ways. The possibility for violence might escalate if there is seen to be no feasible way for rivals to engage constructively, and in order to defuse inter-group tensions. This interpretation of political violence broadly appears in line with Nona Martin and Virgil Storr's (2008) assessment that certain episodes of social violence are, effectively, "perverse emergent orders," arising regardless of the wishes of key authority figures or social movement organizers.

The application of social movement violence is commonly associated with revolutions that swept Europe and North America, and other parts of the globe, over the past few centuries. In general terms, a revolution refers to discrete, often temporally compacted, events in which political and social orders are transformed by their replacement by new arrangements. Greenfield (2018) explains that revolutions often entail physical violence and property damage against a targeted regime that becomes increasingly viewed as illegitimate. Some of this violence, though not all of it in every revolutionary instance, is carried out by participants and supporters of so-called "revolutionary movements," being highly politically engaged movements with an explicit objective of overthrowing an oppressive government (Goodwin and R. Rojas 2015).

One of the more pivotal events in modern history was the French Revolution during the late eighteenth century. This period of upheaval—which saw a transition from absolute monarchy to periods of instability and, then, through to Napoleon's dictatorship—set the stage for one of the famous debates in the history of liberalism itself, between Mary Wollstonecraft and Edmund Burke (Burke [1790] 2006; D. O'Neill 2007; Wollstonecraft [1790] 1996). Wollstonecraft, who spent a short period of time in France during the Revolutionary period, expressed revulsion toward Jacobian violence but, ultimately, viewed the French Revolution as an example of civilizational progress, wherein genuinely won political liberties were gained. In his defense of political tradition Burke criticized Wollstonecraft, and the revolutionary period as a whole. He saw the French Revolution as a period in which "metaphysical" notions of freedom would unleash irrationally exuberant bouts of violent and antisocial behavior, consequently undermining the basis for socio-political cooperation.

Preceding the French Revolution was the American Revolution. This episode stretched from 1765 to 1783, and included armed conflict between secessionist American colonies and Great Britain. Many thousands of people were killed, whether in direct combat or as the result of contagious diseases, and other factors. Whereas this episode will be discussed in detail later, historian George H. Smith (2013) reminds us of the historical and ideational contexts in which the practice of political revolution was justified. In essence, seventeenth- and eighteenth-century political philosophy was immersed with ideas that revolutions are justified if, and only if, political authorities flagrantly abridged individuals' natural rights to life, liberty, and property in a persistent fashion.

Where the dividing line is between legitimate and illegitimate actions to overthrow government is shrouded in subjectivity. As William Gamson (1975) would note, in a social movement theoretical setting, people may be prone to assume violent tactical dispositions if they believe nonviolent means of realizing change are either exhausted, or do not exist. However, it may be the case that revolutionaries may not necessarily reflect the wishes of their fellow citizens. Movement activism to fundamentally, and quickly, transform the sociopolitical environment could be met with backlash, and other kinds of turmoil. Another relevant consideration is that the costs of organizing a political revolution are nontrivial: "Revolutions against a well-organized government require a strong military organization in addition to convincing arguments, pamphlets, speeches, mass meetings, and petitions. The cost of organizing revolutionary movements also tends to be far greater in both the planning and execution stage, because revolutionary campaigns are likely to attract aggressive opposition from the existing government" (Congleton 2011, 155).

Suggestions to the effect there exists a radicalizing, "revolutionary edge" to liberal theorization resembles normative defenses of robust, albeit violent, responses in self-defense against oppressive actors and authorities. These perspectives appear within anti-statist libertarian thinking and, similarly, in the form of anarchist theorems (e.g., Chartier and Van Schoelandt 2021). Jason Brennan (2019) advances moral justifications for self-defensive actions—even those taking the form of lying, cheating, stealing, sabotaging, destroying, attacking, and killing—against political agents. Brennan's refusal to exempt political agents from self-defensive uses of force reflects an underlying value of refusing to dutifully obey governmental authorities. Other, presumably nonliberal, voices have offered similar contributions. An example is the work of Candice Delmas (2018), which attempts a philosophical delineation between just and unjust manifestations of civil disobedience (cf. Moraro 2019). The Delmasian view is that our set of basic political obligations should extend to resistance, dissent, and revolution, in response to the many injustices affecting human relationships.

Additional academic contributions situate violence, or at least the potential for violence, within a broader context of resistance against oppressive forces within society. Coyne and Goodman (2020a) describe the possibility of social movements, and other non-state groups, providing polycentrically oriented defensive services against various aggressors. With respect to anti-racism campaigning in America, it has been noted that the esteemed rhetorician of nonviolence, Martin Luther King, acknowledged the legitimacy of armed self-defense (Cobb 2014; Osterweil 2020). Others have interpreted violent reprisals by Civil Rights movement participants as being the result of an unwillingness by certain racist actors to concede ground (Russell 2010).

We need to be clear that not all revolutionary episodes necessitate large-scale violence and bloodshed. During the late 1980s and early 1990s many Eastern European communist regimes were overthrown by largely *peaceful* revolutionary episodes, involving masses of demonstrators from varied walks of life. The Czechoslovakian "Velvet Revolution" of November–December 1989 was exemplified by mass demonstrations in Prague, Bratislava, and other major centers, but which led to the peaceful transition from a communist to democratic political regime. This event cannot be properly understood without a historical appreciation of the micro- and meso-level forms of dissent and resistance, stretching at least from the 1968 "Prague Spring" protests, the distribution of subversive *samizdat* texts (Machovec 2009), as well as mutual aid efforts for student protestors (Ward 1973). In referring to the effect of relative cultural homogeneity in reducing coordination costs, Olga Nicoara (2018) described the singing of folkloric, patriotic songs by peacefully-protesting Estonians against Soviet occupation. As previously mentioned, the East German revolution of 1989 also proceeded in a largely peaceful manner.

From the standpoint of institutionally-aware social movement theories of Tilly and Tarrow, the peaceful power transition from communism to liberal democracy appears attributable to a range of interconnected factors. The reformist Soviet processes of *Glasnost* and *Perestroika*, which involved greater economic and social openness, arguably intersected with the growing fragmentation of internal governance of the Communist Party. Given the hegemonic influence of the Soviet Union upon its satellite nation-states, pro-democratic revolutionary movements diffused internationally at a reasonably rapid rate. Of course, not all revolutionary impulses at the time succeeded, nor worked out peacefully. The Chinese government murdered peaceful student protestors in Beijing's Tiananmen Square and elsewhere on the mainland, whereas Romania's Nicolae and Elena Ceaușescu were the victims of tyrannicide.

Turning from a macro perspective of violent tactical propensities in certain social movements, it is conceivable that nonviolent or violent tactics emerges as a source of contestation and tension *within* movements. As indicated by Nathaneal Snow (2020), organizers and activists with strong tactical preferences, either way, have the capacity to disassociate from movements who do not fulfill those preferences. Consider the place of violent advocacy in the thought of American Civil Rights activist El-Hajj Malik El-Shabazz ("Malcolm X"), whose views were juxtaposed with Martin Luther King's. Critical of King's nonviolent stance as insufficient to rectify the structural bases of racism in the United States, Malcolm X embraced black separatist ideas. This stance appeared to draw support especially from among young African Americans in impoverished inner-urban environments. While Malcolm X suggested the perpetrators of the violence that is structural racism should be fought, he often framed his arguments in the language of individual (and group) self-defense (Cone 2001). The influence of Malcolm X was evident in several social movements, including Black Power. It has also been suggested that the *threat* of violence—posed by the likes of Malcolm X and his supporters, and other radical groups—assisted in the promotion of racial equality during the 1960s (Nimtz 2016), although the merits of such a statement remain the subject of intense debate.

A recent contribution offers a defense of looting and rioting, as recently witnessed in the streets of Europe, North and South America, and elsewhere.

Vicky Osterweil (2020) argues that there are legitimate reasons for people to engage in looting—the forceful seizure of goods, and other properties, during a period of disturbance—as well as general property damage and rioting. Looting may occur with or without social movement endorsement or involvement. However, Osterweil and other activists, commentators, and researchers claim that violence-oriented tactics, such as looting, may draw public attention, as well as assist with movement mobilization. In any case, Osterweil (ibid., 3) sees looting as a justifiable attack upon "some of the core beliefs and structures of the cisheteropatriarchal racial capitalist society," as well as rejection of "the legitimacy of ownership rights and property, the moral injunction to work for a living, and the 'justice' of law and order."

Given the structural inequalities that modern economic, political, and social systems generate, looting is viewed by Osterweil as an inherently redistributive activity. In her words, it is a form of "proletarian shopping" or "shopping for free" (ibid., 4). Osterweil describes how looting from retailers, and other economic enterprises, removes finished commodities from the circle of voluntary exchange and profit-seeking, and into the possession of impoverished or otherwise marginalized communities. This narrative is taken further, to describe how "goods can be had for free if we all fight together, and that we would be able to live without a wage if we freely shared the products of society. It publicly and communally disregards the store owner's property rights and demonstrates that those rights are only upheld by the violence of the police" (ibid., 16). Contrary to the stereotypes of collective behavior theory of disruptive, yet disorganized, looting by poorly informed masses, Osterweil supports previous research stating that "those who participate in rioting and looting tend to be the most politically informed and socially engaged" (ibid., 8; also, Quarantelli and Dynes 1970). She also speaks of the coordination necessary to enact looting—involving, for example, the staged clearing of business premises, measures to distract law enforcement from looting sites, and so on.

This defense of looting and damaging property poses as a broad-brush critique of nonviolent tactical approaches. Brandishing nonviolence as a "bankrupt concept freighted with moral righteousness but lacking actual content" (ibid., 182), Osterweil considers that pleas to avoid violent orientations in tactical maneuvers places inordinate weight of responsibilities onto protestors, and off repressive police, and other law enforcers, as well as racist, xenophobic, and similar non-state elements stoking societal unrest. In Osterweil's (ibid., 180) words, "[n]on-violence means outsourcing the power you need to meet your objectives to the power or to federal marshals—in other words, to the state."

Osterweil passionately critiques persistent structural hierarchies and inequalities. These are seen to be sustained by legal and political configurations—including increasingly weaponized law-enforcement practices—together with economic restrictions disadvantaging certain minorities. Reflecting upon the 1965 "Watts Rebellion" in Los Angeles, for example, Osterweil (ibid., 200) says, "rather than trying to improve their relations with the community . . . the LAPD increased its military capacity and developed more explicitly counterinsurgent forces." Whereas Osterweil presents a critical (if not hostile) disposition toward capitalism, her critiques also find their place in contemporary liberal scholarship raising issues with governmental surveillance, police militarization, and mass incarceration (D'Amico and Williamson 2019; Coyne 2018; Coyne and Hall 2018), as well as regressive policies which suppress market competition (Lindsey and Teles 2017; Novak 2018b).

A key proposition of Osterweil's is that nonviolence obscures a constructive role for looting, rioting, and other violent tactics to draw attention to a social movement, and to catalyze commitment and mobilization. The 1969 Stonewall riots in New York, for example, is often seen as sparking the rise of a more formal LGBT movement over subsequent decades. The riots were, themselves, elicited by disaffection with police harassment of transgender and gay people, and others seeking to express their diverse gender and sexual identities. Vicky Osterweil reinforces Gamson's (1975) position that violent tactics may be efficacious in attracting attention, including, crucially, from media and policymakers. She also suggests "riots and uprisings can inspire and expand movements that are based around predominantly nonviolent community campaigns for political, cultural, and social power" (Osterweil 2020, 208).

VIOLENT SOCIAL MOVEMENT TACTICS: EFFICACY AND ETHICS

The preceding discussion of justifications for looting provides a pathway to contemplate broader critiques of social movement violence. Indeed, an enduring controversy in social movement studies, and in social science, concerns the efficacy and ethics of violence as a course of action to effect societal reforms. Does violence help secure the outcomes demanded by social movement participants? Is violence ever appropriate to use and, if so, when?

At the outset, we aim to present the presumptive liberal case for nonviolence, both on analytical and normative grounds. The aspirational apex for liberalism is represented by that state of human affairs characterized by productive specialization, and peaceful cooperation, among people, irrespective of their physical or social distance (Mises [1927] 2005; Boettke 2017). As is well represented in liberal theorization, there are links between the economic voluntarism which underpins market-based exchanges and the development of peaceful accord between individuals, as people come to tolerate, and appreciate, ascriptive diversities, and varied cultural and social mores (Montesquieu [1748] 2008; Gartzke 2007). From an institutional economics perspective, the desire for peace also rests in the avoidance of a life-depriving and productivity-sapping Hobbesian "state of nature," epitomized by scaled-up and persistent conflicts.

Liberal political and social philosophy realistically grants the human element of fear associated with violence. In a dynamic process reminiscent of Friedrich Hayek's ([1944] 2006) cautionary tale of the "worst getting on top" in the transition from liberal-democratic toward totalitarian polities, violence tends to select for individuals with an appetite to control and dominate others (Stenner 2005). As also explained by John Meadowcroft and Elizabeth Morrow (2017), certain extremist social movements attempt to attract members by offering access to organized violence. However, to draw upon Adam Smith's ethical considerations of human sympathy, the risk is that violence—including that associated with group factionalization—may reduce the likelihood of agreement-making and coordination between persons (Peart and D. Levy 2009).

It is possible to draw even further from liberal political economy insights in criticism of violent tactical efforts by social movements. Consider the case of looting, characterized by Alex Tabarrok (2019) as "theft plus destruction," or other forms of property damage. The damage, or loss, of final goods and services—as well as intermediate outputs maintained by enterprises—impose what economists dub "opportunity costs," or the costs foregone in replacing inventory or recapitalizing a damaged retail or other commercial site. The notion that "mere" property is somehow instantly replaceable, and at no cost to society, has been refuted by centuries of economic conceptualization (e.g., Hart 2015). The nineteenth-century French economist and publicist, Frédéric Bastiat, outlined his famed example of the shopfront broken window, in which the storekeeper is obliged to wear the costs, in terms of foregone, preferred alternatives, of replacing the window. In the modern era, rapidly growing expenditures on the likes of "guard labor" (Arjun and Bowles 2006), surveillance technology by "brick-and-mortar" businesses, and the pre-emptive (and, sometimes, lengthy) closures of business districts in the expectation that strife will manifest itself on the streets, also impose huge opportunity costs.

Returning to Tabarrok's (2019) looting description, he notes that, in addition to final products for retail sale, "[l]ooters destroy intermediate goods and infrastructure and gain far less than owners lose." To this calculus it should be added the likelihood that violent tactical measures bring forth relatively fewer, perhaps minimal, successes than nonviolent alternatives, as will be described at greater length below. Ethical considerations are never far from the broader picture, either. Bart Wilson (2020) refers to justice norms to describe why we feel resentful when someone tries to despoil valuables considered to be in the rightful, even lawful, possession and use by another. An even broader view of the ethical problematization of social movement violent tactics would introduce the insight that properties are not "mere" things, but significant affordances which can realize human capabilities (Crider 2015) or eudaimonic happiness (Plauche 2009). As one key example, the 1921 race massacre of African Americans by white supremacists in Tulsa, Oklahoma, contributed to long-term declines in home ownership, educational attainment, and occupational status indicators for black residents (Albright et al. 2020), all of which are, surely, suggestive of an unconscionable degradation of life opportunities and well-being.

Another reason in favor of liberalism's nonviolence presumption is that it is oftentimes difficult for social movements to accurately, and justly, identify their targets. The deleterious consequences of incorrectly identifying a target only seem compounded when those wrongfully targeted persons or groups, or their properties, are also subjected to violence, or destruction. In actually existing societies—which are exemplified by entangled economic, political, and other relationships—it is highly challenging to parse out which persons, and whose properties, should be targeted by social movement tactics seeking not only to disrupt, but to damage.

There are numerous reasons to discount the ethical and practical validity of violent social movement tactical choices. A recent study by Feinberg et al. (2020) introduced the "activist's dilemma" concept. Indications of extremity in protest actions include physical violence, property damage, and the vocalization of inflammatory or threatening rhetoric. Extreme protest actions may well succeed in eliciting concessions from movement targets, yet the same extremism may reduce popular support for the movement. One may extend this framework, countenancing the existence of an "activist's reporting dilemma" by media outlets. Extreme movement tactics may increase the probability of receiving media coverage, yet such coverage may be of a *negative* character which, subsequently, fuels negative sentiment toward the social movement.

What does the scholarly literature say about the activist's reporting dilemma? Some studies provide support for the view that violence or extremism conducted by social movements, or even by renegade or fringe elements tangentially related to movements, are likely to attract negative reporting. J. Smith et al. (2001, 1414–1415) investigated newspaper and television reports of protests in the Washington, D.C., area between 1982 and 1991 and found that, "[e]vents characterized by arrests and/or violence were about half as likely as nonconfrontational events to be framed in a way that favored demonstrators. . . . The presence of counterdemonstrators, arrests, and/or violence produced more reporting on the demonstration itself and less attention to the issues at stake." Pearce Edwards and Daniel Arnon (2019) examined various protests in America and Israel. They found that negative media framing of such events increased the probability of their being publicly perceived as violent, and increasing public support for repressing protests.

The May–June 2020 U.S. protests in response to the police killing of George Floyd has raised issues of potential media biases. It is anecdotally observed that the subsequent wave of BLM social movement protests was overshadowed in media reports by instances of looting, private property destruction, and physical violence. This kind of observation is not a new one. Kligo and Harlow (2019, 521) undertook content analysis from various American newspapers and concluded that "[r]ioting and violence were most frequently used to frame anti-Black racism protests, a topic that included the coverage of white supremacist and antiracism protests." In an earlier study, Campbell et al. (2004) described how media portrayed the 1992 Los Angeles and 2001 Cincinnati riots as ineffective, not to mention destructive, events lashing out against societal order, rather than as efforts raising awareness about the need for social change. The manner in which anti-racism movement tactics are reported has significant implications, including with respect to concretely dealing with police brutality and other governmental abuses.

Opponents are likely to take advantage of social movement tactics with violent characteristics. Political actors, for example, may seek to capitalize on social movement violence, real or imagined, by attempting to manufacture societal backlash against otherwise reasonable demands for change. An important recent study by Omar Wasow (2020) considers the empirical impacts of social movement tactical selections upon political behavior during the 1968 U.S. Presidential election. The incidence of violence during the 1960s Civil Rights protests were used by conservative politicians to frame "law and order" political rhetoric which, among other things, exploited white anxieties over civil disorder. This framing process was seen as instrumental in Richard Nixon's victory on behalf of the Republican Party: "[i]n 1968, violent protests contributed to a split in that coalition in which white racial moderates from the Midwest and Mid-Atlantic opted for the 'law and order' coalition and helped tip the presidency to the Republican Party" (ibid., 650). In Wasow's estimation, violent protests likely contributed between a 1.5 percent to 7.9 percent shift among whites toward Republicans in that election.

A wealth of empirical data has been analyzed in the task of assessing the nature, and strength, of association between tactical choice and success. A seminal contribution in this field has been William Gamson's (1975) work, *The Strategy of Social Protest*. This study examined fifty-three American social movements—in Gamson's parlance, "challenger groups"—across ideological and social spectrums between 1800 and 1945. Archival materials, such as newspaper reports, were used to assess the contribution of movement tactics toward gaining advantages, or acceptance, from movement antagonists.

Gamson's overall assessment was that "[u]nruly groups, those that use violence, strikes, and other constraints, have better than average success" (ibid., 87). Rather than seeing violence as arising from psychological frustrations, "[v]iolence should be viewed as an instrumental act, aimed at furthering the purposes of the group that uses it when they have some reason to think it will help their cause" (ibid., 81). Notably, Gamson considered that most of the sampled movements did not consider violence as their primary tactic; rather, violence was incidental to alternative, nonviolent measures. Another important conclusion was that organizational considerations were critical in attaining success—social movement organizations with bureaucratic attributes were seen as more likely to instill the routinized disciplines needed to confront target groups. The Gamson findings have broadly received support from a number of subsequent studies, such as Steedly and Foley (1979) and Frey et al. (1992).

Needless to say, the Gamson study and similar efforts have aroused controversy. Jack Goldstone (1980) confronted Gamson in suggesting the original study was empirically flawed. Recalibrating the original data, and introducing additional empirical information regarding the timing of movement successes, Goldstone estimated that the timing of successes experienced by Gamson's sampled movements were independent of organizational attributes and the use of violent tactical ploys. Other studies have effectually sidestepped the Gamson–Goldstone debate to test the effectiveness of disruptive tactics, such as riots, to movement success. For example, Kelly and Snyder (1980) found no statistically significant correlation between racial violence in the United States during the 1960s and local gains in African American socio-economic outcomes—the latter being a key objective of Civil Rights campaigners. William Collins and Robert Margo also examined the impacts of American race-related riots, on this occasion with respect to central-city residential property values. They concluded that "riots appear to have had strong negative effects on black-owned property values" (Collins and Margo 2007, 877). One factor considered to influence this relationship was the reduced sense of amenity value—such as those pertaining to personal and property security—of residing in riot-affected locations.

Empirical research by Erica Chenoweth and her associates also appears to have tilted the balance of argument toward tactical nonviolence. A key insight gleaned from this work is that the application of nonviolence, in public protest settings, has been relatively more successful in achieving political regime-change than violence (Chenoweth and Stephan 2011). This finding is robust to the kind of political responses to protest events, "including situations in which dissent is typically met with harsh regime repression" (ibid., 220). An explanatory factor behind the success of nonviolence is that, according to Chenoweth and Stephan, "the physical, moral, and informational barriers to participation in nonviolent campaigns are substantially lower than in violent campaigns given comparable circumstances" (ibid.). One of the implications of this explanation is that nonviolent movement tactics incentivize the participation of more diverse, and perhaps a greater number of, supporters (Caplan 1994), rather than participant numbers being restricted to those people physically and psychologically primed for violence. Another matter raised by this research is that there is a greater probability of public backlash against governmental repression of nonviolent movement activities.

Empirical investigations attempting to demarcate social movement tactics as exclusively nonviolent or violent have been challenged. As noted earlier, nonviolent and violent tactical impulses are oftentimes interwoven during the course of real-world contentious events. As an aside, we observe Gamson's (1989) insight that certain nonviolent tactics also prove highly injurious to their targets, especially if public authorities and other supporters of the *status quo* violently react to peaceful contention. There is clear merit in the Ammons and Coyne (2020) plea that researchers continue to explore intersections between movement nonviolence and violence, especially to establish if these two strands of tactics are complements or substitutes.

Our position is strongly in favor of nonviolent tactics in the pursuit of social movement objectives. In his description of process-oriented democracy, G. B. Madison (1998) extols the advantages surrounding "self-limitation" in social movement action. What this means is that movements should vigorously seek to advance their objectives, but not in an unrestrained and violent manner disrespecting the life, property, and equal liberty of others. This includes the freedom of opponents to subscribe to views contrary to those held by social movement participants. The self-limiting tilt in movement tactics seems likely to breed good social movement practice—especially over the need to employ discursive and other novelties in persuading, instead of coercing, people over the desire for dramatic change.

Another advantage of nonviolent self-limitation is that social movements can democratically catalyze the Smithian practice of "open partiality." This concept involves broadening the reach of normative reasoning, and the instigation of morally sympathetic projects, beyond certain subgroups within society toward the general public as a whole (Dold 2019). Reasoning with others in liberal democracy, by presenting mental images of what it is like to live in the position of the repressed, necessarily involves significant investments in socio-cultural labor and epistemic innovation. Such efforts are seen as necessary, given the ethical notion that social movement participants, and others, who speak out against received wisdom must practice moderation more systematically than those who hold received opinions (D. Levy and Peart 2016). This is not to suggest that robust, counter-hegemonic actions and tactics are impermissible, but, rather, to stress the strategic importance of encouraging open-mindedness among those parties identified by social movements as pivotal to economic, political, and social reform.

CONCLUSION

Social movement experience attests to a great variety of tactical positions, aimed at challenging holders of power and privilege, resisting coercion and tyranny, and striving for societal change. We considered tactical choices by social movements within their socio-political institutional context, and tactical innovation as one of many examples of entrepreneurship in a social guise (Koppl 2006). Inasmuch as social movements pursue tactics to encourage change by those outside the movement, it is also appreciated that tactical selections are informed by "internalist" agendas of entrenching commitment to movement collective actions among activists and supporters.

When choosing and implementing tactics, social movements have to engage in trade-offs and make astute decisions. As we shall see throughout this book, an important issue for social movement organizers and participants is to ensure that attempts to change beliefs, norms, practices, rules, and values do not come at the cost of crowding out the capacity of diverse individuals to sort out their own interpersonal conflicts and quarrels peacefully (Gaus 2018a). Liberals look askance upon the application of violent tactical dispositions by individuals and groups. An important underlying reason for this liberal presumption of nonviolence is to maintain economic, political, and social spaces whereby individuals can freely and openly express their views, and to test alternative plans for betterment.

It is a hallmark of real-world liberal actualization that social movements remain free to engage with contentious tactical actions in many parts of the world. The activities associated with tactical selections generate information about the nature, and intensity, of preferences that social movement participants feel about societal problems (Lohmann 1993). It is with respect to this function, together with social movements' strategic commitment and emotional energy (Macmillan 2013), that we come to appreciate Hayek's ([1960] 2011, 174) profound statement that "[i]t is in its dynamic, rather than in its static, aspects that the value of democracy proves itself." As the pains of history attest, however, attempts to enforce all-encompassing, totalizing plans for society, especially through violent means, have, time and again, proven at odds with the premises of individual freedom, and the benefits flowing from it.

We are acutely aware that, in a world stained by the workings of oppression and tyranny, liberalism itself is presented as a revolutionary idea. Efforts by pro-liberty social movements and allies to break free of command and control have often been resisted by those seeking to maintain an illiberal *status quo*. It seems nigh on impossible to avoid conflict and tension on questions of transformative change in society, but it is imperative to better understand these dynamics in the service of advancing liberalizing agendas within actually existing societies. Accordingly, the nature of social movement entanglement with actors within, and across, other domains of human action will be the central theme of the next chapter.

Chapter 4

Social Movement Encounters with Society

Contentious Entanglements

INTRODUCTION

Social movements assume a variety of forms, and partake in numerous tactics in their pursuit of their objectives. The participants, and occasionally supporters, of a social movement risk their intimate relationships with concerned family and friends, their livelihoods, and, sometimes, even their lives. Even so, the sheer number and diversity of social movements points to the widespread thirst for change in varied forms. As indicated already in this book, the changes sought by social movements may be materialistic in nature—involving, say, redistribution of resources—or they may be non-materialistic, concerning, for example, recognition and respect for certain groups.

Social movement participants frequently encounter other people engaging within, and across, various domains. In addition to the movement activation of contentious encounters with legislators and bureaucrats, as well as the judiciary and other political actors, social movements interact with representatives of private corporations, traditional and online media, academia, counter-movements, nonprofit groups, social enterprises, neighbors, and members of the local community, and so on. Many of these encounters may invoke conflictual interactions, but that is not necessarily so in every instance. We have previously discussed the potential for social movements to develop formal alliances and coalitions within a broader network of shared concern. Therefore, there is also room for collaborative, mutually beneficial interactions between social movement participants and other sets of actors.

Social movements are considered to reflect processes and patterns of non-state ordering in their own right. It is true that some movements incorporate organizational forms with clearly identifiable boundaries, together with clear and consistent internal rules and procedures. As research indicates, however, social movements more generally exhibit informal and diffuse network features which distinguish them from entities like for-profit firms, government bureaucracies, nonprofit organizations, and social enterprises. Another interesting characteristic of social movements is that their activities typically abridge institutional boundaries of "market," "civil society," and "state" in the course of their advocacy for change. Social movements have become an important part of that broader tapestry of entangled relations which symbolize modern society.

In this chapter we consider the main attributes of social movement interaction with a variety of other actors operating within economic, political, and social domains. In the next section, we situate social movement activity within a conceptual framework of "entangled political economy." This is followed, in subsequent sections, by discussions about the manner in which movement participants engage with, respectively, certain government actors, business interests, and media outlets. This chapter, then, describes how social movements engage with opposing counter-movements, often giving rise to social tensions due to the contestable perspectives of rival groups. Broader coverage is also presented with regard to the place of social movements within broader civil society. This chapter concludes with brief summarizing remarks.

SOCIAL MOVEMENTS IN AN ENTANGLED POLITICAL ECONOMY CONTEXT

Despite its common usage as a collective noun, "society" is not constituted as an undifferentiated mass. It is, rather, a complex and evolving ecology of individuals engaging with each other, whether on their own accord or through various groups. Some of these groups are mentioned in the introduction to this chapter. We could add the likes of associations, clubs, mutual aid concerns, religious orders, and many more entities whose activities and memberships crisscross and overlap one another. The mentioned groupings differ in terms of geographic scale and their underlying purposes (e.g., civic participation, mutual assistance, recreation, education and enlightenment, political representation, etc.). Furthermore, participation and membership in some of these groups help forge a solid grounding in shared identities.

Social movements are yet another element within the social constellation of human engagements. It is possible to identify in the social movement form the cooperative efforts of large numbers of people dedicated to promoting societal change. Indeed, social movements are among the most luminous of networking activities within society, energetically pushing for transformative changes to our ways of being, doing, and knowing. As noted, movements engage with governmental agencies, private corporations, educational institutions, nonprofit entities, and many other actors, in robust, yet typically (but not always) contentious, ways. Irrespective of the nature of interaction, our account of social movements is in accord with the generic insight that all individuals and groups interface on the same societal plane.

One of the major challenges of social theorization is to aptly recognize and reflect the interactive, even entangled, nature of social coordination. Over the past decade or so, a new framework has been developed by George Mason University economist Richard E. Wagner (2014, 2016) to represent the entangled nature of society in which we live. Unsurprisingly, this framework has been coined "entangled political economy," and it views individuals and groups—whether in private and public sectors, or some domain of civil society—as being intertwined in overlapping exchange relationships, and along competitive and collaborative dimensions. Entangled political economy is inspired by a long tradition in political economy stretching back to Adam Smith and Carl Menger, of a liberal political economy scholarship prior to the twentieth century. Wagner's framework also draws inspiration from contemporary perspectives in complexity and evolutionary studies.

Entangled political economy encapsulates those networked interactions and relationships which are forged between individuals and enterprises, be they of an irregular or regular standing. These entanglements intrinsically exude either the qualities of voluntariness, cooperation, or contract ("dyadic exchange"), or of involuntariness, coercion, or status ("triadic exchange") (Podemska-Mikluch and R. Wagner 2013). In several studies, Wagner has investigated the dense interactivity which undergirds relations between commercial, political, and nonprofit enterprises. Of particular interest is the Wagnerian idea that political enterprises are eager to attach themselves to their typically more productive, and innovative, commercial enterprise counterparts to extract rents and revenues. Such political proclivities have an inclination to create tensions, insofar as there remains sufficient recognition among the members of society that such politically-induced entanglements are inimical to liberal precepts of nondiscrimination and the rule of law.

Social movement participants also activate entanglements, be it with political and commercial enterprises, or other groups within civil society. Movements are complicit in the fluid patterning of connections, and reconnections, as their participants strive to win concessions favoring societal change. They similarly possess a habit of drawing affiliation, and support, from a diverse array of individuals and groups situated among alternative societal domains. Movements might even win support from individuals weakly affiliated with those opposition groups nominally perceived as antagonistic to movement conduct and objectives. This insight is perhaps best illustrated with reference to multiplex networks, used here as an analytical tool to describe multiple modes of interaction (represented by network ties, or connections) among a diverse set of actors (represented by network nodes).

Consider figure 4.1, providing a basic illustrative example of multiplex network structures involving social movement interaction. Panel A illustrates an entire entangled political economy with commercial enterprises (represented by octagonal nodal shapes), political enterprises (triangles), and a SMO (squares). Within each node in panel A are individual actors, represented by circles. Some of these individuals are social movement participants—designated by the shaded circles—whereas nonparticipants of the movement are unshaded. Panel A maps the (non-uniform) meso-level ties between the different enterprises. It also shows the connections among individuals interacting within each enterprise. Those connections are illustrated by the thick, undashed lines in panel A.

Panel B illustrates the network developed by social movement participants. The thin dashed lines indicate how individuals situated in panel A are positioned within the movement network as shown in panel B. Notice, in panel B, the specific connections between the movement participants traverse

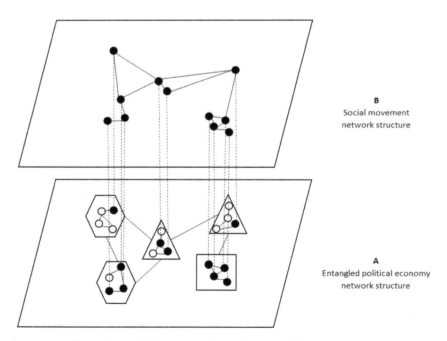

B
Social movement
network structure

A
Entangled political economy
network structure

Figure 4.1   Illustrative Multiplex Network Involving Social Movements.
Source: Author's illustration.

their positions within the varied enterprises displayed in panel A. From a network topographical perspective, this indicates that the social movement involves the participation of people from a variety of backgrounds. In this illustrative example, it is shown the movement has even attracted three supporters—albeit likely to be concealing the full, or true, extent of their movement participation—who act within the political domain of the entangled political economy.

Another feature of the social movement network in the figure is that the SMO in panel A is not directly connected to the majority of movement participants in panel B. In other words, the SMO itself merely represents a subset of the entire movement network, and may not necessarily command widespread legitimacy from the participant majority. Under such factionalized conditions there may be scope for strategic and tactical innovations—given the lack of direct involvement by the majority with, let alone adherence to, the SMO—although this situation also raises questions about the movement's ability to instill discipline among its varied participants (M. Gurri 2018). Even if this social movement lacks organizational rigor, nonetheless it may still be perceived by others as a threat to the established order: "if an informal social group can count as participants a large enough number of people, . . . then the government may have an incentive to avoid policies that could mobilize the informal social group into activities that generate additional costs for government actions" (N. Snow 2020, 40).

Richard Wagner embraces the realist position that entangled relations between and among individuals, and their groups, could be collaborative or competitive, or consensual or exploitative. People will seek to bargain with others in an attempt to pursue their aspirations, desires, and needs. Effective bargaining would entice others with offers which promise betterment economically, politically, or socially, in the short or long run. The same people may alternate their engagement styles with other parties, holding attractive offers off the table and attempting, instead, to threaten others in an attempt to procure advantages. Liberalism normatively advances cooperative aspects of human behavior, including those facets of social cooperation arising as the unanticipated consequence of individuals competing to serve others more effectually (A. Smith [1776] 1999; Rubin 2014). The realism of the liberal project partially rests in its awareness of unproductive and destructive behavior—borne of conflictual relationships between individuals and groups of individuals (Baumol 1990; Hirshleifer 1994)—and its explication of institutional and operational strategies to ameliorate incentives for such conflict.

When considering social movements, it is essential to recognize their irrepressible tendency to entangle with others. Social movement participants may interact, on an intermittent or sustained basis, in a competitive manner against those who are affiliated with counter-movements and other groupings. In these cases, we observe modes of entanglement informed by contestation. However, movement organizers and other participants may discover it is also necessary to collaborate with certain other movements, or with economic, political, and other figures and groups, to amplify their prospects for success. Entanglements embodying collaboration and reciprocity may, therefore, also arise. Whichever relational patterns arise, it is safely said that social movements partake in encounters seen, at least in some quarters, as contentious. Using Wagner's phraseology, social movement participants are suggested to be deeply implicated in "social tectonic" clashes, having the effect of upsetting preconceived notions and established patterns.

SOCIAL MOVEMENTS AND THE STATE

State as Order, Governmental Structure, and Social Movement Opportunities

A voluminous amount of research and commentary points to deep connections between social movements, politics, and the state. Given the predominance of politics in human affairs, it is unsurprising that substantial regard has been directed to the nature of interactions between social movements and those involved in formalized political activities. Indeed, as noted by Hank Johnston (2011), politics, protest, and the state appear to have maintained a co-evolutionary relationship since ancient times. Today, some researchers speak of a "social movement society" wherein the contentious strategizing, mobilization, and tactical operations, as stereotypically associated with social movements, has come to permeate general political practices (Meyer and Tarrow 1998; cf. Jenkins et al. 2008).

Before proceeding any further, it is useful to distinguish between two terms which centrally relate to the domain of politics. These terms are "state" and "government." The state-government distinction matters, given Hayek's ([1973–1979] 2013) observation of widespread confusion between the unintended and intended bases of orderings which both affect, and are affected by, human conduct. Specifically, the proposition that the state is an organization is misplaced. Rather, the state is properly conceived as an emergent order, as suggested in liberal political economy stretching from at least Carl Menger through to Richard Wagner (Becchio 2014). The state, at least in a historical sense, is an emergent by-product of a broader process wherein people engage in forceful, and often violent, contests to control the means of political power. For Max Weber ([1919] 1946, 78), "'politics' . . . means striving to share power or striving to influence the distribution of power, either among states or among groups within a state."

In contrast, government consists of key political organizations populating the emergent order of state. Think of government, in a sense, as interconnected "islands" of conscious political planning situated within an "ocean" of order known as the state. The organizations constituting the government—such as the legislature, bureaucracies and regulatory agencies, and governmental enterprises providing economic and social services—vary along several dimensions. One of these is that government organizations differ in size, from small entities, possessing niche policy and service-delivery influence, through to so-called "big player" agencies maintaining significant discretionary influence and power (Koppl 2002). In addition to the organizational diversity within a given level of government, it is also possible that different levels of government operate within a regional or national political jurisdiction.

Richard Wagner (2016) offers an additional clarifying point to the effect that government is not a unitary, homogenous actor exogenously intervening to reshape the conduct of others within society. Organizational diversity, and the potential for intra- and inter-governmental contestations, suggests that it cannot be presumed that the government strategically and operationally unifies. The non-unitary, distributed network configurations of public-sector organization are an ensemble of relationships which may be classified as bearing "polycentric" properties (V. Ostrom et al. 1961; E. Ostrom 2005; Aligica and Tarko 2012; Aligica et al. 2019). Polycentricity features distributed nodes of decision-making, with a measure of autonomy granted under an overarching set of rules.

In the previous chapter, we referred to the "political opportunity" theories of Tilly and Tarrow. These scholars effectively present a structuralist, as well as exogenously determined, context of social movement engagement with governmental actors. As influential as those theories have been, they have not entirely escaped criticism. The structural interpretation of social movement activity has been seen by some to downplay the creative role of individual agency, not to mention coordinative, networked efforts by movement participants themselves, both of which may push governmental actors toward political positions favorable to movement objectives (e.g., Goodwin and Jasper 1999; cf. Koopmans 1999; Guigni 2009). In fairness, certain social movement researchers have responded to such criticism by further refining the contributions of political activity in models of movement activity. A broader conception of "political contention" is a good example of this, in that it attempts to integrate structuralist and interpretive conceptions of mobilization responses to political developments (H. Johnston 2014; Tarrow 2015).

Modern liberals are deeply attuned to the impact of formal (and informal) institutions upon economic, political, and social activities. Institutions do matter for actions and outcomes, and many studies under the headings of public choice, constitutional political economy, and new institutional economics, seek to affirm this intuitive position. Not only do we think that many of the background institutional mechanisms affecting social movement capacities to drive change are relevant, but we also note that opportunities to manifest change are contingent, non-uniform, and can shift over time and often in unforeseen ways. Accepting the emergent nature of political activities, and the opportunities they bring forth (e.g., Hebert 2019), leads us to an appreciation of the fluid aspects of entanglement between social movement participants and other actors within the political domain.

In addition to a dynamic approach to human interaction, modern liberals emphasize entrepreneurship as a key way in which individuals and groups express agency. Israel Kirzner (1973, 2009) is widely seen as a major contributor to entrepreneurship theory, with his characterization of entrepreneurship centered upon an alert and creative individual, actively identifying potential arbitrage opportunities in market settings. It is possible to broaden this insight to accommodate non-economic activity. Consistent with the inherent capacity of every human being to exercise entrepreneurship, and given the identification of entrepreneurial potentials in non-market settings (e.g., Shockley et al. 2008), social movement participants are also seen as capable of entrepreneurially perceiving (political) opportunities. Movement participants are, potentially, Kirznerian entrepreneurial agents, whose alertness to evolving political opportunities increase the potential for social movement success. Of course, opportunity-identification alone is insufficient to appropriate potential gains; social movements must, *inter alia*, coordinate their key organizers, activists, and supporters to engage collectively (and to do so effectively).

Governmental arrangements exhibiting a high degree of polycentricity provide a useful environment for social movement participants to exercise their entrepreneurial flair. Take the case of federalism, a political arrangement highly esteemed in liberal thought. A federal system consists of multiple levels of government—a central (or national) government, multiple regional governments (referred to as states, provinces, etc.), and potentially other kinds of sub-national governments (such as local or county jurisdictions). Furthermore, the federal system discharges a mix of exclusive, and concurrent, powers and policy responsibilities (including fiscal and regulatory activities) among those levels. Although modern federal systems substantively result from intentional political choices and designs, they, nevertheless, generate emergent political phenomena insofar as the different units of government generate competitive impulses, as well as politically salient learnings, amongst their multiple centers of decision-making (R. Wagner 2005; Candela 2019).

Federalism provides social movement participants with the opportunity to entrepreneurially discover locations wherein their perspectives enjoy strong political receptivity and support. Movements might find ready accommodation of their perspectives in larger jurisdictions, in which diverse cultural, economic, political, and social perspectives and practices flourish. Similarly, a movement may discover stronger support within jurisdictions with a conspicuous, or otherwise identifiable, political tradition for assuming a "first-mover" tradition regarding policy changes. Certain jurisdictions may be the targets of social movement campaigns due to the likes of legislative configurations, political party ideologies, an ability to undertake voting procedures such as public referenda, and so on. Once policy positions preferred by the social movements are implemented by an initial set of jurisdictions, policymakers in other jurisdictions can then benchmark the efficacy of those alternative arrangements, in the interest of potential emulation.

Throughout history, those wielding political power have imposed systems of taxation upon individuals and organizations within their jurisdiction. From an entangled political economy perspective, taxation is represented as a relational act in which political actors forcibly enact a connection with productive economic ventures. This, in turn, is likely to arouse feelings of acquiescence, coercion, and duress on the part of those subject to taxation. Those feelings exist despite the ever-present efforts of politicians—and those supportive of an extensive role for governmental economic activity—to soothe taxpayers by rhetorically claiming that taxes are a justified "price of civilization," or, somehow, necessary for other reasons (R. Wagner 2016).

There is a long history of resistance by social movements, and other groups, against the imposition of tax imposts perceived to be excessive and/or unjust. During the late 1970s in the United States, a wave of anti-tax protests occurred in response to rapidly increasing (or, at least, the threat of such increases in) local and state property tax liabilities. The amendment to the Californian state constitution known as "Proposition 13"—itself the result of a citizen-initiated referendum process in 1978—not only amended the tax base assessment from the market value to acquisition value of property. The Californian constitutional amendments also limited the growth of property tax revenues, as well as restricted the ability of state and county governments to increase taxes in the future (Burg 2004; I. Martin 2009).

The origins of this totemic tax revolt have been the subject of considerable social movement scholarship. Several works by Isaac Martin (2008, 2009, 2013) suggest that the *animus* toward property taxation initially arose as a broad-based concern toward administrative attempts to formalize tax collection based on market values. Given the strong increase in Californian property market values at the time, such changes were seen to expose property-holders to potentially steep increases in tax liability. Grievances about changing property tax assessments were cross-ideologically shared by those concerned about the welfare of low, or fixed, income earners (and young people unable to afford housing), together with those seeking to restrict public-sector growth. In respect of the latter groups, property tax issues enabled long-time tax resisters, such as Howard Jarvis, and organizations devoted to small-government causes to campaign for formal tax-limitation policies.

Our particular interest is with the manner in which anti-tax activists sought to diffuse tax (and expenditure) limitation policies across state and local jurisdictions (Mullins and Wallin 2004). Isaac Martin (2008, 2009) describes how Proposition 13 inspired new movement organizations and networks to emerge in other jurisdictions, pressuring political actors elsewhere to cap property taxes. There was a significant anti-property tax presence in U.S. states such as Massachusetts, Michigan, New York, and further afield. The movement would also take on national proportions, due in part to liberal scholarship articulating the problems associated with excessive growth in governmental size (e.g., Brennan and Buchanan [1980] 2000). The low-tax public sentiment registered as a significant issue, and had proven politically instrumental in Ronald Reagan's successful 1980 Presidential campaign.

It would be naïve to consider that political actors would seek a purely accommodative role to appease social movements. As indicated elsewhere in this book, the relationship between institutionalized politics and social movements is steeped in repression, if not violence—both as movements assertively seek change, and governments assertively seek to hold their ground and quell perceived dissent. In this respect, another engagement option is for political actors to co-opt movement causes, if not movement participants, into conventional political concerns and routines. The aspiration here is to effectively dilute the counter-hegemonic effectiveness of movement activity. Holdo (2019) describes Egyptian military maneuvers to successfully co-opt the agenda of the Arab Spring youth movement (Tamarod), as part of a broader plan by the military to oust the Muslim Brotherhood-led government. According to Holdo (ibid., 451), "[a]s a pro-democratic force, Tamarod was effectively eliminated, since its credibility as such was destroyed. It could no longer credibly claim to be a watchdog for human rights abuse or authoritarianism." Potential for political co-option raises serious questions regarding the capacity of movements to challenge authority, on every occasion, let alone sustain a genuine self-governance inspiring public confidence and trust in the art of contention.

Social Movement Engagements with Judiciaries

We conclude our discussion about engagement between social movements and governmental actors by considering the role of the judiciary. The judiciary generally refers to that branch of government administering justice in accordance with law, including responsibility for officially interpreting and applying law to resolve legal disputes. The judiciary is, on its own accord, an entangled assortment of actors—officials such as judges, lawyers, and bureaucratic and other support personnel maintaining judicial functions on behalf of the state—and organizations—courts and administrative tribunals with different legal limits and procedural powers. Judicial functions are also maintained across multiple levels of government, with differing degrees of geographic coverage and decision powers. The decisions made by the assorted judiciaries are themselves shaped, to some degree, by a complicated array of conventions, discourses, norms, practices, and rules observed by the legal profession (McCann 2004; Ratnapala 2013).

A fundamental liberal principle is that of the "separation of powers" between executive, legislative, and judicial governmental functions. Judiciaries do not make statutory law (as does the legislature) nor do they enforce law (as does the political executive) but, rather, interpret law and apply such interpretations in each disputed legal case. Separation of powers is, from the liberal point of view, to be complemented by the "rule of law." Integral to the maintenance of a constitutional rule-structure for political ordering, the rule of law specifies that law should be formulated in abstract, and general, terms, applicable to everyone in equal measure. Under the rule of law, legal precepts should also be capable of being widely understood by the public, to cultivate broad-scale legal compliance and acceptance (Hayek [1960] 2011; Kasper et al. 2012). Support for these legal arrangements by liberals is, in no small part, motivated by the desire for bounded political behavior which does not spill over into legal discrimination and favoritism, in turn benefiting some over others.

In no uncertain terms, social movements have practically engaged with participants in the political domain. This engagement is often animated by a deep sense of disaffection with existing legal provisions. Interestingly, the political effectiveness of movements is often attributed to favorable judicial decisions in their disputes against governments and other parties (e.g., business), as opposed to the direct attainment of concessions from legislators. There are numerous reasons why social movements would strategically and tactically consider engaging with the judicial branch. An important one is that movement participants perceive a successful outcome in any given scheme for legal redress. Elinor Ostrom observed that American Civil Rights activists fought for racial equality often, though not exclusively, through legal channels. This is because there appeared to be fewer "veto points" associated with judicial decision-making compared against legislative decision-making (also Magness 2020). Specifically, Ostrom (1967, 13) asked: "[d] oes the greater number of potential veto points in the U.S. Congress explain the predominant use, until a few years ago, of the court system by advocates of Civil Rights?" Our suggestion is that the answer to Ostrom's question is in the affirmative. Major social movements which followed—such as the pro-abortion, feminist, gay rights and marriage equality movements, and environmental groups—appear to have learned from the legal-tactical dispositions of the Civil Rights movement, accordingly instigating their own legal challenges in U.S. local, state, and federal courthouses.

Other factors come may influence the tendency for social movements to legally engage their adversaries through judicial processes. A nationwide court, such as the U.S. Supreme Court, provides legal decisions that are applicable across an entire country. This obvious fact might prove attractive to a social movement seeking an all-encompassing decision in their favor, especially if legal procedures through lower levels of government have yielded mixed results, or have been exhausted. However, and depending upon the circumstances, there may still be potential opportunities for victories in sub-national jurisdictional courts. This alternative avenue for legal redress may be more suitable for issues with limited geographical applicability. Another consideration is that legal decisions, themselves, are among the many factors amplifying political pressure for change. The existence of competitive impulses within political federalism, for instance, may ensure that a judicial decision rendered in one jurisdiction is emulated by policymakers (with, or without, the aid of similar rulings in their home jurisdiction) elsewhere. It could also be the case that a successful judicial ruling favoring a given social movement could induce legal mobilizations by similar movements in other jurisdictions (Cummings 2017).

As scholarship intersecting social movement studies and law has matured, questions have been raised about the traits of successful legal mobilization. One factor highlighted in literature is judicial independence, identified as feature encouraging minorities, and other groups, to contest their lack of personal freedoms (Berggren and Gutmann 2020). By presenting an opportunity to mediate disputes between social movements and their opponents in an impartial manner, it is conceived that an independent judiciary provides potentially greater legal access for any given movement (della Porta and Diani 2020). This proposition stands in contrast with the operation of non-independent judiciaries, especially in authoritarian states, which are known to conduct sham trials of dissidents, and pass legal rulings consistently favoring the polity's executive branch and their favored sectional interests.

Another consideration is whether judges, and other participants within the legal infrastructure, are prepared to hear contentious cases put forward by movement participants. This alludes to the role of legal actors as "gate-keepers" with respect to access and, implicitly, the "proper" meaning as to which questions brought forward by potential complainants are legally relevant. As already noted, the existence of multiple domestic jurisdictions for legal redress is likely to incentivize social movement action. In addition, the emergence of international, or transnational, courts and tribunals provide an avenue for social movements to instigate legal challenges (Rajagopal 2003; Lal 2006). Additional issues, such as the costs of obtaining legal representation, may be determinative in social movement legal choices——for example, Vanhala (2012) refers to costs and other facets of "legal opportunity structure" constraining environmental litigation in Britain.

The ability of social movements to engage judiciaries, in so doing side-stepping negotiations with legislators to some extent, has been lambasted over the years. Judicial victories for social movements over identity issues, environmental, and other matters have frequently been met with furious accusations of "judicial activism," portraying judges and lawyers themselves as both partial and powerful arbitrators of societal change. Questions are also raised about the democratic accountability implications of judicial decisions, in that amended understandings of the law are viewed as displacing decisions by elected political representatives. The phenomenon of "cause lawyering" in the dedicated pursuit of some social, or other, end has similarly attracted academic interest, as well as criticism, in recent years (e.g., Sarat and Scheingold 2006; Marshall and Hale 2014).

The perspectives outlined here are not uncontested. There is no assurance of legal victory for movements, and there is a risk that the pursuit of claims may unleash counter-oppositional backlash dynamics (Gloppen 2013). Movement opponents may counter-mobilize to try to weaken the effect of the judicial decision itself, or frustrate its policy implementation in some way. Legal mobilization might, paradoxically, also weaken community support for the social movement, as the movement becomes viewed to merely another cog within those supposedly "rotten" institutionalized structures of politics opposed by the movement's most dedicated supporters.

The extent of social movement engagement with political actors is extensive. Other elements of engagement we do not consider here—for example, movement interaction with bureaucracies, political parties, and so on—warrant attention in lengthier treatises of the political dimension of social movement activity. A consequence of the state as a polycentric order is that it possesses different governmental offices with varying kinds and degrees of influence, if not control. The heterogeneity of governmental structure, in addition to broader issues such as ideological receptivity to movement causes within the political domain, creates opportunities for target selectivity and entrepreneurial claims-making by movement participants. Regardless at which point within entangled space that movements choose to represent their objectives politically, it is, by now, well recognized that political actors can be "simultaneous target, sponsor, and antagonist for social movements as well as the organizer of the political system and the arbiter of victory" (Jenkins and Klandermans 1995, 3). This insight is consistent with Goldstone's (2010) broader assessment that movement activities increasingly generate fuzziness between the boundaries of the formal, institutionalized, if not genteel, politics of the legislator, judge, and bureaucrat, and the informal, non-institutionalized, and muscular politics of the social movement.

SOCIAL MOVEMENTS AND BUSINESS

Nature of the Firm in Entangled Political Economy

The private sector for-profit corporation, or firm, plays a substantial role in contemporary economic organization. The firm is broadly seen as a set of organized, albeit typically hierarchical, relationships that are oriented toward producing goods and services for profitable gain. In an economic sense, owners and managers within a given firm aim to secure, at cost, the right to use and control a range of productive inputs (such as capital, entrepreneurship, finance, land, and labor) which, subsequently, are combined and directed to produce outputs for subsequent sale. Given the extensiveness of the division of labor, and the immensely productive capabilities attributable to globalized accessibility to expertise and resources, the modern economy is characterized by elaborate supply-chain networks among firms, their suppliers, and customers, typically extending across political borders.

Why do firms even exist? An important economic rationale for the firm was proffered by Ronald Coase (1937) who explained that firms exist to economize those "transaction costs" incurred by people interacting in (instantaneous spot) markets. Transaction costs include search costs of identifying suitable trading partners, negotiation costs of establishing contracts, verification costs of ratifying trustworthy counterparties, and the monitoring and enforcement costs associated with maintaining trading relationships. It costs much to engage in market-based economic exchange and, consequently, firms are established to help wear some of the transaction cost burdens. That said, it would be a misnomer to consider a firm to be reducibly equivalent to its production or cost function, given the reality of extensive, entangled patterning of economic and non-economic relationships.

The conduct of private enterprises is conditioned, in no small part, by a complex set of internal standards, as well as corporate regulatory rules imposed by governments. These provisions relate to such matters as the assumption of liability for wrongdoing, the ability to obtain finance from external sources, provisions covering dispersal of profits among the firm's stockholders, and so on. As we shall see, corporations are also influenced by, and they attempt to influence, contentious interactions with social movements (Soule 2009; Rojas and King 2019). Indeed, studies have indicated that social movements strive to directly influence firm economic performance, including through engagement with senior management, workers, and shareholders, as well as indirectly affecting those cultural, legal, policy, regulatory, and social environments in which companies operate (e.g., Soule 2012).

There has been much discussion within economic sociology concerning the extent to which business, and the economy as a whole, is "embedded" within broader social relations. Following Granovetter (1985) one may be suitably aware of both under- and over-socialized conceptions of economic phenomena, nevertheless one might question whether social considerations always influence, and constrain, the conduct of firms (and other economic agents) in a unidirectional fashion. Our opinion about such matters is more in keeping with Peter Boettke and Virgil Storr's (2002) idea of the "rich embeddedness" of economic, political, and social relations on the one plane of human interactivity. Their Weber-inspired conception is also consistent with Richard Wagner's (2016) entangled political economy of improvisational entrepreneurship conducted across all facets of human activity, again, on the same interactional plane. These alternative views enable researchers to consider that corporate conduct may also shape social norms and, more specifically, the conduct of social movements.

From time to time, concerns are raised about the relative economic influence and power of corporations. From a liberal perspective such concerns are valid when corporate dominance results from governmental policies that lessen the economic disciplines of market competition and openness (e.g., Lindsey and Teles 2017; Novak 2018b). As will be described later in this section, there is often a chorus of consternation to the effect that business operations disturbs broader public interest, however conceived, in their social or political guises. Incidentally, such concerns do have the capacity to boil over in the form of protest and similarly disruptive activities—for example, Sarah Soule (2009) characterizes the 1773 U.S. Boston Tea Party protest as an expression of anger toward the politically-enabled influence of the East India Company. Irrespective of one's own position about the consequences of corporations and corporate conduct, the pervasiveness of this organizational form has left few in society untouched by their practices. This has meant, for better or for worse, depending upon one's view, that firms and other economic actors have long been the targets of social movement activity.

Interactions between Social Movements and Corporations

Let us now turn specifically to the interactivity between movement participants and those involved in corporate operations and governance. The manner in which social movements entangle with corporations, especially those of larger scale, will depend, somewhat, upon the proximity of relationship between the protagonists (Briscoe and Gupta 2016). Public imaginary, courtesy of films, newspaper articles, and television reporting, largely projects visions of movement activists descending upon corporate headquarters during a protest or demonstration event. These pictures are consistent an "outsider activism" perspective, conceiving largely nonexistent (or at best, tenuous) relationships between movement participants and firm owners, managers, and, perhaps, even most of the employees.

At the other end of the spectrum, we might find "insider activism" or a sense of "hyper-proximity" between movement participants and those involved in the firm. The activist could well be situated inside the organization itself, as a member of the management team or as a worker, using their insight and knowledge about internal corporate affairs to press for change. Some workers may collaborate, and perhaps even be inspired by social movements transpiring outside the organizational arena, to press for changes such as promotion or better pay for women, enhanced childcare, parental leave , or some other initiative, such as a corporate diversity and employee inclusion program. If we comprehend organizations as reward structures, one may consider insider activism as akin to an internal "social movement" seeking changes in remuneration structures, or striving for workplace recognition and status, all of which having redistributive implications (Tomaskovic-Devey and Avent-Holt 2018).

Social movements have developed an extensive range of tactics aimed at directly enforcing for-profit enterprises to instigate economic change, or otherwise engaging companies to leverage broader cultural, political, or societal change. Movements place legal pressure on firms to enact changes, and they can also petition political actors to enact fiscal and regulatory policy aiming to reform corporate conduct. In addition, movement participants may try to dissuade various stakeholders from engaging with the firm. Brayden King and Sarah Soule (2007) write about disruptive movement entrepreneurship, using data on protests against U.S. corporations between 1962 and 1990. Protestors who successfully targeted key economic relationships maintained by firms, such as workers and consumers, were found to contribute toward falling corporate stock values, thereby limiting the ability of an enterprise to accumulate equity finance. The emergence of "activist shareholder" blocs, with strong conscience adherence, have also challenged certain corporate owners and managers to adjust corporate practices (Davis and Thompson 1994; Michelon et al. 2020).

Although the supposed difficulties surrounding collective action by dispersed individuals suggest otherwise (Olson 1965), consumers are known to adjust their expenditure practices to help achieve some economic, or even political or social, cause. Consumers may form advocacy groups and networks to push for certain spending habits within the population, which may enjoy encouragement and support from allied social movements in doing so. People may also engage in "financial divestments" which is the sale (or removal) of financial assets—such as stocks, bonds, trust and investment funds, and financial relationships—associated with entities considered to be behaving inappropriately. In an interesting reverse case that unfolded in early 2021, amateur investors collaborated through the Reddit social-media platform to purchase shares of gaming merchandise retailer GameStop. This coordinative effort was interpreted as a move to frustrate hedge funds, and certain other established traders, from profiting as a result of "short selling" shares which are expected to decline in value. For some academics and commentators, the efforts of Reddit users to organize in the manner described was seen as a kind of "social movement activity" (e.g., Donovan 2021; Wells and Egkolfopoulou 2021) or a disruptive form of "counter-hegemonic finance" (e.g., Chohan 2021).

Consider the nature and impacts of consumer boycotts. These tactics interrelatedly aim to restrict profits or returns, damage corporate reputation, or raise awareness about how corporate practices are implicated in a problematic issue (Micheletti and Stolle 2015). Consumer boycotts have featured as pivotal contentious activities performed by pro-liberal social movements of the past. Examples include British abolitionists seeking to boycott "slave produce" during the eighteenth and nineteenth centuries, Gandhi's call upon Indians to boycott goods produced by British colonizers, the famous American Civil Rights public transit boycotts of the 1950s, and the South African anti-apartheid movement's divestment campaigns of the 1970s and 1980s. The liberal argument for consumer boycotts unremittingly rests in the freedom of individuals to choose how they spend their disposable incomes. In this context, consumption assumes a "plebiscitary character," as Ludwig von Mises ([1949] 2007) once suggested, but in this case posing as part of a conscientious approach to realize societal change. Similarly, boycotts represent an economic equivalent of free speech, with the corollary that legal and regulatory efforts at prohibiting boycotts are viewed as limitations on speech rights (Berg 2016).

The ethics of consumer boycotting remains controversial to this day. Consider the case of "sweatshop" laboring, in the form of low pay and poor working conditions in textile industries in parts of the developing world. Critics of boycotts point to the potentially unintended consequences of abstaining from purchasing sweatshop goods. In particular, it is said that boycotts disproportionately harm workers, suppliers, and those indirectly involved in textile supply chains that are, more or less, linked to the targeted companies. The concern here is that wealthy owners and managers of firms, who make the production decisions to employ sweatshop laborers, are either relatively unaffected by boycotting tactics or could simply readjust production activities (including relocation to another jurisdiction) to minimize the effects of boycotts.

Others might say that sweatshop conditions are, perhaps, more appealing to individual workers than alternative arrangements in developing countries. The argument goes that efforts to eliminate sweatshop labor may exacerbate unemployment. Displaced former sweatshop workers may need to rely upon the good graces of relatives, or charitable contributions, to survive, or may have to find precarious work within the shadow economy. These arguments imply that workers' choices should be respected—even if the decision to undertake sweatshop work is understood to be, regrettably, couched within a very restrictive choice-set of income generation opportunities (Zwolinski 2007; Munger 2011; B. Powell 2014).

There is no doubt that sweatshop workers in developing countries generally work for much lower absolute pay rates, and operate in appallingly inferior conditions, than their counterparts in developed countries. However, on liberal precepts it would be equally indefensible to disallow movement participants, and others, from persisting with consumer boycotts, if they so choose. We should recall Adam Smith's dictum that production is directed to the interests of the consumer, or *ought to be*. In this context, boycotting signals to producers that sweatshop-produced goods are not preferred by a sizeable (and, perhaps, growing) number of consumers. We also note that complementary, policy-oriented measures could reduce the economic relevance of sweatshops in global labor markets while, at the same time, improve the lives of impoverished workers. Opening borders and easing labor market restrictions could allow people to migrate to wealthier countries, earn a better living, and potentially send remittances back to family and friends. Global information and communication technologies may be used to establish international crowdfunding measures, and expand existing financial inclusion initiatives, to bolster the position of sweatshop workers. Working in sweatshops is often a decision made within a repressed economic climate, such as a lack of access to credit for women (Fike 2018), therefore considerable scope remains to liberalize factor and product markets around the world.

Businesses are not passive in response to social movement pressures. Soule (2018) provides a useful taxonomy of potential business responses, ranging from retaliation (aggressively countering activist critics through policing, repression, censorship, and other counter-tactics) to outright concession (granting advantages or benefits to activists). Within these two polar extremes are a number of potential corporate responses to movement activism. These include: co-opting partnerships; generating pro-social claims consistent with movement messaging; presenting symbolic concessions to movement prerogatives; and providing donations to, and undertaking philanthropic partnerships, with social movements. Georgallis (2017) refers to the evolving interactions between social movements and firms, which invoke reshaping frames, cognitive meanings, and senses of reputation and legitimacy on issues subject to tensions between movements and businesses. It is not necessarily the case that the processes described here are of a conciliative nature, however, given the potential for businesses and social movements to entangle themselves in relations of competition for public attention and support.

Another counter-strategy by economic enterprises is their capacity to establish their own representative, or public relations, organizations. In Australia, for example, the classical liberal writer and politician Bruce Smith established employer associations in the states of New South Wales and Victoria during the late nineteenth century (Hendy 2008). An important motivational underpinning for Smith's initiative appears to have been the desire to countervail the rising influence of labor unions, and related groups, during this period. This strategy seems to have assumed an altogether different form in more recent times, with researchers pointing to the growth of so-called "astroturf" (as opposed to genuinely "grassroots") entities which advance positions consistent with those of industry, or labor unions, interest groups, and other organizations (Walker 2010, 2014). In similar fashion to social movements in general, astroturfing involves efforts "to both amplify pre-existing concerns among the public and also to persuade and mobilize previously unorganized constituencies" (Walker 2014, 6). The key contrast is with the engagement of professional groups—such as strategic consultants, public relations firms, paid lobbyists, and so on—to manufacture contentious activity consistent with the interests of the sponsoring sectional interests. The astroturfing trend described here not only reflects important shifts in the nature of conflictive, if not hostile, entanglement between social movements and the corporate sector, but raises questions about resource mobilization capacities, as well as the institutionalization of movement tactics, in contemporary societies.

Social Movements, Corporate Social Responsibility, and Social Justice

There have been trenchant criticisms, including by numerous classical liberals, concerning the apparent readiness of businesses to concede to, or even embrace, the demands of social movements. In recent years "woke capitalism" has been articulated as a pejorative term describing the tendency of certain corporations to publicize their support for, or sympathy, with various cultural, social, and political causes being waged by perceived adversaries (or enemies) of capitalism itself. Such criticisms are not new, and have been articulated in the past. Friedrich Hayek (1967, 300) argued that corporate affairs would prove socially propitious if it were confined "to one specific goal, that of the profitable use of the capital entrusted to the management by the stockholders." This condition implies the need for corporate cautiousness toward the "political, charitable, educational and in fact everything which can be brought under the vague and almost meaningless term 'social'" (ibid., 304). The risk is that firms believed to be actively engaging in social, and related non-economic, issues are more likely to attract political attention and be captured, guaranteeing effective corporate control by political actors over the long run.

Hayek's views about corporate conduct correspond with his generic critiques of the social justice concept. Hayek seems to comprehend social justice primarily as a political project to realize a preferred, if not idealized, end-state outcome through redistribution (Hayek [1973–1979] 2013; 1988). It is not unreasonable to imagine Hayek to be equally critical about corporate projects invoking the name, if not the spirit, of social justice—as the quote in the previous paragraph suggests. The Hayekian criticism is that any attempt to enshrine distributional equality on social justice grounds would gravely diminish the market-based economic order, the latter tending to progressively lift living standards for all. In one of his more vivid criticisms, Hayek (1988) submitted that social justice embodies a dangerous misapplication of equalitarian sentiments applicable to "micro-cosmos" arrangements—such as families, tribes, and similarly small groups—but working to the detriment of the "macro-cosmos"—exemplified by impartial economic exchanges between non-intimates under the rule of law.

Milton Friedman arguably involved himself even more dramatically into this topic. Writing for the *New York Times Magazine*, he asserted that the responsibility of corporate executives is to "make as much money as possible while conforming to their basic rules of the society, both those embodied in law and those embodied in ethical custom" (Friedman [1970] 1987, 37). Elsewhere, he said that, "[f]ew trends could so thoroughly undermine the very foundations of our free society as the acceptance by corporate officials of a social responsibility other than to make as much money for their stockholders as possible" (Friedman [1962] 2002, 133). If there is any sense in which "social responsibility" may be plausibly assumed by corporate managers, it is to ensure that profits are maintained so that healthy returns are received by shareholders.

Many of the issues discussed here focus upon a host of activities taken up by firms, under the rubric of "corporate social responsibility" (CSR). In practice CSR can assume many forms but, generally speaking, it features the use of corporate funds to promote societal, environmental, and other non-economic goals. Those goals may be facilitated by donating to certain causes, or by firms creating their own initiatives "with a conscience," as it were. CSR practices also entail companies reporting, and representing, their operations in what is perceived to be a socially accountable and conscionable manner. CSR seems a contentious activity with seemingly few ideological proponents. In addition to broadsides by liberals and conservatives to the effect that CSR initiatives are economically wasteful (Henderson 2001; Lal 2006), progressive figures often decry business CSR engagement as a manipulative appropriation of sincerely-held beliefs and goals of social movements and similar groups (e.g., Stark 2015; Vieira de Freitas Netto et al. 2020).

Why have for-profit firms involved themselves with CSR? The main, yet interrelated, reasons are threefold. The first is that corporate owners and managers may genuinely subscribe to underlying CSR causes. This makes them more receptive to using their organizations as vehicles to propel causes nominally shared by potential adversaries, such as social movements. Second, corporate owners may believe that CSR engagement may positively influence a firm's receptivity to social issues, as well as the potential for positive media and public feedback (Soule and King 2015). Third, it is possible that commercial enterprises engage in CSR to deflect public criticism, including from social movement figures, with regard to sensitive issues. Each of those motives, in turn, appear attuned to an underlying motive to avert a depreciation of reputational capital. However, as implied by Brayden King and Mary-Hunter McDonnell (2015) and Sarah Soule and Brayden King (2015), the risk is that a firm publicly banding with certain causes may be susceptible to broader attention cascades and, thus, the target of ever-increasing movement pressure. Connected to this point is the possibility that social movement participants may cynically attach themselves to companies with favorable CSR-related reputations, not only to gain more concessions but to amplify the movement's position on related causes.

Intense criticisms have obviously been leveled at businesses perceived to be veering outside the domain of profitable production. Even so, it is counseled that one may wish to remain cautious about these matters, rather than prejudging all interactions between firms and social movements as being morally indefensible or normatively undesirable. An entangled political economy perspective maintains an ontological basis which assuredly leans *against insularity and separability* on the part of individuals and their entities. In actually-existing societies bearing the qualities of openness, it is almost a foregone conclusion that social movement participants will engage corporate owners, managers, employees, and suppliers. Those engagements will vary from the fleeting to the meaningful, and be imbued with qualities ranging from the combative to the embracing. The deeply laden heterogeneities and overlapping relationships characterizing movement-corporate intertwinements must be recognized, and managed if necessary, but not to be abstracted away or dismissed out of hand.

It is arguable that the Hayek-Friedman critiques were laced with a degree of qualification. Hayek stressed that his preferred limitation on corporations to secure "the highest long-term return on their capital . . . does not mean that in the pursuit of this end they ought not to be restrained by general legal *and* moral rules" (Hayek 1967, 301). Friedman's declaration of the social responsibility of business included, to repeat, reference to legal rules and rules "embodied in ethical custom." Individuals not only maintain a preference for economic flourishing as a means to lead autonomous and fulfilling lives. People maintain heterogeneous ethical and social beliefs, concerns, and values. Customers of corporations maintain such diversities and so, too, do owners, managers, workers, and suppliers of the same-said corporations (Brieger et al. 2019). Significantly, these diverse precepts are not limited to one's own conduct, but may extend to the conduct of others. The non-separability of economic and non-economic dimensions is, after all, reflected in the derivation of corporate financial value from intangibles, such as branding and goodwill (Hammond 2017).

Oliver Hart and Luigi Zingales (2017) suggest that it is appropriate for companies to countenance how their operations and practices affect broader shareholder welfare. This notion is instructive in light of the real-world possibilities that: profitable companies may, under certain circumstances, cause broader ecological and social damages; governments cannot effectively internalize all externalities arising from dyadic interactions; and, finally, shareholders have a capacity to harbor pro-social attitudes. Another constructive contribution toward grasping the broad-scale dimensions of corporate activity is presented by Aligica et al. (2019). Specifically, these authors develop a "polycentric stakeholder analysis" (PSA) paradigm to assess methods of public engagement by corporations with their varied, and competing, stakeholders. PSA may be construed as engagement among diverse actors who share an interest in co-producing resolutions to public problems, with this concept conceivably inclusive of social movement concerns.

Corporate actors may wish to address public problems, and be amenable to approaches from social movements, and other stakeholders, competing for corporate attention and assistance. A PSA approach may be pursued so long as businesses are aware that they absorb the costs of responding to a broad suite of stakeholders about non-economic causes. Attending to social, ecological, and other, problems certainly does not absolve firms from their tasks to produce quality goods and services at reasonable prices for consumers, and to maintain innovative impetus. Far from necessarily inviting the "slippery slope" of governmental intervention at every turn, an important side-benefit of PSA is that "the better that voluntary CSR activities work, the weaker the case is for government intervention" (Aligica et al. 2019 194).

Social movements often assume antagonistic positions relative to corporations, especially larger entities operating at national and global scales. Given the nature of entangled political economy, by no means are social movements insulated from corporate fortunes, or from economic conditions more generally. As noted in the case of SMOs and network structures, movement participants procure many of their resources and capabilities from the marketplace. Entanglement implies interactionism between parties. Therefore, it is unsurprising that contentious movement strategies and tactics would have profound impacts upon corporate reputation, let alone productive activities, along various margins. It is in this respect that the idea that "we are market forces" assumes particular salience, embracing "not only individual buyers and sellers, looking to increase a bottom line, but also our shared projects, when people choose to work together, by means of *conscious but non-coercive* activism, alongside, indeed as a part of, the undesigned forms of spontaneous self-organization that emerge" (Johnson 2011, 393).

SOCIAL MOVEMENTS AND MEDIA

An integral feature of modern life is the availability and use of communication networks through which the populace sends and receives data, messages, and other kinds of information. Communications at the globalized scale we see today have been greatly facilitated by technologies—such as printed newspapers and related documents, radio and television broadcasts, and communication services provided through the Internet—enabling the transference of communicative artifacts and materials. Another feature of the communications environment is the presence of organizational forms—such as private firms and platform infrastructures—assuming proprietary ownership and control over various communication networks. These organizations also assume a "gatekeeping" function determining access to, and usage, of communication technologies by users. In broad terms, the term *media* represents the combination of technologies and organizations providing mass communication.

The nature of intermediated communication services provided by media has significant connotations for the way in which social movements discursively engage with others. As Koopmans (2004a, 368) indicates, "nowadays protesters rarely get to see the addressees of their demands, nor do the latter directly observe, let alone engage, with the protesters. Bystander publics may still be present and occasionally they still cheer and boo, but it is no longer the co-present public that counts most, but the mass audience that sits at home and watches or reads the media coverage of the demonstration." Communication is mainly conducted in the form of indirect, mediated encounters among various parties *through* media organizations and platforms.

In a classic paper in the field of social movement and media studies, Gamson and Wolfsfeld (1993) outline a few broad-ranging rationales for movement engagement with the media. Social movement participants seek to obtain a good standing in the eyes of media participants. In other words, movements want to be taken seriously as a source of information for media outlets with regard to certain public issues. Another reason for movements to partake in media engagement is that newspapers, radio, television, and the Internet help disseminate movement frames rapidly. Finally, social movements would prefer the media to present their issues, and strategic and tactical selections, in a positive or sympathetic light. This could help the movement realize its other plans, such as accumulating resources from potential supporters or building up overall participation.

There are other reasons why social movements should seek workable, if not constructive, relationships with print, broadcast, and online media. It is through media intermediaries that social movements engage in "outside" political lobbying (e.g., Tresch and Fischer 2015), engagement with large corporations, and discourse with other actors. Bennett and Segerberg (2015) remind us that the media also serves as a communications filter through which social movement participants network with one another. Finally, movements use the media to obtain intelligence about their political, economic, and social targets, and about competitor social movements and activist figures.

Social movement participants are likely to consider media outlets as strategically pivotal intermediaries who could assist in publicizing and exerting public pressure upon specific target groups, and opponents more generally. However, media organizations do not necessarily act as impartial disseminators of events, issues, and occurrences, as they unfold, for consumption by undifferentiated masses. They represent a crucial player within entangled political economy as a producer and distributor of opinions, perceptions, and symbols in their own right. What this means, in part, is that social movements and media are commonly entwined in their own interpretive struggles, usually over the meaning and significance of movement tactics and collective actions. As stated by Gamson and Wolfsfeld (1993, 117): "[m] ovements and media are both in the business of interpreting events, along with other nonmovement actors who have a stake in them. Events do not speak for themselves but must be woven into some larger story line or frame; they take on their meaning from the frame in which they are embedded." In this context there are no guarantees that movement efforts to engage with owners, managers, and journalistic employees of media organizations would create positive reportage.

With those issues in mind, social movement participants might, then, perceive they must conduct "dramatic performances" for attention (H. Johnston 2014). The need to supply contentious dramaturgy might push certain movements toward ill-advised actions. Goodwin and Jasper (2015) also observe that the media could misconstrue the conduct of movement activity when, say, journalists and reporters focus on some of the extremist, fringe elements of protests, or when the media identify movement "stars" with a tendency for loose thinking or incendiary language. These possibilities may, in turn, disincentivize social movements from pursuing modest tactics for the sake of providing that "good copy" of attention for media outlets (Gamson and Wolfsfeld 1993).

Boiled down to its essentials, media coverage frequency and sentiment will condition the perceived effectiveness of a social movement's engagement with media. However, this by no means implies that coverage will, or even should, conform to the preferences of movement participants. As noted, there is significant potential that activism will be publicly reported in a negative light. Social movement frames may be misinterpreted, reporting about protests and other tactical selections may be erroneous, and movements might be depicted as a generalized danger and threat to societal order.

Dieter Rucht (2004) identifies a range of strategies available to social movements in reaction to disappointment or frustration with (hostile or inattentive) media. One of these is to seek or create "alternative" media, considered here as a form of communicative self-organization. Movement engagement with alternative media—such as clandestine or "underground" publishing houses, or even "do-it-yourself" pamphleteering—is undertaken with a view to disseminate authentic, unfiltered, messages to already-existing movement participants and to potential supporters. Alternative media can also aid social movements by informing audiences about key values, perspectives, and events (Downing 2001). The outputs of alternative media, whether produced by the movement itself or intermediary producers, are varied—they include journals, magazines, newspapers, pamphlets, posters, radio, and websites, blogsites, and social media.

We agree that alternative media can play its part in expanding the communicative range of "voice" in society, particularly for those promulgating challenger perspectives. From a historical standpoint, technological developments such as the printing press may well have been implicated in the development of the nation-state—due to the paper distribution of official fiscal and regulatory guidelines, combined with the standardization of language and gradual rise of literacy rates (Okun 2020). The effect of the printing press in lowering the long-term relative costs of communications also enabled individuals and groups (including publishers) to print abstract ideas and policy proposals. Some of these outputs conveyed the aim of advancing economic, political, and social freedoms. Indeed, pamphleteering and book production has been deeply intertwined in the story of liberalism's emergence and solidification—from the pamphleteered arguments for fiscal, regulatory, and trade freedoms in eighteenth- and nineteenth-century English and French liberalism, to the distribution of anti-communist material behind the Iron Curtain, and to the alternative literature of black, gay, and women's liberation movements.

It still remains reasonable to ask whether alternative media work by social movements truly succeeds in reaching out to the broader public, beyond the network of strongly sympathetic movement supporters (della Porta and Diani 2020). In practice, it may well be the case that social movements still need to engage with major media corporations and outlets, even if such steps necessitate a need to present a moderate face regarding the direction and speed of desired societal change. The enduring relevance of mainstream media outlets is illustrated by activists publishing "self-help" or "how to" guides to assist movement participants in winning mainstream media attention (e.g., Gitlin 1980; Ryan 1991).

Social movements and traditional media organizations maintain complicated entanglements. Given the position of newspaper, radio, and television networks as key communicative intermediaries, social movements tend to spend considerable time and effort trying to discover how to exploit media opportunities (Gans 1979). As part of this, movement organizers and activists often take concerted steps to attract the attention of media producers, journalists, and reports. Breaking developments in relation to social movement strategies and tactics may, indeed, provide captivating or sensationalist feedstock material for media concerns. However, there is no guarantee that certain media outlets or individual reporters will necessarily report about movement activities in a favorable, let alone impartial, manner.

So far, we have excluded social media, now an important platform for the dissemination of social movement communications. Detailed discussions about the usage of social media by social movements will be reserved for later. Nonetheless, it will be noted here that social media usage has tended to blur the boundaries between senders and receivers of communication, as well as producers and users (Bennett and Segerberg 2015; della Porta and Diani 2020). This trend has significant implications for the capacity of social movements to organize against their targets, and to encourage participation in public demonstration and other tactical maneuvers.

SOCIAL MOVEMENTS AND COUNTER-MOVEMENTS

We have previously read that social movements are capable of building constructive alliances with other groups. Social movement organizational practices, tactical behaviors, and forms of collective action may also be emulated by other movements, reflective of a process of social learning. In referring to the legacies of twentieth-century feminism, Nancy Whittier (2004, 531) suggests that movement success "helped to spawn other challenges around gay and lesbian liberation, child sexual abuse, and intersections of race, class, and gender." In societies respecting freedom of assembly, expression, and of speech, it should not be surprising to learn that social movements also exist in opposition to one another. So-called "counter-movements" attempt to thwart the capability of initiator social movements to achieve the latter's objectives. In doing so, the counter-movement, in effect, works to defend some element of the *status quo* on principle, or for expediency.

In social movement literature, there are several conceptualizations of counter-movement features and behavior. Inspired by the political process approaches of Charles Tilly and Sidney Tarrow, Meyer and Staggenborg (1996, 1631–1632) refer to a counter-movement as "a movement that makes contrary claims simultaneously to those of the original movement . . . [counter-movements are] networks of individuals and organizations that share many of the same objects of concern as the social movements that they oppose. They make competing claims on the state on matters of policy and politics . . . and view for attention from the mass media and the broader public." That a counter-movement attempts to stymie others is reinforced in earlier work by Mottl (1980, 620), describing counter-movements as "a particular kind of protest movement which is a response to the social change advocated by an initial movement."

Social movement and counter-movement interactions are both complex and dynamic, and the nature of such interactions vary depending on case and context. Limiting our considerations to movement activities within the political arena, we can imagine that political concessions gained by a given movement instigate counter-responses. A counter-movement may react by exerting pressure upon policymakers to reverse legislative or policy victories of the initial movement. Assuming the counter-movement successfully reverses the political concessions won by the initiator movement, the initiators return to the political scene in an effort to reinstate the initial reform. As noted by Dorf and Tarrow (2014), the formulaic, to-and-fro process outlined here is an oversimplification of interactional dynamics between movements. The authors refer to the possibility of "anticipatory counter-mobilization," wherein counter-movements mobilize prior to a social issue or problem receiving mainstream attention. Even here the success of pre-empting the emergence of a movement for societal change is not assured: "the successes of 'anticipatory countermobilization' are often temporary because they can trigger social movements to mobilize against them" (ibid., 453).

Counter-movements are usually depicted as instigators of "backlash dynamics," which appear to have gripped social policy in recent years. For feminist scholar Ann Cudd (2002), a backlash is couched within a broader socio-psychological context of group-based stereotyping. This stereotyping, in turn, prescribes an oppositional response to movement-enabled concessions to perceived out-groups. Lest the impression be given that counter-movement activity is entirely a reflex response, Clarence Lo (1982) suggests that counter-movements may be informed by ideological commitments. Furthermore, counter-movement activity often reflects a considerable measure of strategy and careful planning. The core idea of a counter-movement, then, is that it is contestably engaging with its social movement opponents strategically and tactically, and not necessarily in a reactive fashion.

It is obvious that social movements and counter-movements entangle in a largely conflictual and turbulent fashion. These protagonist groups engage in competition for publicity, finances, material resources, human participants, and social esteem. Movements and counter-movements may clash on the streets, occasionally bursting into violent activities, but their conflicting relations can also be manifested indirectly. Indirect engagements of mutual influence between movements and counter-movements have been described by Zald and Useem (1987) as "loosely coupled conflict." For example, a study by Vann (2018) indicates that social movements and counter-movements attempt to encourage their supporters to vote in electoral contests in order to nullify the voting intentions and strength of their opposition.

Another indirect means through which social movements and their opponents interact is through rhetorical and framing debates. Such debate is usually colored by efforts to perpetuate negative images of their opponents throughout media, or elsewhere. Engaging in argument and counter-argument, the two sets of opponents implicitly aim at increasing coordination and other costs upon their opponents (della Porta and Diani 2020). For Whittier (2004, 532) movements also "may alter the form that another movement takes—its frames, discourses, collective identity, goals, tactics, and organizational structure" (also Dillard 2013). While social movements and counter-movements do vary organizationally and ideologically, they most assuredly aim to detrimentally impact one another on most occasions.

Societal tectonics, as expressed by social movement interactions with counter-movements, have become evident over many public issues. New counter-movements of a reactionary nature—some of which have coincided with the emergence of populist, anti-democratic, and authoritarian political figures globally—have emerged to challenge liberal freedoms (e.g., Hawley 2017; Main 2018; Meadowcroft and Morrow 2017; Morrow and Meadowcroft 2019). Counter-movement participants have expressed a yearning for a resurrection of economic nationalism and anti-immigration stances, together with a reversal of individual and human rights along racial, gender, and sexual orientation lines. These groups have come on the heels of earlier movement activities that vigorously challenged pro-globalization policies during the late 1990s and early 2000s. A major task for proponents of liberal ideas over the next few years will be to intelligently and robustly respond to illiberal counter-movements.

SOCIAL MOVEMENTS AND CIVIL SOCIETY

We now turn to consider the place of social movements with civil society, the latter generally understood in liberal theorization as those spaces of association beyond economic and political domains. Far from being represented as a singular, undifferentiated entity, civil society encompasses a complex and evolving ecology of individuals engaging one another through various groups. These groups include associations, clubs, neighborhoods, religious orders, professional interest groups, nonprofit organizations, social enterprises, mutual aid, and many other activities and entities. Irrespective of whether any given social movement attends to a cause congruous with our own personal preferences, we subscribe to the view that social movements are, also, an important part of civil society. As stated by Rucht (2010, 1444), "one has to acknowledge that democratically oriented social movements, along with a broad range of nonmovement related voluntary associations, are a constitutive element of a vibrant civil society."

The key theme of this chapter is that social movement participants typically stand ready to assertively engage with, and mobilize against, a variety of actors. This cross-domain activism by social movements is, in our view, comprehensible through the lens of entangled political economy. Recall that entangled political economy explicitly encapsulates the relationships and interactions forged between individuals and groups, and these can transcend specialized domains of human action. In other words, the profundity of entangled political economy is its dethronement of strict separability assumptions for the study of civil society:

> Society cannot be captured by simple addition across independent entities denoted by state, market, and civil society, for the resulting patterns of social activity depend significantly both on interactions among its various participants and on the institutional framework that governs those interactions. The relation between polity and economy is not separable and additive but rather is entangled. State agencies and offices act within society as part of the self-organizing motion of society, and do not stand outside of society and act on it. (R. Wagner 2010, 163)

As explained in this chapter, and elsewhere, social movements are, themselves, actively entangled with political and commercial enterprises, as well as alternative groupings within civil society, in their pursuit of societal change.

By virtue of their oppositional stance toward many issues and problems, social movements are seen by some to necessarily threaten the functionality of civil society. However, it is our view that such a perception is mistaken. Whereas contractarian theories of society and politics ideally hold that the attainment of civil society, and institutional rules underpinning it, requires consensus on the part of all participants, it is unreasonable to expect in a world of heterogeneity and its deep diversities of interests, perspectives, and values that such consensual conditions will necessarily be met. Taking a realist approach, disagreements should be presumed to exist in various economic, political, and social contexts, and over any given period of time (Sleat 2013; Sabl 2015). It is in these contexts that social movements will aim to rally people to express their problems through various means. Rather than contend that disagreement automatically signals deterioration of civil society, one may recognize civil society as a space wherein "individuals, primarily less powerful challengers but also dominant interests, come together to collectively act and to legitimate their interests to the broader public" (S. Klein and Lee 2019, 67).

For a certain train of civil societal thought, the very notion of a social movement sits uneasily for other reasons. Scholars who equate civil society with normative standards of *civility* among intimates and strangers alike (e.g., Shils 1991) criticize the proclivity of movement participants to embrace disruptive conduct in challenging the societal *status quo*. While social movement activity may now be largely seen as a subset of contentious politics populated by many claim makers and takers (McAdam et al. 2001), social movements are typically seen as an exemplar of acting in opposition, and often stridently so, against the interests and values of other agents within civil society. The potential for social movement disruption seems amplified when considering that disputation applies to differing notions of value and worthiness (Dekker and Kuchař 2017).

The critical characterizations noted earlier should be couched within a broader perspective appreciating the dynamic basis of societal change. For a start, the presence of conflict between social movements and those whom they entangle with today does not necessarily entail conflict tomorrow. It is true that social movement activity may expose significant inter-personal and inter-group tensions, but if parties are willing to discuss and exchange ideas such a stance may help "promote alternative, and prospectively improved, ways in which people *can cooperate and align their prerogatives*" (Novak 2018a, 6; emphasis added). When social movements assume a self-limiting stance of reasonableness, nonviolent methods of dispute resolution, and respecting others' rights and liberties (Madison 1998), their proposals for societal alternatives remain objects of choice (in some instances, compellingly so), and not of imposition. As de Bakker et al. (2013) have noted, engagements between social movements and other groups can often be accompanied by a blurring of the senses between "contentious" and "collaborative" forms of managing conflict. Taking a broader point from those same authors, such blurriness implies that "social movements cannot solely be understood through the lens of contestation and civil society cannot be reduced to collaborative association" (ibid., 575).

Much of the focus of social movement theory is upon the contentious engagements between activists and actors within the governmental domain, such as legislators, regulators, and policymakers. Liberals, too, devote much of their intellectual focus upon government. This seems underpinned by concerns that growth in the scale and scope of public-sector activities displace productive market-based economic activities of material provisioning, as well as those diverse, polycentric, and voluntary civil societal arrangements of mutual support and care. It is not at all unreasonable that liberals should critically glance toward social movements, to the extent they pursue illiberal projects with the effect of diminishing the exercise of freedom and liberty. Even so, a key claim in this book is that there is more to be said about social movements and their activities, and constructively so, from liberal perspectives. At the very least, not every social movement assumes an illiberal approach toward public issues or the means to pursue societal change.

The development of identity-sensitive and culturally-sensitive "new social movements" theory has the potential to interpret social movement activities in a new light, specifically in ways that are seen as amenable to civil society (and, perhaps, liberal) theorizations. The reason for this, as scholars such as Alain Touraine and Alberto Melucci have explained, is that social movements can be seen as arenas for reshaping cultural norms subscribed to by non-state actors, as opposed to merely petitioning government for formal policy concessions at every opportunity. Jean Cohen and Andrew Arato (1992) indicates that new social movements theory focuses upon reforming the cultural substructures of civil society, to achieve greater autonomy recognition and rights for minorities and otherwise forgotten, or repressed, groups. In this light, the work of social movements, in creating expanded spaces for toleration, respect, and acceptance among diverse individuals and groups, would appear to affirm some high-level liberal objectives.

Reference to new social movements, and their cultural works, is merely a starting point. The history of liberalism is shaped by the efforts of people organizing for, and demanding, liberation from undue governmental restrictions, and certain social movements have played their part in the struggle for a better, freer world. Admittedly, much of the focus of this book concerns those movement efforts obtaining political concessions in a pro-liberty direction. Recognition should, nevertheless, be given to those perspectives about movements which reflect a "non-state-centric" view of the world. This view is distinct from a "state-centric" movement conception, which is the subject of detailed critique by Jeff Shantz. In a recent work, he submits that "[s]ocial movement theorists . . . emphasize movement characteristics . . . that are geared to better influence decision makers. This obscures movements that seek capacities to make their own decisions and not rely on authorities to better decide for them" (Shantz 2020, 44). Whereas Shantz is critical of liberal paradigms which he believes dominates movement theorization, and that (arguably, in contrast with entangled political economy) government is caricatured as closed and hierarchical, these readings should not deter liberals from conceptually advancing a genuinely "non-state-centric" interpretation of social movements. Indeed, observations to the effect that social movements provide opportunities for self-governance, and non-statist avenues for social change, should be of great interest to civil society scholars in liberal perspective.

CONCLUSION

Social movements have a major bearing on the processes and patterns of human association. The influence of social movements upon other actors—who focus their attentions within and across economic, political, and social domains—is both extensive and profound. They seek to recognize the existence of symbolic resources, draw attention to shared commitments concerning identity and values, and leverage networking relations to build major, cross-cutting constituencies supportive of societal change. Regardless of our position over the appropriateness of social movement activities, what is surely widely agreed is that movement entanglement with multiple groups has a major impact on our lives, including the capacity of our institutions, organizations, and practices, to absorb change.

This chapter restricted its coverage to movement interactions with certain elements of government, business, media, as well as counter-movements. While actors within these domains will be referred to in the case studies presented in subsequent chapters, we acknowledge that movement participants contentiously engage with additional members of society involved in certain activities, functions, and roles. Social movement researchers have produced important literature surrounding the attributes and implications of movement engagements with academic institutions (e.g., Rojas 2007), and religious orders (e.g., Morris 1984; Hannigan 1991), to name two additional examples.

The discussions outlined in this chapter, not to mention elsewhere, are predicated upon an endorsement of Richard Wagner's entangled orientation to liberal political economy. The terms of entanglement between social movements and government agencies, business organizations, media outlets, and counter-movement organs, and networks, necessarily suggests that as social movements influence, they, too, are influenced. Many of the aforementioned entities assume outsized roles within contemporary civil society, possessing the authority and logistical prowess to severely limit social movement influence in many parts of the world (including in liberal-democratic societies). The effectiveness of social movements in translating their demands into reality will not only depend upon the issue carried by the movement itself, but by the organizational-institutional responses of other actors in business, politics, media, and elsewhere. An ongoing challenge for social movements is to ensure they can win hearts and minds outside of their core activist and supporter bases.

Social movements, like many other groupings within civil society, upset patterns. Many social movements seek to upset patterns intentionally. The breadth and intensity of social movement engagements underline the very plasticity of the movement form, the determination of movements to advocate for meaningful change, and the capacity of diverse movement participants to undertake cross-cutting engagements across domains of human action. Social movement involvements in emancipation, and with the broader realization of liberties, are appropriately conceived as *co-evolutionary* processes between movement participants and others located in civil society, wherein some measure of mutually-agreed reform opportunities have been discovered or are being negotiated. This broad insight will be illustrated in the following chapters, using a number of historical and contemporary case examples.

Chapter 5

Social Movements and Liberty

Case Studies in the Modern History of Freedom

INTRODUCTION

A key claim we seek to advance is that social movements can be understood through the prism of liberal political economy. In this chapter we proceed a step further, applying liberal reasoning to interpret movement conduct, figures, and key events in its modern historical context. The very conception of a social *movement*, in our view, is established within a broader architecture of societal change (McGee 1980; Popper 1944), and this, in turn, gives credence to the historical examination of movements. Of particular interest is that arguments, and direct action, for reform in a liberal direction have been advanced and propagated by social movements over decades, if not centuries.

In remarking that social movements have contributed to freedom in varied guises, we do not wish to present a hagiographic account. A vast number of projects fail, and the history of social movements is littered with errors, failures, missteps, and unanticipated consequences. Similarly, historical development refuses to unfold in a determinist manner. However, the project of liberalism in actually-existing societies is unmistakably affirming of freedom as an economic, political, and social aspiration. As the English politician, academic, and lawyer Walter Lyon Blease (1913, 11) once remarked, "[i]n practical politics the work of modern liberalism has been to alter the conditions of society so that this freedom of growth may be secured for each member of it. . . . Against a privileged race, rank, creed, or sex liberalism must fight continually." It is in this spirit that social movements often serve as crucial historical elements in struggles to expansively realize liberal opportunities in the real world, as the cases put forward in this chapter will attempt to convey.

Bringing the historical contributions of social movements to light serves as a useful application of what has been recently described as "liberal history." Challenging state-centric, or overly politicized, accounts of the historical record (Garín 2017), liberal history methodologically emphasizes the individual, and the voluntary groups they initiate, as primary agents in historical episodes. Given the aversion to political, and other forms of power which threaten to constrain the exercise of individual freedom, "classical liberal historians are especially attuned to examining the economic, social, political, and cultural conditions, and institutions that preserve the widest sphere for human liberty" (Douma and Magness 2017, x). Furthermore, this liberal historical approach is conducted with an appreciation that society is properly understood as an evolutionary process, "of interactions and institutions emerging from similar human problem situations rather than in terms of a 'genetic' or internally determined process of development" (Ealy 2017, 7).

As this chapter shall illustrate, social movement participants have been active contributors to expanding economic, political, and social freedoms. While the sections constituting this chapter are categorized along those dimensions of freedom for simplicity, we want to make clear that the studied movements (and, by and large, others, for that matter) acted *across* domain-specific boundaries. Movement organizers, activists, and participants generally understood that their schemes were not solely economic *or* political *or* social in intention or in effect. In our descriptions of pro-liberty propensities in the following movement case studies, we remain mindful of the explanatory "messiness" underlining historical analysis and investigation.

The next section of this chapter describes the contribution of social movements toward certain economic liberalization episodes. Specifically, we reflect upon movement activities for the right to own, control, and trade property, which includes activism to minimize government infringements of property rights. This is followed by an account of social movement involvement in realizing democratic political reforms—in this case, empowering political participation by, and representation for, women. In addition, this chapter provides a description of the development of civil liberties, human rights, and related manifestations of social freedom. We provide specific reference to the struggles for racial equality. This chapter concludes with a set of brief remarks.

SOCIAL MOVEMENTS FOR ECONOMIC FREEDOM

Property Rights, Free Trade, and Taxation

A hallmark of liberal thought is its normative priority upon the freedom of individuals to interact with one another in economic contexts. The presumption here is that people should enjoy the ability to produce, distribute, and exchange goods and services, on the condition that people respect the equal rights of others to conduct similar activities. In addition to undertaking speech acts, said Adam Smith, human beings are inclined to exercise their innate desire for sociability through trade. Empirical evidence supports the judgment that allowing people to economically participate more freely is associated with economic growth, and related material benefits (e.g., Berggren 2003; Hall and Lawson 2014). As noted by Geoffrey Brennan (2018), however, the freedom to undertake economic exchange does not connote ethical-moral entitlements to insulate agents from losses stemming from any ill-conceived ventures.

It is a truism that there must exist certain kinds of resources, known as property, to enable economic exchanges to occur. Indeed, there are numerous things—animal, vegetable, or mineral, as well as intangible items—in the world. On what basis are individuals conceived to own, control, and use such things, in ways that secure economic value in trades? Over the centuries liberal thinkers have outlined a conception of *property rights*, describing the possibilities of managing things owned, controlled, and used in a manner consistent with ensuring extensive individual freedoms. The seventeenth-century philosopher John Locke ([1689] 1988) outlined a system of "self-ownership" in property. This confers a right to the ownership, control, and utilization of one's own body, labor, and other resources, and with the prevention of such rights being coercively realized by others without consent.

It follows from this discussion that institutional and practical arrangements, according esteem and respect for property rights, are pivotal to upholding key liberal economic commitments. In particular, property rights are seen as a necessary, but not sufficient, condition to facilitate decentralized exchanges in market economies. Following the insights of Hayek, decentralized exchange ensures that adjustments to property rights reflect the distributed insight and knowledge among the population, concerning opportunities to add economic value for the benefit of others. The ability of property rights to distil such epistemic diversity provides a spur for entrepreneurs to propose new economic solutions. Affording individuals and groups the freedom to voluntarily own, control, and use property incentivizes them to economize on resource use, because users bear the costs of their actions (B. Powell 2002). The widespread dispersion of property—which tends to occur in market-based economic systems respectful of property rights—also serves as a bulwark against the accumulation of political power and influence over the economy (Halliday and Thrasher 2020).

At this juncture, we seek to offer some clarifications surrounding the nature of property rights. At the outset, property rights feature a range of benefits and duties which are not reducible to the fact of physical items being in possession: "[a] property right is a liberty or permit to enjoy benefits of wealth—in its broadest sense—while assuming the costs which those benefits entail. . . . It will be observed that property rights, unlike wealth or benefits, are not physical objects nor events, but are abstract social relations. A property right is not a thing" (Irving Fisher, quoted in Kasper et al. 2012, 188). In taking care to make the distinction between property *qua* things and property rights, Bart Wilson (2020) also clarifies that rights (in property) are not abilities. Repeating our earlier reference to Geoffrey Brennan, property rights do not serve as entitlements, or guarantees, of economic success. Indeed, a critical facet of the association between robustly-performing markets and the presence of, and respect for, property rights is that competitive economic processes work to ameliorate commercial failures—in so doing, dynamically reallocating properties from lower to higher valued uses.

Liberalism is known for its forthright arguments for minimizing expropriation of property rights by malign private and public actors. A longstanding liberal proposition is that individuals have extensive, indeed on some accounts, *innate* or *natural*, rights to own, control, and use property. For liberals the fulfillment of such conditions rests upon appropriate economic, political, and social conduct, institutions, and practices. Much of modern liberal political economy stresses the importance of formal rules, ensuring that political actors do not enact fiscal, legal, and regulatory policies in a manner abridging rule of law precepts. Formalized political rules need to be supported by cultural affirmations regarding the importance of property rights. Indeed, as noted by Wilson (2020, 19), "[t]he justice and temperance of *mine* and *thine* are necessary conditions for prosperity and human flourishing." In this sense, institutions and norms go together in the liberal scheme.

The liberal critique of politics responds to the observed proclivities of political actors to diminish the economic value of property, if not subverting property rights altogether. Governmental predation of property rights is portrayed in so-called "leviathan models"—such as those outlined by Brennan and Buchanan ([1980] 2000), and Levi (1988)—wherein political actors are assumed to maximize revenues and rents. However, it does not take one to assume the dynastic organizational form of leviathan to appreciate that political action can pose as a significant risk to property rights. Governments promising to protect property rights, *ex ante*, but which renege on such promises, *ex post*, can stifle private investments and other relevant productive activity (Higgs 1987; Voigt 2020). Legislators, bureaucrats, and other political actors may try to elaborate justifications for such conduct, often involving affective and moralizing rhetoric to garner public acquiescence (R. Wagner 2016). Nonetheless, knowledge and incentive problems dictate that the governmental circumscription of the rights to own, control, and use, property is likely to come at a hefty cost to economic growth, productivity, and living standards (Pennington 2011).

The American Revolution

Taxation arrangements have been identified by economists, historians, political scientists, and sociologists as central to the formation and persistence of the modern state (e.g., Schumpeter [1918] 1954; Levi 1988; Olson 1993). Taxes have commonly been used to finance public (and other) goods, and to redistribute private-sector resources. Whereas the ethics and morality of this fiscal practice is covered extensively elsewhere (e.g., Huemer 2017; Lomasky 1998), we merely wish to highlight that taxation is widely understood to affect property rights. Indeed, orthodox economic policy literature openly suggests that governments impose, and adjust, tax bases and rates in a bid to reshape the parameters of private ownership, control, and usage of property, or to influence the rate of return on values generated by, properties, in the name of broader policy purposes.

The entangled political economy perspective indicates that taxes have the effect of parasitically attaching governmental authorities onto certain individuals, commercial enterprises, and other entities, as well as the gainful activities pursued by the latter assortment of actors. Richard Wagner (2015, 2016) outlines how tax impositions foment tectonic clashes between commercial and political interests, as political considerations and prerogatives become interwoven with market exchanges. When taxes are perceived to be excessive or unfair in some way—whether on the part of those statutorily liable for their payment, or those indirectly affected by such exactions—the social tectonics described in entangled political economy literature potentially take on a dramatically contentious hue.

Social movements have often organized as a response to growing public animosity toward punitive, unfair taxation policies. The likes of Adams (2001) and Burg (2004) have exhaustively cataloged the manner in which people have peacefully protested, and sometimes rioted, as an expression of grievance against punishing taxation. That political actors have all too-frequently abrogated property rights, through unpopular tax measures, attests to the realities that political desires for revenue—typically coupled with weak feedback mechanisms informing rulers that their measures are being received as contrary to public interest (A. Martin 2010)—have long colored the historical relations between citizen and state.

The American Revolution is held by many liberals as a laudatory example of the cumulative effects of tax resistance toward institutional change. Detailed chronological accounts of the revolutionary period are amply covered elsewhere (e.g., Ramsay [1789] 1990; Knollenberg [1975] 2003; G.

Smith 2017). These additional treatments detail the existence of numerous additional factors informing the colonial revolt, and subsequent war, against British rule in the eastern American mainland colonies. Our particular interest is in the organized resistance against the imposition, or threat of imposition, of punitive tax measures upon colonial residents by the distant British parliament.

Considering the American Revolution as a tax revolt presents, on a *prima facie* basis, something of a puzzle. The relative lack of British state capacity—particularly in respect of tax collection administration, and related law enforcement, among its colonial offshoots—suggested considerable tax evasion. Historical accounts point to evidence of evasion through goods-smuggling trades within a vibrant shadow economy, which was accompanied by local corruption by customs and other officials (Andreas 2013). If there existed ample means for American colonists to sidestep the application of British laws, then why did taxation brew active resistance against colonial rule? An answer to this question may lie in the deterioration of British public finances. This deterioration is attested by ballooning public debts, and rapidly increasing interest expenses, during the first half of the eighteenth century, consequent to periods of conflict with other European powers (especially, but not limited to, France) (Salsman 2017).

To defray the costs of war debts, British parliamentarians assented to a raft of new and increased taxes upon the colonies, including those in North America. The British Exchequer swiftly imposed new and additional taxes on international trade, on such products as imported coffee, cloth, indigo, and wine. In 1765 the *Duties in American Colonies Act 1765* (or "Stamp Act") was introduced, obligating the colonists to pay a direct tax upon printed material (e.g., legal documents, newspapers, pamphlets), and to have that tax payable in British currency. A year earlier, legislation was passed to impose duties, and stricter customs enforcement functions, in an effort to repress the illicit molasses trade from the Caribbean to the United Kingdom via the American colonies. In 1767, the British Parliament introduced yet another measure—the "Townshend Acts" approving taxes on certain imposed commodities, such as glass, lead, paint, paper, and tea (J. Powell 2000). These measures, all in all, were egregiously received by the colonists. Although the British measures, in isolation, might have appeared reasonably modest, there were concerns in the American colonies that the tax measures established a precedent for an even greater taxation burden in future (G. Smith 2017). After all, the dramatic accumulation of public debts by the British Exchequer signaled the prospect that subjects under British domestic and foreign political dominion would be held liable to repay them.

Concerns about political representation were not far from the minds of restive American colonists who opposed the new raft of British taxes. Tax opposition was complemented by a growing colonial disquiet over their lack of direct representation in the British Parliament (or, at least, inadequate carriage of their concerns through to the ruling British authorities). A prominent exclamation of colonial concerns was advanced by James Otis in 1764:

> I can see no reason to doubt but that the imposition of taxes, whether on trade, or on land, or houses, or ships, on real or personal, fixed or floating property, in the colonies is absolutely irreconcilable with the rights of the colonists as British subjects and as men. I say men, for in a state of nature no man can take my property from me without my consent; if he does he deprives me of my liberty and makes me a slave. If such a proceeding is a breach of the law of nature, no law of society can make it just. The very act of taxing exercised over those who are not represented appears to me to be depriving them of one of their most essential rights as freemen, and if continued seems to be in effect an entire disfranchisement of every civil right. For what one civil right is worth a rush after a man's property is subject to be taken from him at pleasure without his consent? If a man is not his own assessor in person or by deputy, his liberty is gone or lies entirely at the mercy of others. (James Otis, cited in Burg 2004, 255)

As the months and years passed, groups emerged to conduct displays of resistance against British taxes upon American colonists. One group, known as the "Sons of Liberty," protested against the Stamp Act. The Sons of Liberty were noted for helping to organize the dramatic contentious performance of dumping a cargo shipment of tax-free, imported tea into the Boston Harbor (Ness 2004). This protest event, famously known as the "Boston Tea Party," was met with immediate political repression by the British government, together with a longer-term program of British militarization in the colonies. With little prospect of reconciling sharpening disagreements, a conflict dynamic between the thirteen American colonies and the British government escalated into what is now known as the American War of Independence. After a few years of war, with thousands of casualties on both sides during the military conflagration, the British officially conceded in September 1783 and eventually decolonized North America (Conway 2013).

There seem little doubt tax grievances made a catalyzing contribution toward revolutionary impulses in the American colonies. In his assessment of the American Revolution, George Smith (2013) suggests the organizers and activists who challenged British rule would not have succeeded in their efforts without a critical mass of public support within the colonies. There is certainly ample anecdotal evidence to the effect that subscription to liberty ideals—such as Lockean notions of self-ownership and the inherent human right to property, more generally (e.g., Hartz 1955)—infused the cultural-social configurations of colonial America. Other researchers point to the espousal of civil disobedience frames during the colonial era (Thierer 2020) though, in fairness, research points to similar rhetorical strains in numerous other societies, including Britain itself (Carter 2010).

Perhaps even more significant than ideational influences were the democratizing effects of institutional colonialism in North America. Congleton (2011), as well as Tarko and O'Donnell (2019), outline the relatively high costs attached to centralized public governance of the colonial outposts. An interpretation of this research work is that the costliness of ruling the original thirteen American colonies from Westminster not only contributed to establishing localized political authority, as an institutional convenience to the British colonizers. The so-called "tyranny of political distance" facilitated a taste for local political representation, and engagement, among the colonial residents in the numerous townships and municipalities (also Tocqueville [1835] 1998). Unpopular fiscal directives seen as unjustly diminishing property rights attached to private production and trade, and which are unilaterally imposed in a manner appearing to single out colonial outposts, incentivized resistance in the shape of counter-colonist agitation and, ultimately, American revolutionary fervor.

British Corn Laws and the Anti-Corn Law League

The desire that tax policies do not unduly abrogate property rights need not necessarily create revolutionary turmoil. It is possible to detect historical examples of anti-tax mobilizations within existing political institutions, and prosecuted by precursors of what might be labeled today as "moderate" or "reformist" social movements (Berberoglu 2019). A distinguished case example of this can be found in nineteenth-century Britain. In particular, we draw attention to the successful campaign against British agricultural tariffs (the so-called "Corn Laws"), whose success relied upon a blend of organization, insider political lobbying, and the arousal of popular agitation for economic reform.

The British *Importation Act 1815* imposed tariffs upon the importation of various basic grains, such as barley, oats, and wheat. This measure, and subsequent amendment legislation, effectively served the interests of those aristocratic landowners wishing to limit the effects of import competition in the grain trade. Economists such as Thomas Malthus expressed support for the Corn Laws, suggesting that lower import prices would mean that "farmers would be unable to pay their way, labourers would have their wages lowered, and manufacturers would suffer from a fall in the purchasing power of land-lords and farmers" (Woodward 1962, 61). This arrangement, and other pro-tective policies subsequent to the 1815 tariff imposition, did not win uniform support across the British population. Key sources of opposition included liberal, free-trade intellectuals and political figures—such as David Ricardo, who represented himself in both capacities during the early nineteenth century—as well as certain business interests seeking an expansion in trade.

The tariff resistance of parliamentarian Richard Cobden was particularly notable, as was that of his colleague John Bright, both assuming leadership roles in the Anti-Corn Law League. As indicated by Pickering and Tyrell (2000), the League established multiple "sub-branch" associations across the United Kingdom, providing an organizational focus for anti-tariff activism. As noted by Stephen Davies (2015), restrictions of democratic participation and representation raised the relative costs of counter-hegemonic organization. However, the representation of Cobden, Bright, and other free traders, in the British Parliament provided a strategically vital platform for the political production of anti-tariff discourses. What is more significant, however, is the manner in which anti-Corn Law agitators utilized an impressive array of tactics to rally public opposition against the agricultural tariffs.

What techniques were used to arouse opposition against tariffs? For its part, the League encouraged and facilitated the generation of thousands of parliamentary petitions. The number of petitioned signatures against the Corn Laws, in the years leading up to eventual reform, were said to have regularly exceeded one million (Miller 2012). Numerous public meetings in halls and other spaces were also arranged, with the League providing financial and logistical support for Cobden, and other notable public speakers, at those meetings (J. Powell 2000). Morley (1914) referred to the persuasive style of argumentation contained in League pamphlets, and other campaign literature, which disseminated throughout townships and districts. The production of anti-tariff media, and other tactics, were supported to some extent by financial aid from individual supporters, and from mercantile interests and other groups. The growth in financial support led Cobden to remark: "[t]here is something very English in the fact that money should have so material an influence in a struggle of this nature. In France, the machinery would be likely to be that of musket; and in America that of the ballot-box. Italy would organize a secret society. But here we are all for money" (Cobden, cited in Pickering and Tyrell 2000, 33).

Cobden and the Anti-Corn Law Leaguers were not hesitant in stressing the right of individuals to be able to use their own properties, and produce, to facilitate cross-border economic exchange. In addition, this movement creatively drew upon economic precepts to highlight the detrimental tariff effects—especially upon low-income consumers and downstream processors of imported grain. In one instance, Cobden mentioned the number of wedding rings pawned by women to procure sufficient funds for bread (Prentice [1853] 1968). It is suggested that the manner in which anti-tariff economic ideas were communicated eventually persuaded the British political executive, even those sensitive to the interests of well-connected agricultural interests, of the need for reform (Irwin 1989).

The League's organizational prowess and financial acumen attracted the ire of varied opponents. One of those opposition groups was the Chartist working-class movement, which alleged that Cobden and his associates were beholden to Manchester manufacturers and related concerns. The Chartists, ironically, became something of an oppositional counter-movement, engaging in public criticism of the League, as well as partaking in efforts to disrupt and "de-platform" League speakers and public events. The irony was that both the Chartists and Leaguers proclaimed to promote the interests of working people. In correspondence with Joseph Sturge, an activist with an interest in both camps, Richard Cobden stated, "[t]he Chartists don't seem to comprehend their real position. They direct all their attacks agst [*against*] capital, machinery, manufactures, & trade, which are the only materials of democracy, but they never assail the feudal aristocracy & the state church which are the materials of the oligarchical despotism under which they are suffering" (Cobden, cited in Guelzo 2015, 395; emphasis added).

Sustained agitation eventually yielded fruit, when the government led by Prime Minister Sir Robert Peel abolished the Corn Law provisions in 1846. The economic effects of the Corn Laws repeal remain the subject of investigation, however a recent paper suggests that the reform worked as it intended. The "repeal was a progressive, "pro-poor" policy: the welfare of the top 10 percent of income earners falls by about 1–2 percent and the welfare of the bottom 90 percent increases by about 0.5 percent" (Irwin and Chepeliev 2020, 4–5). There is little doubt that this reform example had continued to inspire economic freedom movements, as well as think tanks and pressure groups, to this day. The example presented by Codben, Bright, and their associates highlighted that incumbent governments can be challenged to eliminate privileges that they, or their political predecessors, establish (Lips 2020).

SOCIAL MOVEMENTS FOR POLITICAL FREEDOM

The Struggle for Liberal Democracy

Throughout recorded history, politics has played a critical part in shaping the human condition. Despite its historical significance, a harmonized intellectual conception of politics remains elusive. For our purposes, politics is interpreted as the management of power relations within the context of public governance—specifically, between those in status positions of *rulers* and *ruled*. We cast this definition broadly, given the capacity of political activity to spill over into economic and social domains via relationships of influence, if not control (R. Wagner 2016). Another salient attribute of politics, raised by Richard Wagner and by realist political thinkers (e.g., Sleat 2013), is that politics not only presents opportunities for cooperation but also conflict, because individuals legitimately disagree over preferred ways to govern themselves, and others.

The liberal mode of thinking focuses upon the need for political affairs to be conditioned in ways that respect individual freedoms. A basis for this position is that the history of actually-existing politics is littered with instances of coercion and oppression—not only over perceived out-groups, and those with minoritarian views, but over entire populations. At its extreme, political control has morphed into genocide, war, and other forms of physical violence. Liberal theory indicates that the potentially predatory appetite of the holders of political power, and of those striving to obtain access to the political means, is to be best avoided. Therefore, liberalism offers "a theory of politics in which political power is controlled and directed in a manner that ensures the ruled are not oppressed or tyrannized at the hands of those who rule over them" (Sleat 2013, 21).

Careful theorization and empirical observation indicates that democratic systems are more likely to uphold liberal principles of public governance. Contrary to the opinions of its critics, liberals are ardent, impassioned democrats (e.g., Buchanan 2005b). Liberal political principles are not only relevant to the design of constitutions (Buchanan and Tullock [1962] 1999), and related fundamental working rules of politics, but to the effective and proper conduct of post-constitutional politics. In regard to the latter, liberals seek institutional and organizational arrangements for the dynamical turnover of political representation and policies, as circumstances and public opinions change (Buchanan 1954b). They also favor a politics which maintains an expansive "public realm in which citizens can freely and peacefully seek to mediate their social-political differences" (Madison 1998, 13), a situation consistently proven to be impossible under authoritarian and totalitarian forms of government. It is on the basis of these principles that a categorical class of public governance, distinctly known as *liberal democracy*, represents a hallmark of political thought.

We will be considering the struggles of the early British feminist movement for adult women to attain the right to vote. Voting may be considered one of many forms of collective choice technology—which also include: unilateral or executive decisions by leaders; policy decisions negotiated between government ministers, bureaucracies, and interest groups; and judicial decisions. In practice, there are significant variations in method to ratify approved, or winning, choices arising from a voting event, for example, a general election determining the composition of political representatives to sit in a legislative assembly. This observation has facilitated an expansive public choice literature surrounding the efficiency of alternative voting decision rules (Tullock 1998).

Over the years, many questions have been raised about the utility of the vote motive. Scholars versed in public choice theory have suggested that the probability that any given person would cast the decisive ballot choice in a general election is vanishingly small. This proposition raises concerns about the effective ability of individuals to democratically restrain political power. Other theorists assess that the act of voting alone is insufficient to hold governors in check, therefore the likes of exit (via interjurisdictional mobility) and additional voice mechanisms (including social movement activities, such as protest) are necessary to complement the voting function in promoting political accountability. However, the often protracted, and sometimes fierce, social movement struggles to extend the voting franchise does not seem to square with the theoretical lack of instrumental value attached to voting. Therefore, a key question to be answered is: Why has the desire to vote been so pressing for so many?

James Buchanan (1954a) perceptively indicates that individual choices in markets and politics differ on a comparative institutional basis, largely for reasons concerning perceived interdependencies weighing upon vote motives. One of the more persuasive rationales for voting rests in the desire to equalize power differentials in a democratic political context. Politics provides one means through which interdependent, collective interests are realized, but it remains important to configure the relations between citizens, who are governed, and those personnel who are democratically elected to govern the organizations of state. According to Chris Berg (2015, 149), "democracy has, as its moral foundation, the presumption of political equality—all individuals are morally equivalent. . . . There is no fundamental or natural hierarchy that places one individual or class above another."

The right to vote is a derivative of a broader political rationale in support of democratic equality. If people are held to be politically equivalent—and are not to be coerced, or dominated, against their will by governors—it stands to reason they have an equal right *to participate* in the affairs of public governance. Participation in this sense is inclusive of the right to vote. The availability of universal democratic franchise, in particular, represents a marker of the equal standing of all individuals to participate politically. As stated by Judith Shklar (1991, 388), "people who are not granted these marks of civic dignity feel dishonored, not just powerless and poor. They are also scorned by their fellow citizens." Consistent with this, the historical lack of voting rights eventually sparked vigorous responses by disenfranchised groups. Many social movements organized to promote democracy, and the right to vote, on the basis of eliminating systemic power differentials between rulers and ruled.

Female Suffrage in Nineteenth-Century Britain

Prior to the establishment of universal voting rights in 1928, Britain endured a gradual, and often fraught, process of democratization. Prior to the modest iterations of democratic liberalization, commencing from the *Representation of the People Act 1832*, parliamentary representation was effectively restricted to men with significant property and wealth holdings. Whether an individual male person was eligible to vote depended upon various factors. These included if one resided in a county or borough area, and the value of their property. These restrictions contributed to extreme variations in House of Commons parliamentary representation. Newly-formed industrial towns such as Manchester and Birmingham were minimally represented, or not at all, yet certain "rotten borough" areas, mainly in the south, were. An infamous example was the Old Sarum electorate, which had merely *seven voters* yet *two parliamentary members* (O'Brien and Quinault 1993).

In the years leading up to the 1832 reforms, a variety of social movements agitated for improved parliamentary representation and an expansive set of voting rights. This period was exemplified by significant levels of social unrest, and other forms of counter-hegemonic contention, in both urban and rural areas. These activities were supported, if not organized to some extent, by nascent working-class movements, such as the Birmingham Political Union (Archer 2000; Aidt and Franck 2015). Charles Tilly (1981) noted the frequency of rioting by Britons over the issue of democratic reform, and many other matters. Additional contentious opportunities were catalyzed over such matters as restrictions imposed upon Catholics, and working conditions borne in agricultural and industrial districts. Extending voting rights to women were the subject of an even lengthier struggle between social movement activists and the British government. The 1918 suffrage reform accorded partial voting rights to women (specifically, in favor of propertied female householders), but the realization of comprehensive female adult suffrage had to wait yet another decade.

The struggle for British female suffrage was prosecuted by several large SMOs, alongside smaller groups and their networks. By the turn of the twentieth century there were numerous organizations competing against one another for political and public attention. The largest group was the moderate National Union of Women's Suffrage Societies (NUWSS), established in 1897 as the result of multi-body amalgamation. In 1903 a militant suffrage group, known as the Women's Social and Political Union (WSPU), splintered from the NUWSS. Many other groups existed during the period—including the WSPU splinter group (Women's Freedom League), and the Women's Liberal Federation attached to the Liberal Party. Drawing the connection between taxation and representation, or the lack thereof in the case of women, a number of tax-resistance groups were also established. Jane Unwin (nee Cobden) notably provided support to the Tax Resistance League (Crawford 1999).

Feminist organizational capacity was complemented by an elaborate array of friendship networks and ideological alliances. Personal networks were forged between the leading figures of American and British suffragist movements (Holton 1994, 1995), whose collaborations assisted in formulating international activist campaign infrastructures (Mead 2013). Women with suffragist sympathies would also develop discussion clubs, meeting one another in halls and restaurants (Crawford 1999). These networks, and the emergent transnational feminist movement more broadly, exchanged insight and knowledge about how to respond to political targets and counter-movements. In similar fashion to their British counterparts (Hollis 1979), for example, McCammon et al. (2004) found American suffrage movements used pro-liberal equality and justice frames to persuasive effect. Diffusion of intellectual arguments supporting women's right to vote, and for gender equality—such as those provided by Britons Wollstonecraft, Bentham, and Mill—fueled inspiration and motivation among social movement participants on both sides of the Atlantic.

The NUWSS and WSPU were the two largest, and most prominent, British suffrage movements of the early twentieth century. In a reflection of the growing popular support for extending voting rights, both organizations gained additional members prior to World War I. NUWSS membership rose from about 13,400 in 1909 to 26,000 in 1911, and to at least 50,000 members by 1914 (Hume 1982; Purvis 2019). Researchers suggest that the WSPU also experienced membership growth (Lance 1979), but that its relatively small aggregate member size (estimated at between 2,000 to 5,000 in 1914) was conditioned by public antipathy toward its disruptive, and at times violent tactics (Garner 1984; Purvis 2019). Inter-organizational tactical variations compromised overall movement capacity to present a united front (Rubio-Marín 2014), enabling anti-suffrage counter-movements to more easily promote their case against enfranchisement (B. Harrison 1978; Lind 1994).

Participants in the British women suffrage movement utilized an impressive array of tactics to publicize the case for democratization, and to pressure politicians over voting rights matters. Following the footsteps of many other social movements during the period, suffrage movements petitioned legislators to instigate change. It is estimated that from 1868 to 1918 approximately 17,000 petitions (containing 3.3 million signatures) for women's suffrage were directed to Britain's House of Commons, with other petitions sent to the House of Lords, the Prime Minister, and the ruling monarch (Miller and Stewart 2018). Movement organizers and activists would also coordinate public demonstrations and marches. These tactics would symbolically illustrate the level of public support for the female suffrage agenda in close proximity to the "political action space" of Parliament in Westminster, London.

The early suffragists notably undertook "insider" lobbying, and related activities, within the political domain. Organizers, activists, and supporters provided campaign support for pro-suffrage political candidates—primarily those in the "radical" faction of the Liberal Party, in the first instance, and, later, Labour and other parties. Activists such as Barbara Bodichon, Emily Davies, Elizabeth Garrett, and Helen Taylor formed the Kensington Society group in 1865 to discuss gender equality. This group organized a petition of 1,500 signatures—including those of Florence Nightingale and Harriet Martineau—to enfranchise property-holders, regardless of their gender (though excluding married women) (Purvis and Holton 1998). The newly elected legislator John Stuart Mill agreed to present this petition to the House of Commons, and during the parliamentary debates over the 1867 Reform Bill he tabled a proposed amendment to allow a "person" (not merely a "man") to vote. This amendment was unsuccessfully carried, but the movement's strategy to identify supportive politicians in Westminster helped elevate female suffrage as a mainstay issue.

As support for expanding voting rights grew, and as women themselves gained an independent economic capacity to provide financial aid, the suffrage movement moved to finance their cause. A notable example of this was the NUWSS election fighting fund of 1912, with expenditures slated to support Labour political candidates. Needless to say, this initiative failed to command unanimous support among the relatively moderate, and traditionally Liberal-voting, NUWSS membership. However, the fund was considered by Garner (1984) as an initiative of strategic importance, insofar as it encouraged Liberal Prime Minister H. H. Asquith and his colleagues to reaffirm their support for franchise reform. In effect, the NUWSS and the suffrage movement was able to leverage growing inter-party rivalry within the British Parliament to advance the case for voting rights, which became a reality after World War I.

The ensemble of demonstrating, lobbying, and petitioning may be classed as moderate, or "constitutional," tactical styles of social movement activity. However, the esteem for such tactics decayed over the years as parliamentarians continued to stonewall on voting rights. The political intransigence contributed to an eventual breakdown of social movement unity, leading, in turn, to a distinctly militant, counter-hegemonic brand of feminism. The so-called "suffragettes" established groups, such as the WSPU, and were led by charismatic (and oft-perceived by their detractors as "authoritarian") figures such as Emmeline and Christabel Pankhurst. It is true that WSPU participants engaged similar tactical efforts as their moderate rivals, however they also undertook disruptive and unconventional practices to attract public attention. Emmeline Pankhurst rationalized her group's militant tactics in the desire to wage "civil war" against men who refused to extend the vote franchise to women (H. Smith 2010). The tactical sense of militancy was also aimed at rousing commitment from the most dedicated, or perhaps fanatical, movement supporters.

The scope of militant tactical actions by the WSPU and the other suffragettes was extensive. Property damage was a central feature of disruptive tactical selection. Prior to the First World War, "suffragettes burned down churches, libraries, houses, railway stations, seaside piers, race course and cricket pavilions and boat houses. They set off street fire alarms, cut telephone wires, destroyed post, slashed paintings in art galleries, attacked exhibition cases at the British Museum and planted bombs. Bombs were found beside reservoirs, at waterworks, at a lighthouse, in trains, and in churches, including St Paul's Cathedral and Westminster Abbey" (Purvis 2019, 1221). Jailed suffragettes, including Emmeline Pankhurst, wished to signal their willingness to be maimed, or even to die, for their cause by engaging in hunger strikes (van Wingerden 1999). Disrupting public meetings by Liberal and other politicians, in something of a tactical precursor to today's "cancel culture," was another aspect of their militancy (W. O'Neill 1969). Finally, the WSPU suffragettes convened public protests which had a tendency to descend into violence. The infamous "Black Friday" protest of November 1910, for example, ended with many arrests as well as reported accounts of police mistreatment of female protestors (Pankhurst [1914] 1971; cf. Bearman 2009).

The distinction between "constitutional" and "militant" modes of female suffrage activism was practically blurred. Moderate and radical movement organizations were known to opportunistically draw upon repertoires of contention informally considered the preserve of their rivals (Holton 2019). Furthermore, emphasis upon tactical choices tends to obscure high-level commonality between different organizations, and networks, with respect to their ends (Ph. Levine 1987). Publicity surrounding high-stakes suffragette militancy also tends to overshadow the genuinely innovative nature of tactical development by suffrage movement organizers and activists, of the likes, nowadays, synonymous with culture-oriented new social movements. This includes the usage of artistry and pageantry (K. Collins 2012; Rolley 1990; Tickner 1987), and the prolific production of contentious feminist media during a period featuring a dramatic reduction in communication costs (Congleton 2011; DiCenzo et al. 2011).

The emergence of the WSPU, with its rallying cry of "Deeds Not Words," marked a significant shift in social movement tactics in late-nineteenth and early-twentieth century Britain. How effective were violent tactics in persuading government to yield on franchise extension? Destruction and disruption signaled frustration by suffragettes with a lack of progress toward reform. At the same time, according to some historians, the Pankhursts and their allies motivated new waves of activism (e.g., Lance 1979). In addition, the WSPU efforts attracted media and public attention, even if the reported reception to their tactics were denigratory and hostile in nature (Vessey 2020). Radical tactics were seen by suffragette supporters as a legitimized manifestation of resistance against political tyranny (Mayhall 2000), and they served a broader function of diminishing cultural stereotypes to the effect that women are demure, submissive, and ready to acquiesce to perceived injustices (Garner 1984).

As noted in this book, the moral disposition of liberalism clearly disfavors the utilization of tactics destroying property, injuring or killing people, or causing harm in other forms. It is possible to find historical analyses questioning the efficacy of suffragette militarism, implicitly lending some support to this liberal view. Anecdotal evidence abounds that the militancy campaign by the suffragettes antagonized certain movement activists and supporters, and the British public more broadly (e.g., Rosen 1974). These effects arguably also undermined the efforts by participants in the moderate feminist social movements to present themselves as rational and reasonable political negotiators.

Another issue concerns property damage. There would seem little question that damaging and destroying assets, and personal effects, could magnify a sense of animosity between property owners and those movement participants campaigning for female suffrage. Estimates vary about the financial and economic costs of suffragette property destruction, but Bearman (2005) submits a damages figure of up to £2 million in 1913–1914 (roughly £232 million—or U.S. $297 million—in today's terms). Garner (1984) criticizes the lack of suffragette tactical nous to select so-called "hard" economic targets for destruction—such as the factories and other establishments owned by proprietors linked to Liberal Party activities—depicting this as evidence of a lack of strategic forethought by the suffragettes. On the other hand, Bearman (2005) notes the existence of substantial guard labor (Jayadev and Bowles 2006) protecting key premises from suffragettes, radical unions, and other potential saboteurs. The selection of smaller, somewhat unguarded, private properties may not only reflect a rational interest in evading apprehension, but it appears to reflect the suffragettes' belief that entangling the public in an intimidation campaign could swiftly deliver desired political concessions (Bearman 2007).

Extending the voting franchise is, ultimately, a political issue. It seems reasonable that social movements, and other actors seeking political change, logically ought to devote the lion's share of their attention toward political actors. There is some suggestion that suffragette militancy turned British political sentiment against movement participants, reinforcing the *status quo* position of disenfranchisement of women. The moderate suffragist Millicent Fawcett (nee Garrett) complained of Liberal Prime Minister Asquith's rhetorical indistinction between militants and non-militants. Senior Labour figures shared in the political inclination to publicly disavow the legitimacy of the suffrage movement (Purvis 2019). The use of militant, even violent, tactics probably had the effect of encouraging the ruling Liberal Party to reframe suffrage as a law-and-order issue, contributing to the censorship and harassment of feminists (Holton 1995).

Finally, the engagement with militant tactics by the suffragettes also struggled to overcome collective action problems. The prospect of violence disincentivized support, certainly from among the more moderate sympathizers of the WSPU, and, quite possibly, from the bulk of the community as a whole. Along certain margins, such disincentives might have also translated into reduced participation in peaceful-yet-contentious activities (if there was no guarantee that initially peaceful activity would not turn violent), the curtailment of campaign finance, and so on. Another consideration to bear in mind is that violent movement work is necessarily risky. Bearman (2005) suggests that WSPU bombers and vandals were paid professional staff, or were given retainers for future mobilization. Even so, there were relatively few people (perhaps 300–400 people at most) estimated to willingly engage movement targets violently. The difficulties associated with sustaining violent collective action were also evidenced by the degree of strategic disunity within WSPU—those members questioning militancy were said to be routinely expelled, or silenced, by the organization's centralized leadership (Holton 1995).

The historical record duly shows that adult British women gained the ability to vote from the period 1918 to 1928. Some historians consider that World War I promoted national unity and political bipartisanship, undermining subsequent legislative hurdles to suffrage reform. Mono-casual explanations are probably insufficient to present something of an accurate telling of the history. For Bearman (2005), World War I presented something of a "structural break" allowing the suffrage movement to strategically retreat from its controversial militant tendencies. In this context, we should consider Congleton's (2011) view that the suffragette slouching toward "civil war," if not "revolution," lacked logistical and political credibility. The general assessment is that the WSPU experience illustrated it was difficult to sustain, if not scale up, violent social movement campaigning. This is because such tactical postures are susceptible to abstention, and similar forms of free riding, and are amenable to repressive counter-tactics by governmental authorities. In the final analysis, it seems that incremental, and peaceful, political bargaining between the political establishment and pro-franchise reform individuals and groups, including key social movements, likely delivered the goods on British democratization.

Democratization, including its constituent element of vote franchise extension, is suggested to enhance public sector quality in the long run. Expansion in the eligible voting population is posited to effectively "depersonalize" political activity, "because the number of voters increases and fewer voters personally know the candidates running for office" (Congleton 2011, 175). An implication of this, by way of casual observation, is that "[g]overnment in the 1880s to 1940s became less corrupt, less a tool of exclusive or extractive elites, more predictable, and more effective" (Fawcett 2014, 143). Social movements have been important participants in the drama that politics ought to work more effectively for the people at large. In stating this claim, we recognize the broader economic, political, and social processes likely to tilt the political agenda in favor of enfranchisement. These include industrialization, which facilitated female labor market participation and upward economic mobility for lower and middle classes, the growth of inter-party competition for electoral support, and, finally, ideational subscription to pro-liberal ideas of political equality and justice (Congleton 2011).

SOCIAL MOVEMENTS FOR SOCIAL FREEDOM

Equality and Justice for All

Throughout modern history an identifiable strain of social movement activity also appears informed by the desire to advance liberty in its social dimensions. This element of liberal theorization foundationally rests in the belief that each and every person is equal, due to their shared humanity. Consequent to this belief in equality is the principle that everyone should be afforded due dignity, and respect, to undertake their own initiatives and projects, provided that these do not coerce or harm others. Given adherence to the non-harm proviso, actions may be conducted freely by any individual on a solo basis, or in association with others to benefit from the fruits of social cooperation.

Just as is the case for liberalism in its economic and political dimensions, a liberalism appreciative of the social undergirding of freedom robustly defends individuals' rights to voluntarily engage one another in mutually beneficial ways. Preventing others from undertaking their own actions and to discover their preferred "experiments in living," through legalistic coercion, or non-governmental strategies of conformity, is to intolerantly privilege one's own prerogatives over others, and is, thus, regarded as unjust. A consequentialist interpretation of such matters would lament the epistemic (and other) costs associated with prevention of association, circumscription of diversity, and so forth. Considered in tandem, these reflections lead to an appreciation of *social liberalism* as "an emancipation doctrine—from dogma of the altar, from repression by the crown, from violence by the sword, and from exploitation by the privileged mercantilist class" (Boettke 2019).

A significant hindrance to the realization of socially liberal conditions is the scourge of racism. Racism is the viewpoint that human beings are, somehow, divided into separable categories (labeled as "race"), and that individuals and groups are innately identified as being superior or inferior to one another on the basis of racial categorization. According to Bolick (2008) racism is associated with the discriminatory treatment of individuals or groups, on the basis of their perceived racial status. Racism extends to instances of bigotry, prejudice, and stereotyping. A growing body of research has identified a range of individual and societal-wide maladies arising from racist attitudes. These include reduced opportunities for economic and social participation, adverse psychological impacts, and other manifestations of compromised well-being. In short, racism damages health and wealth along several dimensions.

Popular, "folk theorems" of race tend toward racial distinctions based upon physical characteristics, such as skin color, or, perhaps, behavioral traits allegedly associated with different groups. Work by social scientists has increasingly come to the view that race is inherently a socially constructed phenomenon, emerging from the intertwinement of cultural, legal, political, scientific, social, and other considerations (e.g., Tate and Audette 2001). A key element of race as a social construction are those twisted rhetorical investments which perversely attempt to depict members of certain racial groups as somehow inferior, or otherwise incapable of standing in a position of equality with other human beings (Grynaviski and Munger 2017; Novak 2018b). Recent scholarship reinforces this nuanced understanding of race, highlighting the existence of numerous factors influencing constructions of racial identity (Sen and Wasow 2016).

The liberal view is that personal interactions should provide a basis to dispel racism and, in so doing, quelling discriminatory attitudes and revising stereotypical perceptions. Interaction between persons enables communication, learning of norms, perspectives, and values held by each other, and how to act moderately and sympathetically when responding to the needs of one another. It is for this reason that liberals believe that frequency in contact is associated with social toleration, if not mutual acceptance, among heterogeneous individuals and diverse groups. This insight finds support in socio-psychological literature, such as the seminal Allport (1954) study showing diminution of discrimination and prejudice due to more frequent contact between diverse individuals. The liberal perspective can, however, be traced much further back to French philosopher Montesquieu ([1748] 2008) and his nomination of the pacifying effects of trade.

Competitive and open markets are seen by liberals as institutional spaces conducive to breaking down racial, and other, barriers (Storr 2008; Berggren 2014). One of the reasons for this, as described by Becker (1971), and given empirical support by the likes of Pager (2016), is that, to put it simply, *discrimination costs*. Economic agents harboring discriminatory attitudes toward those they potentially hire, work with, or purchase from, are likely to bear the costs of their discrimination in competitive market settings. As the American Civil Rights movement, as described later, illustrated, social movement pressure is capable of increasing the costs of social illiberalism, in part by specifically targeting discriminators and disrupting their economic operations. To the extent that social norms also influence economic conduct (Ikeda 2018), movement communication supportive of basic liberal values— such as dignity, equality, and justice—could also be applied to raise the costs of racism.

American Civil Rights

One of the regrettable features of history is that racism has been afforded much (though not all) of its malign effect through the authority and force of governmental legislation, in addition to political moral suasion and policy development. Where innate human tendencies toward sociality, freedom of association, and exchange work to help corrode racial stratification, the politics of division, and statutes of segregation, work in the opposite direction. This reality poses problems in any place but, it seems, especially acute for a country such as the United States, having been established on the principles of constitutional liberty yet, paradoxically, indulging in colonization, slavery, and racism. This American difficulty was poignantly described several decades ago by Frank Knight:

> Equality before the law means that there is equal opportunity for everyone to find or make his own place in society. This ideal was dishonored in the breach rather than honored in the observance for some time into the age of liberalism, notably by this country in the matter of racial discrimination. We were from a generation to a century behind the main civilized world in getting rid of slavery nominally based on race, but actually a caste distinction, and then had to do it by one of the most terrible wars in history. (Knight 1960, 136)

Although racism against African Americans prevailed since the colonial era, its most brutalizing and formalist expressions were found throughout the Southern states. Many thousands of African Americans were forced into slave labor primarily to undertake arduous agricultural work and, subsequent to the 1860s Civil War, they found themselves increasingly subject to discriminatory rules and regulations. Racially discriminatory legislation and ordinances were maintained at both county and state levels, and became collectively known as "Jim Crow" laws. Creeping formalization of racial discrimination also found legal support, such as in the shape of the infamous 1896 U.S. Supreme Court "separate-but-equal" ruling in the *Plessy v. Ferguson* case. Ira Berlin (1988) recounts the many acts of civil disobedience by blacks. These included anti-slavery insurrections and riots as early as 1739, in combination with the small-scale, everyday refusals to defer to whites. Notwithstanding such micro-level acts of resistance, the pervasiveness of racially-charged governmental restrictions meant there was simply no period wherein African Americans experienced a "golden age" of freedom (Gregory 2017).

During the nineteenth century, activists and thinkers of classical liberal persuasion, such as William Lloyd Garrison and Frederick Douglass, opposed slavery. For these figures slavery represented an egregious deprivation of basic liberties, including with respect to bodily autonomy and free association (Sandefur 2018). Prior to the twentieth century, abolitionist organizations were established to not only engage with "insider" political lobbying, but to rally members of the public in support of the anti-slavery cause. So, too, did a host of social movements emerge to challenge American slavery and, later, governmental policies restricting education, employment, private and public services access, and voting on racial lines (Ness 2004). As the decades wore on, and as local or national political concessions were sporadically won, African Americans and their allies increasingly mobilized to liberalize the statute books, and engage in cultural-social works promoting racial equality and dignity for minorities.

Black America was, arguably, able to find its most prominent voice for freedom in the shape of the Civil Rights movement during the 1950s and 1960s. The tendency of historical accounts is to imbue this movement with a sense of unity and coherence; however, it is more appropriately conceived "as a continuum of interrelated events, leaders, and ideologies" (ibid., 107), entangled in both competitive and complementary respects. Composed of people of varied backgrounds, situations, and tactical preferences (ranging from liberal moderation to socialist/radical militancy), there was the ever-present risk of systemic failure to gain anti-racism concessions from policymakers.

Organizational capability has been seen by researchers as pivotal to the successes obtained by the Civil Rights movement during the mid-twentieth century. To organize anti-racist campaigns necessitated an ability to draw upon already-established social networks to organize activists, and to procure the necessary finances and other materials to sustain collective action (McAdam 1982; Olzak and Ryo 2007). One of the more notable organizations is the National Association for the Advancement of Colored People (NAACP). Much of its focus then, as it is today, was to promote political lobbying, public advocacy and, most notably, litigation efforts to overturn formal segregation policies (including the 1954 *Brown v. Board of Education* schooling desegregation case). Established in 1909, the NAACP is a multiracial organization originally organized and led by such luminaries as sociologist W.E.B. DuBois, liberal activist Moorfield Storey, and feminists Ida B. Wells and Mary White Ovington.

Following the establishment of early-mover organizations, such as the NAACP, a plethora of actions were undertaken during the 1950s and 1960s to repel racial inequalities. The Montgomery, Alabama, bus boycott campaign was instigated by Rosa Parks's refusal to surrender her bus seat to a white person, subsequently leading to a year-long boycott by African Americans of the local bus transit system from December 1955 (Morris 1984). A legal decision ruled that segregated bussing was unconstitutional under the Equal Protection Clause of the 1868 Fourteenth Amendment to the U.S. Constitution. In the wake of the Montgomery events, theologian Martin Luther King, Jr., and numerous other Christian black ministers established the Southern Christian Leadership Conference (SCLC) in 1957. The SCLC aimed to promote Civil Rights through explicitly nonviolent means, such as consumer boycotts and peaceful protests.

Social movement organizations were able to draw a considerable measure of localized support from the communities they aimed to represent and serve. Even so, bodies such as the NAACP and SCLC were criticized for their moderate stances when confronting racists, and in seeking concessions from pro-segregationist authorities. Dissatisfaction with "mainstream" Civil Rights organizations contributed to the establishment of groups with robust civil disobedient, and even militant, tactical objectives (McAdam 1983). In the wake of "sit-in" campaigns at segregated retail department store restaurants in Greensboro, North Carolina, and elsewhere, the Student Nonviolent Coordinating Committee (SNCC) was formed in 1960. An earlier-established organization, the Congress of Racial Equality (CORE), organized student "Freedom Rides" through segregated passenger transit facilities in the American South. Other groups, such as the Black Panthers and the Nation of Islam, vigorously advocated self-defense and the right to bear arms in confrontation with police and white supremacists (Rhodes 2007).

Civil Rights organizations also sought to procure finances to aid activists. An important element of fundraising was aimed at bailing out jailed protestors. There were many examples of such "bail funds." The NAACP, for example, funded the release of student sit-in protestors in Greensboro, and provided attorneys to legally represent the students. CORE and NAACP collaborated on funding in 1965 to bail out jailed protestors in Springfield, Massachusetts, meanwhile the SNCC assisted in establishing the Mississippi Bail Loan Fund for jailed Civil Rights protestors in that state (Steinberg et al. 2018). Funds to support Civil Rights activists were drawn from a range of sources, such as church congregations and other local community gatherings throughout the South (Morris 1984). Other groups in the U.S., such as members of the growing black middle class and white sympathizers, contributed financial aid and in-kind support to Civil Rights organizations (Oberschall 1973). As noted by Chong (1991), Civil Rights figures, such as King, were frequently solicited by organizations to engage in fundraising, and to draw attention to the mistreatment of blacks, especially in the South.

Participants in the Civil Rights social movement were not merely confronting segregationist politicians and their law enforcement officials. They challenged deeply-entrenched organizations and social networks which legitimized racist norms, and aimed, through their actions, to depreciate malign forms of social capital privileging white Americans (Carden 2009; Cunningham 2012; C. Harrison 2018). The efforts of Civil Rights movement organizations, and individual campaigners, were buttressed through networks involving black church congregations, educational establishments, and other sites, where African Americans could interact and plan tactics in the name of anti-racism (e.g., Calhoun-Brown 2000; McAdam 2014; Morris 1981). As previously mentioned in this book, networks often provide oppressed minorities opportunities to build solidarity that overcomes collective action problems. Discursive exchanges among networked participants, which recall campaign successes and failures, provide avenues for social learning as well as for building shared senses of identity.

Researchers generally agree that framing strategies and collective narratives also assisted the Civil Rights movement. Much scholarly attention has been directed to the rhetorical techniques of Martin Luther King in mobilizing Civil Rights movement participation. Two strains of rhetoric may be identified in King's public speeches. One is the identification of black Americans' struggle as one grounded in nonviolent confrontations with the purveyors of segregationist public policies and white supremacist privileges. Another identified pattern in King's communicative strategy, as mentioned previously, was the use of Biblical references, which referred to American racism as a collective sin to be purged (Williams 1995).

The construction of a sinful racism was coupled with narratives by King, inspired by the Biblical Book of Exodus, to solicit participation in a movement struggle that would eventually deliver freedom for African Americans (Selby 2008). Biblical references also served to connect with historical, and other familiar, narratives. Specifically, the oppression felt by African Americans was part of a larger collective narrative about how people have been mistreated on racial grounds, and that social movement struggle is a necessary (but not sufficient) condition for emancipation (Mayer 2014). Finally, an ability to draw upon the Bible was couched by activists as a strategic measure aiming to weaken the resolve of those racists who professed to draw upon Christian teachings.

Much reflective scholarship has focused upon the entrepreneurial qualities of King's strategic and tactical involvements in Southern protests. Indeed, King has been often described as a "norm entrepreneur" pivotal to expanding the size, and deepening the influence, of the Civil Rights movement (e.g.,

Sunstein 1997; Ellickson 2001). In this context it has been stated that, "King must be seen as a man who solved a technical problem that had stumped Negro leaders for generations. As a powerless group living in the middle of a powerful majority that hated and feared them, Negroes could not stage an open revolt. . . . King and the sit-in students solved the technical problems by clothing a national resistance movement in the comforting garb of love, forgiveness, and nonviolence, a transformation that enabled Negroes to stage an open revolt without calling it an open revolt" (Lerone Bennett, cited in Oberschall 1973, 222). Chong (1991) refers to the use of motivational rhetoric as being often intermixed with cajoling and shaming pressures, as part of a broader strategic ploy to encourage additional people to join their peers in the anti-racism struggle.

We have already referred to an array of tactical measures. Let us now consider the economic ramifications of selective contentious tactics organized by Civil Rights movement groups. According to Luders (2006), the ability to cause economic disruption is a key tactical choice used by social movements to push for societal change in their favor. Although the *prima facie* motivation of Civil Rights movement tactics is to substantially raise the relative costs of indulging in racist practices, Luders suggests that a balance must, nevertheless, be struck between "disruption costs" (i.e., costs arising from movement activities) and "concession costs" (i.e., costs arising from movement success). Economic disruption must encourage the pro-segregationist targets of movement activity to come to the bargaining table, so to speak, but in a way that does not prohibitively raise subjectively-perceived costs of conceding to anti-racist activism.

The Luders study found that businesses in competitive market settings, and typically with relatively small profit margins, tended to be more sensitive to disruptive campaigns. These included retailers, hoteliers, restaurateurs, and proprietors of tourism facilities. The Greensboro lunch counter sit-ins by African American students deterred regular customers from dining in, inducing hefty financial losses for the affected Woolworth's retail outlet in the process. This outcome induced the lunch counter to desegregate, in the space of a few short months (Luders 2006). Incidentally, economic studies of separate cases, such as that presented by Roback (1986) in the case of streetcar transportation, point to the resistance of certain service providers to enforce segregation laws, due to the additional costs of racially separating customers.

Another way that Civil Rights activists made racism expensive was through mass protests, which threatened to deter investment and trade in affected localities. In addition, movement tactics risked frustrating broader economic development objectives for those disrupted counties and states. These considerations appeared relevant in the case of Birmingham, Alabama, in which both young and old Civil Rights protestors were brutally attacked by a local police force led by Eugene "Bull" Connor. Negative publicity directed toward events in that city, and the concomitant losses in business turnover, contributed to an eventual arrangement between the local government and downtown business interests to eliminate segregation (McWhorter 2001; Luders 2006).

Even if movement participants had successfully pooled labor and other resources, especially in economically deprived locations, severe challenges confronted organizers, activists, and supporters. Movement recruitment and participation were perennially threatened by severe repression against contentious movement displays by law enforcement agents—especially in the U.S. South with the most stringent racial segregation laws. Police brutality was frequently meted out at Civil Rights protestors, including during the 1963 Birmingham protests and the Selma-to-Montgomery, Alabama, march of 1965 (Ness 2004). There was also the genuine threat of white supremacist vigilante groups attacking Civil Rights protestors, which was disconcertingly evidenced during the CORE-inspired Freedom Rides campaign of 1961.

The disincentive effects of government repression were at tension with another strategy: coax the police and vigilantes into physically abusing protestors. The organizers of certain events—such as the 1961–1962 Albany, Georgia, protests assisted by King and the SNCC—sought a complementary strategy of tempting law-enforcement officers to jail protestors, and to overstretch prison capacities. Another rationale for this strategy was to try to win media and public attention, as well as sympathy, over to the Civil Rights cause. Brutal attacks on nonviolent Birmingham protestors in 1963 by local police has been largely viewed as a pivotal moment, given that reporting by media outlets induced an increase in public sympathy for the movement.

The American Civil Rights movement is noted for its preparedness to institutionally arbitrage between levels of government. To circumvent the baleful consequences of local- and state-level segregation policies, movement participants petitioned the Kennedy and Johnson federal administrations to legally reinforce longstanding constitutional provisions aiming at racial equality. The federal *Civil Rights Act 1964* prohibited racial (and certain other forms of) discrimination in education, employment, housing, and public accommodations, while the *Voting Rights Act 1965* prohibited racialist legal barriers preventing people from exercising their right to vote. Whereas this legislative agenda affirmed the ability of African Americans to exercise their rights on their own accord, it provided such affirmation by effectively eliminating the ability of lower-level legislators to subvert the principles of racial equality. In effect these legal reforms straddled the divide of negative and positive liberties, insofar as such a divide can be neatly identified (Gregory 2017).

As for the Civil Rights movement itself, internal fractionalization, and shifting public priorities arguably led to deviations in strategic and tactical orientations after the mid-1960s. In the wake of legislative victories eliminating formal racism, King and other key movement figures sought to tackle the manifestations of ingrained structural racism in American society. These concerned differential economic opportunities, in terms of employment, access to private and public services such as health care and housing, as well as the inequalities of treatment within the criminal justice system (Loury 1998).

Deeper disaffection within some movement factions with "merely" legislative wins, and the mainstream lobbying and nonviolent activism (Osterweil 2020) led to new groups. One of these was the Black Power movement, which aspired to directly confront their racist opponents. A number of researchers have argued that rioting in urban and other areas from the late 1960s provided agency for the racialized "law and order" politics which came to dominate U.S. politics during the last quarter of the twentieth century (e.g., Flamm 2007). It is not entirely clear, however, that the moderate successes of the Civil Rights movement faded away. Aside from the entrenchment of legislation, many scholars argue that the Civil Rights movement provided the quintessential template whereby other oppressed groups—for example, disability, feminist, and LGBT communities—could claim their rights and, through it, strive to expand the domain of liberty (Skrentny 2002; Kymlicka 2007; Welzel 2013).

CONCLUSION

Are social movements and their activities amenable to historical interpretation? This chapter provides cases attempting to illustrate that this is so. Are movements implicated in the trajectories of liberalism, and if so how? Our argument is that social movements are important, yet, still, somewhat overlooked, participants within critical episodes of liberal history. Movements have not only been implicated in the development of the "Great Enrichment" of modernity (McCloskey 2010). They have also been involved in the struggle to garner respect, and amplify participation and voice, for the oppressed, and even have had their hand in political democratization and the downfall of unaccountable, even despotic, rule.

For the sake of clarity, we indicate that social movements cannot take all the credit for the realization of freedom's possibilities. Nor can movements endure all of the blame arising from a lack of success in ushering liberty during times past. In daring to dream of a freer future, and being prepared to partake in risky collective actions, demanding the involvement of people, resources, strategy and, above all, patience, social movements have helped to close the distinction between liberal theory and reality, and belief and practice. In the case of movements pushing a freedom agenda, we can think of them as liberalism's faithful-yet-rebellious tinkerers, seeking to fix both unfree and outdated ideas, institutions, organizations, and practices, with the intention of securing a freer future for all.

We readily acknowledge there are a great additional number of case studies which deserve explanation, and which may be subjected to future research. Social movement causes of a liberalizing nature, and those whose activities exerted the broadening the boundaries of human freedom, can be found across the broad gamut of entangled economic, political, and social domains. Entanglement is a key factor in the liberal history of social movements, because of the way in which contentious strategies, tactics, and activities have been aimed simultaneously at the economic, political, and social interests of movement supporters, and their opponents. As circumstances change, movement participants have shown an impressive capacity to adjust tactics, which can impact various domains of human conduct. One might suggest the history of successes and failures of social movements have shown tendencies, and often unintentionally so, to "spill over" into additional, or broader, domains of human action.

Our attentions are, by and large, restricted to reformist social movements which sought change given the constraints of existing institutions, organizations, and practices. This chapter also provides a consideration of the cultural and social belief systems of people within those communities that movements sought interaction. Furthermore, the attention of this chapter was trained on pro-liberty reforms facilitated by social movements, and similar groupings, in the United States and United Kingdom during the nineteenth and twentieth centuries. It goes without saying that social movement influences have also been felt across continental Europe, and in Africa, Asia, Latin and South America, and Oceania during this period. While admitting the limitations of our coverage, we submit that our analytical focus allows for an appreciation as to how social movements work, what they aim to achieve, and the opportunities and challenges associated with their efforts.

Social movements have played a critical role in diffusing ideas of equality and justice for peoples oppressed by customs, traditions, and laws. Under certain circumstances, social movements have also helped build polycentric structures within the polity and civil society, thereby encouraging "experiments in living" that have demonstrated the values of diversity and socio-political recognition to the broader society (Mill [1859] 1985). We have also described the contribution of social movements, or at least precursor kinds of movement activity, toward economic liberties. In fact, numerous contemporary social movements—including those "new social movements" centered upon identity recognition and respect—find their antecedents in economic struggles. As will be noted in the next chapter, movement activities across key dimensions of human activity continue to profoundly reshape our lives, even to this day.

Chapter 6

Issues Raised by Contemporary Social Movements

INTRODUCTION

During the course of the early twenty-first century social movements have challenged a wide-ranging assortment of institutions, organizations, practices, and values. Social movement activities have been prosecuted over a vast number of issues, attending to all manner of perceived abuses, injustices, and lack of opportunities affecting human beings. Movement participants have also mobilized over such matters as the mistreatment of animals and neglect of environmental amenity. Many of the movements which have emerged impact understandings of, and esteem for, liberal values in their economic, political, and social aspects. Some notable examples include the turn-of-the-century anti-globalization protests, OWS, Tea Party, the 2010–2011 Arab Spring, BLM movement, and climate-change protests. The crescendo of contention activated by social movements has, likewise, renewed scholarly interest in social movement theory.

Social movement encounters with their primary targets, and opponent groups, have become particularly fractious in recent years. On a speculative basis, these developments may be informed by a sense, felt by many people globally, of hardship and strife attributable to multiple crises and institutional rupturing. Certainly, the lack of contentment over the quality of life felt in many countries seems to have been cynically manipulated, if not amplified, by prominent-yet-divisive political figures. Adherence to sound governance and the rule of law has steadily whittled away, along with the essential economic, political, and social freedoms necessary for human flourishing. On this score, social movement activity and participation might be seen as an obvious response to the troubles that have arisen. However, it may also be the case that growth in movement activities is contributing to widespread feelings of anxiety and strain.

Anecdotal and empirical evidence has suggested that social movement activities, such as protests, strikes, and boycotts, have grown. Activists and supporters of social movements are also applying a range of innovative techniques to bring their causes to public attention, and to invite responses from policymakers and other actors within society. Chief among techniques is the use of the Internet, social media, and associated information and communication technologies (ICTs) to propagate communication within, and among, social movement networks. Important research questions are currently being asked about the effectiveness of digital technology in organizing movements, and the consequences of digital activism for achieving transformative changes in the world.

This chapter provides an account of a selective, yet interconnected, range of contemporary issues raised by national and global social movements. The next section examines the responsiveness of social movements to contemporary economic problems. This is followed by an examination of governmental repression of movement activities, enabling a critical perspective about the appropriateness of law-enforcement and surveillance tactics in repelling protest and other forms of activism. Following that, we will discuss the use of digital technologies by social movements. This chapter will be concluded with some brief remarks.

SOCIAL MOVEMENTS AGAINST THE CAPTURED ECONOMY

A number of researchers and analysts have declared that we live presently in an "age of protest" (e.g., Bahgat et al. 2018; Brannen et al. 2020). Whereas the issues and topics animating social movement activities differ across time and space, a working hypothesis has recently emerged that growth in contentious collective action by movements is, at least in part, attributable to increasing public disaffection with economic conditions (T. Cowen 2019). Severe economic and financial repression since the 2007–2008 "global financial crisis" (GFC) has left in its wake an unedifying legacy of substandard economic growth, contributing toward constrained mobility with respect to income and living standards. The decade-long period of relatively weak growth had been closely followed by the Covid-19 pandemic with devastating consequences from the standpoint of maintaining human life, not to mention the economic livelihoods of individuals, families, and communities.

Returning to a point made earlier in this book, the author and legal scholar Butler Shaffer argued that policies tend to have the effect of restricting economic activities in the name of order. In his words, "'order' is no longer solely perceived in terms of the 'hygienic' function of eliminating acts or threatened acts of aggression and violence, but instead is perceived as including the organization and structuring of human relationships in order to permit some men, through the use of state coercion, to make the behavior of other men more predictable for their objectives, and more conducive to their control" (Shaffer 1975, 737–738). Attempts by policymakers and law-enforcement agents to limit voluntary, productive entanglements of an economic nature, according to Shaffer's thesis, induce frustration among community members. This frustration potentially sets the scene for protests and other anti-hegemonic courses of action, but could also risk public acts of aggression. The Shaffer analysis resembles collective behavior theories of the twentieth century which, as noted earlier, tended to be superseded by subsequent social movement theories. Nevertheless, this study provides a reasonable account as to why people grievously respond to persisting material hardship. Shaffer's conceptualization appears consistent with subsequent research effort identifying a sense of autonomy, or being in control of one's own life, as important to happiness and life satisfaction (Bavetta et al. 2014). Adding to this, there is some, albeit equivocal, support in empirical literature that worsening economic conditions (or perceptions of economic deprivation, or hardship) and contentious activity are connected (e.g., Grasso and Guigni 2016; Kurer et al. 2019).

To the extent that Shaffer's propositions are correct, then social movements have surely capitalized on the discontent experienced by the many. As Tyler Cowen (2019) noted there has been a perceptible turn toward protest, and other contentious activities, in response to economic pressures. Expressions of economic grievance have frequently occurred in the Middle East, North Africa, and Latin America, but have even become more prevalent in developed countries. In respect of the latter, this has been illustrated by the OWS and Tea Party movements in the United States, as well as anti-austerity protests in southern Europe. A particular flashpoint for contemporary contention appears to be increasing relative prices for essential items, such as food, fuel, and housing. Utility prices for services such as electricity, transportation, and water supply have also risen sharply in recent years, sparking public demonstration and rallies in numerous locations globally. Negative reactions to rising prices may be directly motivated by the material hardship caused by such phenomena, as well as by general anxieties that cost-of-living pressures might constrain future opportunities to enjoy upward socio-economic mobility.

In a study of the protests and riots in the wake of price increases in Burkina Faso, Engels (2015) found that the rising prices provided a lagged opportunity for social movements to frame arguments, and mobilize opposition, against the ruling political regime. Movement participants were also able to exploit price hikes to demand greater freedom of assembly and expression, as well as raise public awareness over the need for anti-corruption political reforms. This strategy thus helped metastasize a multipronged cycle of contention (McAdam et al. 2001) throughout Burkina Faso, placing immense political pressure on government. Maccatory et al. (2010) similarly noted social movements in Africa established coalitions with consumer groups, labor unions, human rights organizations, and other concerned groups, in an effort to magnify the scale, if not the potential effectiveness, of food-price protests.

There are other examples whereby rising prices for staples, and other essential goods and services, have galvanized social movement activities. A host of "joined-up" protests embodying a measure of social movement organization have been experienced in Latin and South America (Walton and Seddon 1994). There have been other cases in which price increases have been met with largely improvisational contentious actions, some of which have been destructive in their effect (Auyero and Moran 2007). In some instances, certain ethnic or racial minorities have been unfairly blamed for cost-of-living pressures and related economic hardships. An example of this has been the periodic harassment of Chinese storekeepers and traders in south-east Asian countries during food riots and other economically related events (e.g., H. Johnston and Lio 1998).

The Middle East and North Africa (MENA) region is another flashpoint for economic protest. Despite its hydrocarbon bounty, the region has struggled to provide an economic climate conducive to entrepreneurialism, innovation, and inclusive growth for many of its peoples. The lack of economic buoyancy in the MENA region appears to stem from an underlying lack of economic freedom enjoyed by ordinary citizens, especially for women (Al Ismaily et al. 2019). A combination of burdensome regulations, difficulties faced by business entrants, and a significant economic presence for state-owned enterprises stifle private economic opportunities and promote crony entanglements. The combination of those malign tendencies serves to maintain corrupted, privileged economic-political elites. It should also be said that military misadventures by Western powers have compounded the misery experienced by the over half-billion populace within the region.

It is against this background of immense hardships that the Arab Spring social movement emerged. The origins of the Arab Spring are largely attributed to the self-immolation of Tunisian street vendor, Mohamed Bouazizi, in response to police harassment over the legality of his trade (A. Gurri 2020; and for recent assessments of fatal forms of protest, see Hafez 2006; Greenland et al. 2020). Bouazizi's action underscored the restrictive economic environment faced by many in the region, and it mobilized a wave of protest in Tunisia, followed by similar activities in Algeria, Jordan, Egypt, and Yemen. Eventually the Arab Spring protests spread throughout the MENA region, and became entwined with a broader range of issues such as political corruption and repressed civic freedoms. One of the countries within the region, Lebanon, has subsequently been gripped for years by protests by citizens frustrated with economic closures, resulting from a combination of political patronage and untrammeled rent-seeking conduct. Social movement researchers have also illustrated how collective action framing, political opportunities, network interactions, and the use of low-cost digital technologies have contributed to the Arab Spring uprising (Durac 2015; Leenders 2013; Lafi 2017).

Turning now to trends among developed countries, there has also been a strain of contemporary social movement activity devoted to alleviating living-cost pressures. In a previous chapter, we referred to the contributions of individual tax activists, think tanks, SMOs, and other bodies in impelling property tax and other fiscal limitations. Resistance against certain tax measures has been evident elsewhere. In Australia, increases in electricity prices during the early 2010s, which were attributed to the effects of a national carbon taxation scheme, led to rallies and protests organized by conservative groups (Copland 2019). In more recent times, a group of activists in France—referred to as the "Yellow Vests" movement—have protested over concerns initially related to fuel taxation as well as generally rising costs of living.

Arguably the best-known modern case of a movement devoted to a systematic liberalizing agenda is the U.S. "Tea Party" movement. Coined after the original colonial-era protest movement resisting the imposition of tax on imported tea shipments, the modern Tea Party coalesced during the Obama Administration. Many of its activists appeared to be primarily concerned, at least initially, about the need to lower American tax burdens and reduce governmental size. Broader issues of budgetary sustainability also motivated movement participants, leading key movement representatives to call for public-sector debt reduction and the limitation of government expenditure. Another cornerstone issue for the Tea Party was its resistance to President Barack Obama's agenda to substantially extend health coverage using public policy measures. The concerns of this movement in the health policy space related to the costs of health mandate initiatives, as well as the perceived risk that growing public-sector involvement would crowd out health insurers and other non-state actors (Pipes 2015).

Scholars investigating the Tea Party social movement found a diverse array of individuals and groups sharing intellectual, financial, and other resources. Tea Party chapters were organized to encourage attendance at public rallies and related contentious events. Activists of this movement drew upon the research and advocacy efforts of free-market think tanks, linked with media outlets such as Fox News, and, during the Obama Presidency, elicited political support from Republican Party politicians (Skocpol and Williamson 2012; Roberts 2018). During the formative years of the movement's existence, it was able to create a collective narrative of being a political "outsider" (Heaney and Rojas 2015). This imagery captured the imaginations of those who wished to express grievances over post-GFC economic conditions, as well as to signal opposition against President Obama himself (Maxwell and Parent 2012).

For a relatively short period of time, the Tea Party was able to command significant mobilization potential. According to some estimates, Tea Party "Tax Day" rallies in April 2009 were attended by over 300,000 people across 340 American cities (N. Silver 2009). Whereas criticisms had been leveled at the movement regarding their authenticity as a grassroots concern, with claims of astroturfing conduct (e.g., Fetner 2012), the Tea Party nonetheless demonstrated an ability to influence the American political stage—as evidenced by the election of supportive Republicans during the mid-term election (Tufecki 2017). However, as is the case with most things, the momentum of the movement could not be sustained. Popular support for the Tea Party, based on opinion polling, declined roughly from the period of the 2010 mid-term election through to the 2016 election of Donald Trump as U.S. President (Yoder 2017). The number of active Tea Party chapters declined by as much as 40 percent from 2010 to 2012, with the suggestion that many participants had been co-opted into the broader Republican Party at the time (Almeida and Van Dyke 2014).

Contemporary economic conditions suggest that the need for economically liberationist social movements remain. The aftermath of a devastating global financial crisis and, recently, a global pandemic has exposed deep economic inequalities. From a liberal standpoint, much of these inequalities stem from political departures from generality precepts in fiscal and regulatory treatment (Buchanan and Congleton [1998] 2003; Novak 2018b). Specifically, Lindsey and Teles (2017) refer to these inequalities to be the result of a "captured economy" of fiscal and regulatory advantages enjoyed by relatively few, but which constrain future income growth and upward mobility for the majority. Redressing economic inequalities arising from policy choices, therefore, appears to be a desirable candidate for social movement strategy and mobilization (Geloso and Horwitz 2017). A new wave of activism in this direction would clearly resonate with fundamental liberal ideas, of breaking up power structures by harnessing voluntary association, competition, and choice. An additional benefit of such an agenda is that redressing inequality in a "liberty-consistent" fashion may draw, at least in theory, crucial support from preexisting social movements, civil societal associations, and business and political organizations, whom otherwise would not find cause to build alliances.

Efforts by social movements to counter the restrictive effects of regulation upon medicinal drug provision are an intriguing case study of functionally pro-liberty activism. The provision of drugs for people living with HIV/AIDS in the United States, and elsewhere, were (and continue to be) subject to two regulatory conditions. First, the retail sale of drugs was conditional upon health regulatory approval based on criteria regarding drug safety and efficacy. An overly lengthy approval process, or delays in providing final approvals for drug sales, is likely to prolong the pain and suffering of those needing the pharmaceutical treatments. Second, intellectual property (IP) provisions, such as patents, applied to drug manufacture. A patent holder enjoys an exclusive authority, license, right, or use of the product (in this case, HIV/AIDS treatment drugs), and this precludes others from imitating, or using, the product without the prior consent of the patent holder. Whereas the appropriateness and consequences of IP remains contentious, the economic principle is clear that effectively monopolistic granting of IP rights to patent holders raises the price, and restricts the quantity sold, of pain-relieving, if not life-saving, drugs, all else being equal.

During the early years of the HIV/AIDS epidemic the cost of available treatments were largely unaffordable for sufferers. The azidothymidine (AZT) drug, produced and patented by Burroughs Wellcome under the brand name Retrovir, had, during the late 1980s, cost a patient U.S. $8,000–10,000 per annum (Molotsky 1987). Another issue of concern to members of the LGBT community, and others living with HIV/AIDS, was that the cumbersome regulatory approvals regime of the U.S. Food and Drug Administration (FDA) prevented swift and widespread access to experimental drugs. In the face of such obstacles to treatments, and against the background of moral panic and discrimination against people living with HIV/AIDS, and gays and lesbians generally, activists directly challenged corporations and governmental authorities. Social movements were established to also raise awareness about the harmful consequences of inattention to the HIV/AIDS crisis.

One prominent social movement group is the AIDS Coalition to Unleash Power (ACT UP). Formed in New York City in March 1987, ACT UP developed a reputation for robustly direct actions against their targets and using confronting techniques to gain media attention (such as their "Silence=Death" motto) (Finkelstein 2017). Among the initial targets for ACT UP was Burroughs Wellcome. In arguably their most notable protest of September 1989, several members of an ACT UP subgroup (known as "Power Tools") entered the New York Stock Exchange in Wall Street. They chained themselves to the VIP balcony overlooking the trading floor, and unfurled a "SELL WELLCOME" banner. An estimated 1,500 protestors followed this initial group, blasting foghorns to drown out stock-exchange activity and handing literature to floor traders explaining the impact of the

AZT patent upon people living with HIV/AIDS (H. King 2010). In response to the publicity generated by this protest episode, the company subsequently announced a 20 percent reduction in the price of AZT treatment (ibid.).

ACT UP also engaged in a range of actions against the FDA. Several demands were elucidated by this social movement entity. This included the desire to: expedite drug approval processes; end double-blind placebo trials involving people with life-threatening illness; establish a "parallel track testing" process in which individuals with advanced cases of HIV/AIDS could participate in drug trials; and allow people to import experimental drugs for personal use (Crimp 2011; Ness 2004). In October 1988 ACT UP organized a demonstration outside the FDA's Maryland headquarters, effectively shutting down the facility for a day (Eigo et al. 1988). In response to movement pressure, the FDA introduced regulatory-relief measures—including streamlined approvals processes—having the effect of easing drug access to people living with HIV/AIDS. It is noted that actions by ACT UP and similar groups within the HIV/AIDS activist space were not limited to the American situation. Movements in Europe and other developed regions, as well as developing countries, continue to work toward reducing restrictiveness in drug availability associated with IP arrangements (e.g., ACT UP n.d.; Kapstein and Busby 2013).

An interesting contemporary example of a collective, whose objectives challenge the maintenance of the "captured" economy, is the pro-housing "Yes, In My Backyard" (YIMBY) social movement. A major driver of cost-of-living pressure, especially in Anglosphere countries, is a lack of housing affordability. Several measurements of housing affordability (or, in this case, a lack thereof) are available, with one of the major studies in this field assessing affordability in terms of median housing prices as a ratio of median annual income (Cox and Pavletich 2020). The finding that median house prices exceed median income in many metropolitan housing markets is widely attributed to the existence of restrictive supply conditions—such as governmental zoning regulations, planning and land development approval processes, and related policies (Glaeser and Gyourko 2003; Glaeser et al. 2005; C.-T. Hsieh and Moretti 2019).

New examples of movement organization and activity have emerged in locations affected by extremely high housing development and residential rental costs. In the San Francisco Bay Area several YIMBY advocacy groups have been established, including the Bay Area Renters Federation, GrowSF, and SF YIMBY. These groups, and larger entities such as California YIMBY, not only seek to build a base of supporters at the neighborhood level but actively engage with local-state politicians and bureaucrats in calling for relaxed housing regulations (Warburg 2017). This political engagement involves presenting petitions to policymakers, formulating policy submissions in response to legislative developments, undertaking direct lobbying, and raising finances for pro-YIMBY political candidates and officeholders (Dougherty 2020). Similar movement activities have emerged in other high-cost U.S. locations, such as Boston, Seattle, and New York, as well as in places such as Toronto and London (e.g., J. Myers 2017).

A number of researchers have discerned an intergenerational characteristic informing YIMBY involvement. In particular, the Millennial generation (i.e., those born between the early 1980s and the mid-1990s to late 1990s) are seen to be actively promoting additional dwelling construction in well-established districts (Holleran 2020). Arguments in favor of density promotion, and relaxing zoning and other land-use restrictions, are mixed with cultural, economic, and social frames and related rhetorical dispositions. These additional considerations refer to the need for people to be closely situated to well-paying jobs as well as culturally enriching activities and events (ibid.). Opponents have accused YIMBY groups of being little more than astroturf entities, advancing the pro-building interests of construction and real-estate lobbies (McCormick 2017). In contrast to such claims, there is some suggestion that the movement for affordable housing is capable of attracting widespread support—as illustrated by the existence of YIMBY groups subscribing to both liberal and progressive orientations (Dougherty 2020).

No one should be under the illusion that any social movement dedicated to *promoting* economic freedom would be conducted effortlessly or without opposition. Individuals possessing economic advantages due to deep political connections, and possessing the social skills and competencies to lobby for, and protect, their privileges, will fiercely resist proposals in favor of economic openness. The challenge facing social movements advocating pro-equality *and* pro-liberty economic reforms is compounded by enduring cultural-institutional environments that portray rent-seeking as an acceptable practice (Choi and Storr 2019). Even so, the reality of economic antagonism and discontentedness evidenced around the world cannot be denied, with hardship likely to motivate social movement challenges against the captured economy into the foreseeable future. It seems a potential key to future success will be to recall precedents from the not-so-distant past, when movements pushing deregulatory agendas helped win critical, pro-liberty policy concessions against the purveyors of fiscal-regulatory privilege (e.g., Audretsch and Woolf 1987).

THE VISIBLE FIST:
REPRESSING AND CRIMINALIZING DISSENT

Earlier in this book we discussed the types of engagements between social movements and those agents affiliated with political functions and roles.

Given the extensive degree of governmental entanglement in contemporary affairs, it is obvious that social movements would often direct their efforts toward fiscal, legal, regulatory, and other policy changes. Historical and contemporary experiences illustrate the potential for significant gains that social movement participants could achieve for their causes, should they successfully apply pressure against political targets.

It should not be taken from the preceding commentary, however, that political actors remain inert in the face of social movement activity. In autocratic polities, and even in liberal-democratic societies maintaining a great measure of freedom of assembly, association, and of speech, governments are known to vigorously respond to social movement activities. To some extent, especially in democratic settings, legislators and bureaucracies will attempt to accommodate and placate social movement demands. This disposition appears consistent with political attempts at reconciling competing policy prerogatives and diversity in stakeholder viewpoints. There is also a school of thought that social movement activities in their own right generates valuable information and knowledge, which may be advantageously acted upon by those operating within the political domain.

Social movements and, indeed, all members of society are subjected to an array of governmental activities in accordance with a so-called "protective state" function (Buchanan [1975] 2000). To ensure that individuals strike contractual arrangements, carry out economic exchanges, and live together with a reasonable degree of accord, it is held that governments should provide policing, justice, and related services. These services are seen as necessary to uphold domestic law and order. The logic of the Weberian political perspective seems to dictate that policing and defense are manifestations of the state, and its organizational apparatus of government, maintaining a monopoly of coercion within a certain geographical space.

The views outlined above are emblematic of a typical classical liberal position with respect to the appropriate role of government. There are alternative views as to whether governments ought to exclusively protect individuals and groups from any harm potentially meted out by others. It is in this vein that we recognize the existence of an anarcho-capitalist and libertarian tradition—attributable to such figures as Gustave de Molinari, Murray Rothbard, and David Friedman—suggesting that governmental activities in these areas may be displaced by competing, polycentric security services organized privately and communally. To be sure, conditions in the real world are obviously far removed from the anarcho-capitalist scenario. Nonetheless, the concerns raised by this libertarian strand of thought about the potential for governments to abuse (monopolistic) protective functions holds weight, and seems to have applicability with regard to the treatment of social movement participants.

What attracts significant attention in social movement scholarship is that relationships between social movement and political actors are repeatedly fractious. History is marked with governmental entities and law-enforcement authorities seeking to repress movements, often responding to movement tactical measures with coercive force. Governments also proactively seek to limit movement networking and, in so doing, deprive contentious elements of society of the benefits from being able to get together—such as social capital accumulation and trust-building, knowledge sharing, and practicing internal self-governance. Repressive counter-tactics by public-sector actors often curtail the ability of movement participants to congregate, creating internal tensions among key movement organizers and activists, or even splintering dissident groupings altogether. Another frequent tactic deployed by government is to project an unfavorable public image onto social movement actors, denigrating those who protest, or otherwise press for societal change, as "anarchists," "radicals," "terrorists," "enemies of the people," and so on.

Law-enforcement officers will often maintain a presence during a protest event, or a similar public episode of contention enacted by movement participants. The police who watch over, or physically encounter, social movements may be construed as "street-level bureaucrats" that "represent" government back to the activists (as well as observing supporters and bystanders of the general public) (della Porta and Diani 2020). The level of police presence at public social movement activities will vary, depending upon factors such as spatial attributes, the size of the protest, numbers of counter-movement protestors and supporters present at a given event, and the potential for physical harm and property damage that may be caused by protestors (Earl et al. 2003). Nonetheless, images of police personnel standing shoulder-to-shoulder in formation, wearing protective gear, and handling protective shields, as well as combating protestors with weaponry, are seen by many sociologists as performative displays not only to intimate protestors but to arouse media, political, and public attention (e.g., Chesters and Welch 2006; D. Martin 2013).

Interactions between social movements and law enforcement may be construed as social dramaturgy. Nonetheless, there are real, sometimes life-and-death, consequences attached to how protestors and police interact. As described earlier, social scientists have applied game theory to describe the payoffs associated with varying styles of interaction between social movement protestors and law-enforcement personnel. There is a distinct possibility that any pre-emptive tactical "plays" or "moves" by social movements could break down—whether it be due to overzealous, repressive policing, or destructive actions by fringe (or other) protestors and movement supporters. To the extent that the game is interactive, the potential for surprises and other unanticipated developments may yield learnings and innovations by the varied protagonists interacting in public places.

It is far from guaranteed that severe crackdowns upon public mobilization will succeed. Indeed, severely repressive policing responses to protest and related activity could motivate social movement participants to persist with their extra-institutional agitations. Studies of the 2011 Arab Spring movement found that rumors and news of police, and governmental, oppression of political dissidents encouraged *additional* protestors to take to the streets, as a way of signaling opposition to unjust treatment (Atak and della Porta 2016; Lawrence 2017; Jumet 2018). Hank Johnston (2014) generically points to the collective dimension of movement activity as signaling a commitment to fellow movement participants, and to society, to pursue their specific cause, in the potential face of imprisonment, torture, or even death. Oftentimes in response to police brutality and the use of the military against civilians, a movement evolves from a focus upon a given, specific issue to far broader "meta-issue" concerns about the quality (or lack thereof) of the relationship between individual and the state (della Porta and Diani 2020).

Stereotypical political analysis and commentary regarding police treatment of social movement activists often tend to focus upon variations in treatment under autocratic versus democratic political regimes. An autocratic regime (of communist, fascist, or some other, variety) tends to be greatly intolerant of critiques directed toward the concentrated exercise of political power. Accordingly, life under such regimes:

> are often characterized by Orwellian penetration of the state into realms of private life and civil society, ongoing monitoring and social control through a highly developed and extensive police apparatus, strong ideological socialization, and continual propagandizing. Totalitarian states often employ *state terror* to limit opposition. Extensive and arbitrary arrests and executions quash ideological or policy disagreement within the ruling party, and instill fear among citizens. (H. Johnston 2014, 46)

In contrast, democratic politics are presumed to maintain commitments to the liberal rights of assembly, expression, and speech. A strain of scholarly research indicates that police interactions with social movements in liberal democracies have developed over the course of the twentieth century, into a set of practices known as "negotiated management" (e.g., McCarthy and McPhail 1998; Baker 2019; Della Porta and Diani 2020). Negotiated management refers to an increasingly formalized regime of legal, and operational, standards governing the patterns of interaction between protestors and the police. This regime is exemplified by dialogue and negotiation over expected behavioral standards to be applied by both parties—say, a commitment to nonviolence by protestors, on the one hand, and restraint by the police, on the other.

Reality is decidedly more complex than is presented by the autocratic-democratic binary. Using the political process approach Charles Tilly (1978, 106) writes, "[t]he repressiveness of a government is never a simple matter of more or less. It is always selective, and always consists of some combination of repression, toleration, and facilitation. Governments respond selectively to different sorts of groups, and to different sorts of actions." Donatella della Porta and Herbert Reiter (1998) highlight a range of factors determining the actual degree of police repression against social movements. These incorporate the degree of police adherence to laws and regulations, extent of application of force, legitimacy of police response to protestors, discrimination with respect to treatment of different protestors, responses to changing protest situations, and so on. In short, the response to social movements by law enforcement can vary from case to case.

The political interest in repressing movements could be traced to a fundamental "seeing like a state" (Ja. Scott 1998) imperative, rendering the political order legible, comprehendible, and, thus, stable, for (among other things) revenue- and rent-extraction purposes. In recent decades there have been growing concerns about the extent of entanglement between policing, private security services, militarization, and a rapidly expanding national security apparatus. This development suggests a "monstrous hybridization" of the values of governmental law enforcement, defense, intelligence, and security agencies, and the non-state actors they engage with, to pursue ventures of joint interest (R. Wagner 2016).

In her description of an emergent "surveillance capitalism," Shoshana Zuboff (2019) describes the monstrously hybrid commercial-political interfacing between digital surveillance firms and law-enforcement authorities. Zuboff refers to law-enforcement agency client-listings of digital surveillance companies, including those which monitor the social-media activities of various movement campaigns. Illustrating the pervasiveness with which entanglements between private and public sectors occurs, Coyne and Goodman (2020b) identified the intertwinement of public-sector security agencies and private surveillance firms in respect of managing U.S. cross-border movements. The significance of this form of entanglement is that the contentious public activities of social movement participants are, also, at greater risk of being severely repressed. This risk is certainly pertinent in the case of liberal-democratic societies, whose ideals of an underlying presumption of the right to express disagreements—including through challenges to political authority and other holders of power in society—worryingly appear to have been backsliding.

Some of the most compelling contemporary research regarding the repression of freedom of association and speech is being undertaken by George

Mason University economist Christopher Coyne and his associates. Coyne and Hall (2018) have accounted for the unhappy tendency for domestic law-enforcement agents to appropriate heavy-handed, and often lethal, tactics and technologies waged in foreign battlegrounds. Repressive and forceful policing techniques have been applied against domestic minority groups with alarming frequency (Coyne and Hall-Blanco 2016). In response to protests following the tragic August 2014 police shooting of African American teen Michael Brown in Ferguson, Missouri, police officers entered the town with armored vehicles, military-grade rifles, and combat uniforms. This tactic by those carrying out the putatively "protective function" of the state was designed to intimidate protestors, and to repel them, representing a far cry from the reasonable demands of BLM protestors for law enforcement to treat people of all races impartially and nonviolently.

The ceaseless evolution of the public sector has manifested itself in the form of the "national security state." Technological developments increasingly allow for the mass surveillance of human populations, and these have been eagerly deployed by governments to monitor social movements (even those of a peaceful, orderly nature) and their participants. In recent years, for example, news reports pointed to the use of digital surveillance against key BLM activists, together with informants and police officers embedding themselves within BLM activities (e.g., Levin 2016; Joseph and Hussain 2018). As foreshadowed by James Buchanan (2005a), the deployment of technologies and techniques for surveillance purposes—such as artificial intelligence, closed-circuit television cameras, drones, facial recognition, Internet metadata snooping, spyware, and so on—have enabled long-held standards of liberal constitutional and liberal proceduralism to be corroded, if not traded away, for the sake of (real and imagined) security imperatives.

Governmental use of technologies to monitor their own citizens, including those involved with social movements, is not new. During the Cold War period, from 1945 to 1989, many Western countries expended vast resources on espionage and intelligence-gathering to track suspected communist political sympathizers. This included spying upon labor union members, and other groups, suspected of maintaining subversive alliances with the Soviet Union (e.g., Cain 1990, for a description of union surveillance in Australia). It did not take a great deal of effort for governments to extend their surveillance to cover allegedly "deviant" social movement participants, who were campaigning on matters as diverse as environmentalism, feminism, gay rights, the rights of indigenous peoples, and peace and nuclear disarmament. Information accumulated about movement participants were drawn from background identity checks and published sources. In addition, governments used photographic and sound recordings, drew testimonies and materials from informants, and obtained information through impersonation and other forms of deceit (Marx 1979; Cunningham 2003; Boykoff 2006; Salper 2008).

In the presence of repressiveness, social movement participants tend to clandestinely organize away from the prying eyes of the policeman and the camera. Scholars such as James C. Scott (1990) and Timur Kuran (1995) refer to the differentiation between conformist, and non-conformist, communications in public and private spaces. Numerous resistance movements—including those engaged in the struggle against North American slavery and European fascism—organized in ways which evaded detection by law enforcement and intelligence agencies. The existence of a "concealed commons," through which social movement participants can self-organize and, on occasion, launch successful campaigns for societal change, often surprise unsuspecting political elites, participants in the security apparatus, and law-enforcement personnel. Putting those contentious innovations aside, a liberal perspective would maintain the demand for thoroughgoing reforms to policing and national security operations. The objective of such reforms would be to enable social movements, and all individuals and groups within civil society, to canvass their views and perspectives peacefully, and without undue inhibition.

Social movement participants may seek to evade governmental repression, and even to use technologies to counter-monitor, and publicly expose, abuses by police and related personnel. Is it possible to advance systemic reforms to quell the abusive capacities of state actors? Contemporary liberal thinkers have been at the forefront of realistic possibilities for substantial policing reform, freeing up the potential for genuine social movement engagements with governments and other actors.

An obvious route for reform is to prevent the militarization of police forces. In the most immediate sense, this suggests prohibiting the purchase of military equipment. Furthermore, police should refrain from the use of military-grade vehicles, aircraft, and weaponry when engaging in operations to maintain domestic law and order. Reformers have also demanded the end of deployment (or, at least, the significant de-escalation in the use) of "special weapons and tactics" (SWAT) police teams, as well as military or paramilitary troops, to quell domestic disturbances (Balko 2013). Liberals have long called for the cessation of legal punishments for "victimless crimes," such as recreational drug use and prostitution, which have, for too long, presented law enforcement with plentiful opportunities to use excessive, and often lethal, force against citizens. In the view of Coyne and Hall (2018) there is a risk that operational adjustments, of the nature described here, may not be sustainable in the face of reform inertia, thus it is also necessary to engage in cultural revitalization in favor of anti-militarism and individual liberties.

There have also been renewed calls to "defund" the police. The principle of defunding varies, with suggestions ranging from redirecting finance from certain aspects of police operations (such as military-style equipment procurement, and weapons and personal combat training) through to reducing budgetary appropriations for policing in general. Savings procured as a result of police defunding may be redirected into social support or investment programs for marginalized communities, the development of conciliation and restitution functions to resolve disputes, or for some other related purpose. Others have suggested a return to non-state forms of policing—for example, Coyne and Goodman (2019) propose decentralized and polycentric (non-state) solutions of self-defense against aggressors. They indicate that movement participants have a legitimate right to defend their own supporters against violent opponents, which was a tactic occasionally deployed by American Civil Rights campaigners against white supremacists and others who threatened their lives.

Inspired by the works of Elinor and Vincent Ostrom, modern liberal political economists have studied the disconnection between police and the communities they purport to serve. In the American context, researchers have expressed concerns about the effects of increasing federal financial, regulatory, and related entanglements with local and state policing operations (e.g., Boettke et al. 2016, 2017). One of the more concerning consequences of this trend is the potential for increasing inattention by local-state police to the localized—and often tacitly appreciated—needs of communities for public order and safety, including by way of degradation of community policing activities (cf., Goodman 2018). As described by Boettke et al. (2016, 321): "[m]ilitarization and centralization of the police make it increasingly difficult for individuals within a community to exert any sort of influence in the local provision of public safety. Instead, control rests in the hands of officers who are accountable to external forces rather than individuals within the community they are intended to serve."

For those who are reticent to lend their support to police defunding or other kinds of structural reform, there remains ample scope to train a spotlight upon the ethics of contemporary policing. This topic appears salient in light of anecdotal evidence that police have, on numerous occasions, perversely responded to BLM activists, and related protestors, with excessive force (Bouie 2020). Law-enforcement personnel should remind themselves that individuals and groups have constitutional and moral rights to free assembly and speech, and that legitimately includes collectively voicing displeasure against the economic, political, and social *status quo*. Individual police officers should also consider applying much higher thresholds of propriety in response to emergencies and other incidents. Jake Monaghan (2017) outlines the proposition that law enforcement officers have several moral obligations to refrain from killing people. These include the notions that: (a) police are well-situated to aid, rather than harm other people; (b) the assumption of a monopoly of force by government implies law-enforcement officers are causally responsible for another person's vulnerability to aggressors; and (c) police officers have voluntarily committed to an obligation to serve and protect others.

It is important to recognize that the national security state operations firmly raise doubts over the realization of the idealized protective state, the latter seen as requisite to protecting individual liberty. As evidenced by Coyne (2018), U.S. intelligence and security agencies have swelled in terms of budgetary appropriations, staffing, and the procurement of surveillance technologies. This expansion—usually justified by political actors under the banner of protecting members of the community from extremists—has been coupled with an accumulation of sweeping legal powers to monitor the general population. A reasonable liberal approach to such developments would be to seek curtailment of any tendencies to abuse surveillance powers. To do so would be to diminish political fears associated with openly expressing alternative (and possibly contentious) viewpoints of potentially significant informational value (J. Levy 2018). On civil liberties grounds, there are other credible arguments favoring greater accountability and transparency of national security agencies to legislatures and, through them, the general public who are compulsorily obliged to finance such entities through taxation and other revenue-raising instruments.

It should be obvious that social movements that destructively engage their targets and opponents should be subject to proportionate law-enforcement controls and legal sanction. The reality is that rapid governmental expansions in the fields of policing and security have contributed to cases of unwarranted repression of social movement participants. In no plausible sense can be it presumed in a liberal framework that our compatriots, who so happen to be involved in a social movement, are "enemies of the public" who must be watched and controlled, and, on occasion, brutalized. We are in agreement with Jacob Levy's (2018) characterization of philosopher Judith Shklar's work focusing upon restraining the abuses of armed agents of the state, as well as with Fiona Jeffries (2011) on the imperative of resistance against the political perpetuation of fear. It is on the basis of such arguments that the reform of the "visible fist"—that is, an increasingly repressive law enforcement and national security—is elevated to become an issue of paramount importance.

CONNECTIVE ACTION:
DIGITAL ENGAGEMENTS BY SOCIAL MOVEMENTS

Previously we considered the relationship between social movements and conventional mass-media outlets specializing in print and broadcast journalism. Social movement participants often relied upon the media outlets to communicate their immediate demands, and longer term aspirations, to adversaries and target groups, and to draw broader public attention to their cause: "[t]he symbolic worlds of recognition, power, and legitimacy in which these organization-based movements operated were largely constructed through the mass media that enabled distant citizens to include or exclude one another in 'imagined communities'" (Bennett and Segerberg 2015, 367). For their part, proprietary media organizations possessed great capacity to filter and interpret information about social movements—often in ways which diluted esteem for movement objectives, tactical decisions, and even participants. Relationships between social movements and traditional media were contentious, in perhaps the truest sense of the word.

One of the most significant developments of the past quarter-century or so has been the structural change of the media and communications landscapes. In no small part, such change has arisen thanks to the emergence and relatively rapid adoption of the Internet, smartphones, and other ICTs. Individuals and groups that wish to challenge manifestations of the *status quo*—from cultural norms through to public policy positions—could communicate their oppositional, or extra-institutional, stances through digital technology almost instantaneously, at scale, and at relatively low cost.

To better appreciate the significance of digital technologies and their online affordances for social movement activity, we should briefly revisit collective action theory. An Olson-inspired, rational-choice perspective suggests that social movements would have difficulty sustaining large-scale campaigns over a lengthy time period. This is because of the temptation to free ride on others' contributions, in tandem with the obstacles of noticing who has made their genuinely fair and reasonable contribution. The solutions to the collective action problem, as Olson (1965) saw them, were either to coerce individuals to contribute to the movement, or organize the provision of selective (material) incentives to entice contributions.

Most social movement researchers agree that digital technologies have reshaped collective action possibilities. Reflecting upon the changes that have occurred, Bennett and Segerberg (2013, 2015) have coined the notion of a "connective action" that is operative in online spaces. The conventional collective action agenda is centered upon contributing to one's preferred cause, involving expenditure of resources and "socially engineering" high levels of shared identity, and culture, among participants within the social movement network. In contrast, under connective action, individuals are no longer bystanders waiting to be incentivized or coerced into collective action but are, instead, capable of becoming active producers and consumers of online communications and information. In the view of Bennett and Segerberg (2013, 35): "[i]n place of content that is distributed and relationships that are brokered by hierarchical organizations, connective action networks involve co-production and co-distribution, revealing a different economic and psychological logic: peer production and sharing based on personalized expression."

The notion that collective action exudes a highly entangled co-involvement by both suppliers and demanders was an important feature of Elinor Ostrom's (1993) scholarship with respect to public services. Our proposition is that Ostrom's insight can be easily transposed to the case of connective action by social movement participants. Protestors can use smartphones and other devices, for example, to gather photographic and video counter-surveillance evidence of police brutality and other abuses (Carty 2015). These images may be filed in databases or cloud computing stores (Politi 2020). This ability to produce footage of police responses has been instrumental in raising awareness about brutality against African Americans, indigenous peoples, and other oppressed groups around the world. Taking the co-production theme one step further, the dissemination of police brutality footage may be used to encourage policymakers to interact with movement participants, with a view to constructively develop strategies for law enforcement reform.

The success of connective action does not merely rely upon the ability to capture attention, and to enable people to carry news and information throughout their trusted online networks. Jennifer Earl and Katrina Kimport (2011) describe the onset of online protest, and other forms of digitally enabled social change activism, whose success rests upon two additional features. The first is that the Internet and other digital technologies facilitate a significant reduction in organizational and participation costs for a social movement. The second idea is that online engagement allows group-oriented actions to launch without the need for organizers and other key personnel to be physically present on any given occasion. These insights have potentially significant implications with regard to the ability of movements to procure sufficient resources. Researchers are turning their attention to crowdfunding practices, with digitally enabled payment mechanisms facilitating transfers from potentially large numbers of people to movement organizations and networks. An intriguing, albeit tentative, insight from the literature is that crowdfunding initiatives by social movements and similar collectives, such as welfare organizations, have the potential to generate feelings of solidarity, to the extent that pledgers believe they are participating in a shared cause (e.g., R. Davies 2015; H.-C. Hsieh et al. 2019; Nielsen and Binder 2020).

Social researchers are yet to draw definitive conclusions about the implications of digital technologies for movement activities, such as those hypothesized a decade ago by Earl and Kimport. However, all indications are that the impacts have been profound. If co-presence is no longer a requirement for organizing social movement activities, this changes the dimensions of the action space (Ikeda 2012) necessary to develop and refine movement tactics, and to engage targets. From the standpoint of Earl and Kimport (2011, 11), digital technologies could alter small, localized concerns into "actions that are spread out across time and space into major collective, coordinated actions." Related to this is Zeynep Tufecki's (2017, 10) observation that "many people have the opportunity to seek connections with others who share similar interests and motivations," breaking down the social influence of homophily grounded in shared characteristics such as race and gender. Martin Gurri (2018) similarly refers to the contribution of digital technologies facilitating active, meso-level online networks incorporating people with shared interests or themes—which he labels "vital communities."

In addition to creating a larger pool of connections among movement organizers, activists, and supporters, it appears that the Internet and related digital technologies can facilitate major tactical events. Tufecki (2017) contrasts the lengthy and meticulous processes involved by American Civil Rights campaigners in organizing the 1963 March on Washington with the markedly compressed period of time needed to organize the 2011 OWS protests or the Arab Spring. A comparison of movement activities of today with those of yesteryear anecdotally suggest that online communications could help scale up movement tactics, and do so more rapidly. However, there is a remaining question to be asked: How durable are digitally enabled movements? Whereas these movements "can scale up quickly and take care of all sorts of logistical tasks without building any substantial organizational capacity before the first protest or march" (ibid., 70), a lack of culture or infrastructure for collective decision-making risks tactically immobilizing a movement when conditions change. Organizational fragility on the part of a rapidly scaled, digitally enabled movement may be discovered by their opponents (including governmental authorities), who will respond either by repression or dismissal of the movement participants.

There is a school of thought that digital technologies have reduced the significance of movement organizational activity, and that such a trend is, in fact, desirable. This reflects a view that populations are increasingly distrustful of organization, preferring to engage with online movement activities because they foster "leaderless" tactics, either on the web or the streets. For example, impressions of "leaderless-ness" have characterized pro-democracy protests in Hong Kong, which relied upon social media and smartphone apps to communicate tactical information in real time. The benefits of leaderless-ness are said to include decentered entrepreneurship, and high levels of tactical improvisation. It is also claimed such a movement may be sustained beyond the apprehension of any single individual, or small groups, perceived by governmental authorities as central to the protests (Serhan 2019). However, online engagement does not guarantee immunity from intra-group tensions, or the disentangled splintering of a social movement into smaller, yet potentially less cohesive, subgroups (N. Snow 2020).

There have been growing concerns about censorship and repression faced by digital technology users. According to Freedom House, which presides over the production of a regular global Internet freedom index, Internet usage is becoming increasingly restrained by "digital authoritarianism." This not only includes website and social-media platform blocking, and connectivity restrictions, by governmental agencies, but it also encompasses cyberattacks on anti-government targets, and the dissemination of false or misleading information by state actors (Tufecki 2017; Freedom House 2019). In addition to this, governments around the world have stringently persecuted whistleblowers and dissidents, both of whom effectively redress the age-old principal-agent problem by alerting the general public to abuses of political power (Coyne et al. 2019).

Martin Gurri (2018, 42) speculates that the fervor for governmental repression of digital freedom of action partly rests in the discomforts experienced by elites in reading, hearing, and watching "the alien voice of the amateur, of the ordinary person, of the public" *en masse*. For repressive political regimes, in particular, digital technologies are something to be controlled and restricted. The underlying basis for such a desire is that open use of the Internet and related technologies are perceived to threaten the "tranquil" state of pluralistic ignorance among the populace, regarding different, and better, ways of being, doing, and knowing under freer institutional conditions (Tufecki 2017). Similarly, an implication of research work by David Karpf (2016) would be that authoritarian political actors possess incentives to suppress the free-wheeling use of digital technologies which, inter alia, enable social movement challengers, and anti-authoritarians generally, to experiment and test out which tactics can be used to undermine government.

The Internet is frequently slighted as facilitating messy and contentious, if not dangerous, chatter. Online interactions are also widely claimed to contribute toward societal divisions in the form of factionalism, polarization, and tribalism (Sunstein 2008), even if the temporal veracity of such a claim is contested in certain situations (e.g., Hargittai et al. 2008). There is no denying that contestation, and even conflicting, perspectives are illuminated as a result of widespread use of digital technologies. Nevertheless, a compelling case *against* extensive Internet censorship and the suppression of digital freedoms can be made.

The first point to make is that valuable insights are not *concentrated* and *monocentrically* ordered among the few. Instead, those insights are *distributed* and *polycentrically* ordered among the many. To be able to discursively share such insights with others, who may be closely or distantly situated from oneself, aids in the discovery of innovations and ideas to improve one's own life, as well as the lives of members in the surrounding community. Robustness in communication also allows people to register and hopefully, better still, to understand perspectival diversities. Liberalism is firmly associated with the architecturalization of the premise that breaking down communicative barriers among diverse peoples will enable them to better appreciate the reasons for their different viewpoints. While the ability to freely express oneself is not presumed to lead to consensual agreements, free speech and expression (both offline and online) is necessary to defuse inter-personal, and inter-group, tensions, and craft pathways toward social toleration.

Regardless of the reason, censorship on the screen is an anathema to liberal principles and sensibilities, just like censorship in the speaking hall or out on the streets. In no small part, restricting harmless, albeit occasionally contentious, uses of digital technologies is to be presumptively opposed, in order to avoid limitations upon the social discovery of valuable new information, knowledge, and perspective. From the perspective of social movement studies, what is crucial about digital technology is that it provides an additional avenue for people to signal their preferences for change. Within this, the likes of the Internet, social media, smartphones, and similar technologies provide a potential basis for movement growth and development, reflective, in turn, of latent demands for societal change within communities (Earl and Kimport 2011; Tufecki 2017).

CONCLUSION

The first two decades of the twenty-first century, pockmarked as it has been by rolling crises, appears to rebut Francis Fukuyama's famous (or infamous, depending upon one's view) "end of history" argument. For context, recall his suggestion that the cessation of the Cold War, and the passing of communism as a reputable organizing principle, represented "the end point of mankind's ideological evolution and the universalization of Western liberal democracy as the final form of human government" (Fukuyama 1989, 4). Fukuyama does not rule out that alternative forces, such as religion and nationalism, may arise as challengers to liberalism. Nonetheless, he takes guidance from "[m]any of the wars and revolutions fought . . . in the name of ideologies which claimed to be more advanced than liberalism, but whose pretensions were ultimately unmasked by history" (Fukuyama 1989, 15).

One might disagree with the determinist impression of Fukuyama's declaration, arguing that he declared victory for liberalism perhaps a "little too soon." Others may respond by claiming that Fukuyama was never incorrect with the suggestion that liberalism still remains the vital idea for humanity's future (McCloskey 2019), or, similarly, that the "end of history" is the closest approximation to the Durkheimian "social fact" traceable in actually-existing societies. In the eyes of those living in the troubled early twenty-first century, the esteem of Fukuyama's insights seems to have been diminished, at least for now. Economic freedom has waned, minorities and many other groups around the world are victimized by violent, reactionary backlash dynamics, and, increasingly, we are meeting the end of a police baton or are being haunted by the constant eye of the surveillance state. All in all, the disturbing trend is that illiberalism appears, again, on the rise.

What we do not contend is that the tumult of the early twenty-first century spells the death knell for liberalism. Manifestations of illiberalism gripping the world are undoubtedly of great concern. Nevertheless, it is our position that great encouragement should be taken from the demonstrated self-organizational abilities of ordinary people, worldwide, to formulate social movements to demand their liberties and human rights. A most unheralded aspect of liberalism's endurance is the ability for its fundamental principles to resonate and stir within the breasts of humankind. This has been manifested in mobilizations and tactical responses to resist injustice, inequality, and illiberalism. The troubling events of recent times have reinforced an age-old truth. As the English Levelers of the 1600s initially recognized, and subsequent generations of liberals have come to know, liberty is a struggle against the holders and proponents of authority of all stripes.

This chapter illustrates how a variety of social movements are standing up to the abuse and brutality by those who seek to dominate and subjugate others economically, politically, and socially. Movement participants have relied on age-old tactics to get their point across, but have also been willing to create novel repertoires of contentions, including with the aid of new means such as digital technologies. Be it the Arab Spring, BLM, YIMBY activists, and so on, we see a colorful assortment of social movement participants effectively pursuing the ends of liberalism, reconfigured for our times. The question as to whether Fukuyama spoke too soon, or spoke out of turn altogether, remains to be answered. Our view is that the conduct of social movements, of a liberalizing and emancipatory nature, might have an important say in the final answer.

Chapter 7

Meanings and Methods of Social Movements

Further Implications

INTRODUCTION

A cornerstone of this book has been the application of liberal political economy to social movement activity and conduct. In doing so, we have studied movements through the conceptual and analytical filters provided by Austrian, Bloomington, and Virginia political economy. All put together, these respective sub-branches of liberal political economy are seen to shed light on social movements in three interrelated ways. The first consideration is that social movement participants play a part in entrepreneurially discovering, and communicating, public issues. Social movements engage in practices of self-governance, and small-scale democratic artisanship, in the process of building their respective cases for societal change. Third, and finally, movements undertake collective actions in their efforts to challenge political and other forms of power.

The nature and consequences of social movements are by no means limited to investigation from a political economy perspective. Indeed, the quest to comprehend how social movements operate, as well as how, and to what extent, they impact society as a whole, poses additional research questions. One is these is: how do social movements fit with key normative commitments seen to be held by the proponents of liberal thought? Some of liberalism's greatest figures have explained that liberalism is welcoming of evolutionary impulses, including in the form of societal change (Hayek [1960] 2011). On the other hand, much of liberal theorization from its earliest days appears concerned with the circumstances under which economic, political, and social orders may be sustained. On the surface, the latter concern with order may be suggestive of an appetite for stability, but such a state of affairs is potentially undercut by forces of change. Since the advent of collective behavior theory during the first half of the twentieth century, social movements have been conceptualized as a threat to those institutions and structures which are said to give rise to orderly patterns of human conduct.

Additional normative claims have been made about social movements, and the conduct of their participants. Social movements are seen to be intentional, yet proactive and even insistent, collective agents for changes in society. In addition, movements are seen to be prone to advance their goals in a disruptive fashion. At the arguably extreme limit of concern is that social movements are believed to undermine democratic political procedures and systems—and the degree of community trust placed in these arrangements—by promoting rent-seeking behavior in the quest to attain special privileges. Finally, even the most ardent defender of the social movement form of engagement might concede that a plethora of these groups are effectively seeking to *undermine*, rather than support, freedom of individual action in a range of (entangled) human domains.

In light of these issues, it appears reasonable to ask: What are liberals to make of these claims? When considering the aforementioned matters, the argument is reinforced that it is impossible to restrict the scope of inquiry to political economy. This reflects, to some degree, the reality that social move-ment studies are increasingly embracing a growing number of social scientific disciplines (Roggeband and Klandermans 2017). Liberal political economy itself, it may be argued, represents an antidote to epistemological ring-fenc-ing (Fuller 2016). This has been aptly demonstrated by the inclinations of Hayek, the Ostroms, and Buchanan to connect their political economy stud-ies to broader philosophical, and related, constructs. More recently, a vibrant research agenda for cross-disciplinary inquiry has taken shape in the form of Philosophy, Politics, and Economics (PPE) (e.g., Hanley 2017; G. Brennan 2018; Dekker and Kolev 2019). The point we are making here is that liberal political economy is an intellectually entangled enterprise and, consequently, this chapter shall outline social movement traits which are interpreted as being inclusive of extra-economic interpretation.

This chapter is structured in the following manner. The next section considers the role and contribution of intentional actions undertaken by social movements, within a broader context of entangled domains featuring emergent ordering processes. Following this, we consider the place of social movements within an expansive conception of democratic political interac-tion. This allows us to explicitly incorporate discussion, and other aspects of voice, which may be used to present stern challenges to hegemonic power positions and structures. This is followed by a critical assessment as to what extent those living in liberal-democratic society should accommodate social movements, given that many participants involved with the latter actively seek to undermine the liberal order. This discussion is followed by a set of concluding remarks.

SOCIAL MOVEMENTS AND
CONSTRUCTIVISM ON THE MARGINS

Modern liberal thinkers are forthright critics of extensive governmental involvement in economic relations, not to mention other aspects of life. Hayek, in particular, refuted the agenda which he labeled "rationalist constructivism," which reductively conceives all aspects of society as (figurative or real) objects amenable to comprehensive design or reform (Burczak 1994; A. Martin 2015a). The liberal temperament firmly refutes the planner's desire for consciously constructed "blueprints" for wholesale societal change, which are imposed upon others without consent. Friedrich Hayek's objections to rationalist constructivism belong to the same vein of liberal skepticism concerning the utter *re*modeling of emergent, or spontaneously, ordered processes, the latter regarded as a "composite of all the separate striving of individuals to realize their purposes and plans" (Boettke 2018, 186).

Whereas Austrian economists detected erroneous doctrines rooted in the fascist and communist economic planning regimes of their times, Hayek philosophically traced the constructivist notion back further, to the French Enlightenment rationalism of Descartes and Rousseau (Hayek 1948). The "false individualism" of the French Enlightenment is informed by presumptions of an exaggerated human capability to amend evolved institutions, and relationships, in the shape of one's own choosing. To commit to the constructivist fallacy, in Hayek's view, leads one to fall under the spell of a *"synoptic delusion . . .* the fiction that all the relevant facts are known to some one mind, and that it is possible to construct from this knowledge of the particulars a desirable social order" (Hayek [1973–1979] 2015 vol. I, 12). One of the more famous imageries of liberal critique was forwarded by Adam Smith, in the guise of a "man of system" who conceitedly treats their compatriots as chess pieces in a greater game of societal control. As perceptively noted by Karen Vaughn ([1994] 2018), some of the worst horrors of history that have befallen a society are attributed to politically totalitarian missions to reform the populace and their activities, to, chillingly, create a "new people."

A standard-bearing position of liberalism is that the regularities of human affairs are often not the product of deliberate human contrivances but are, instead, the unintended consequences of human actions (Barry 1982; Horwitz 2001). These include patterns of interaction between individuals labeled as "social" in character, and which are generically referred to as instances of "emergent" or "spontaneous" orders. The generic character of such orders is famously described, by Scottish Enlightenment figure Adam Ferguson ([1767] 2007, 119), as "the result of human action, but not the execution of any human design."

Throughout this book we refer to emergent and spontaneous orders as distinct categories. As the likes of Lewis (2011) and D'Amico (2015) indicate, this distinction between the two terms is more than purely semantic. Emergence relates to phenomena whose properties are ontologically distinguishable from, or irreducible to, the properties of those components complicit in generating the phenomena. This conception potentially incorporates elements of *intended*, directed action by individuals or their groups. A spontaneous order, by comparison and in contrast, refers to the *unintended* consequences of human action. Thus, the emergent order concept implicitly relates to a broader range of phenomena than does its spontaneous counterpart.

It is widely recognized that Friedrich Hayek extended emergent and spontaneous order theorizations in several ways, including from epistemological and philosophical perspectives. In an original contribution, Hayek indicates that such orders are the manifestation of coordinative activities by people who possess some specialized spatial or temporal knowledge about efficacious ways of being, doing, and knowing, but whose knowledge is necessarily partial and incomplete, due to their ignorance about all aspects of society in its totality. Indeed, no *single* individual bears cognitive or other capacities to possess knowledge pertaining to *all* of societal processes. What is pivotal to the overall efficacy of spontaneous orders is the ability of people to adhere to abstract, generic rules simplifying the scope of discretionary action in a complicated world, and helping to (inter-subjectively) converge expectations among diverse individuals about what are appropriate modes of action.

At first glance, the efforts of social movements to intentionally motivate agendas for societal change might appear to run afoul of liberal commitments to embrace emergent and spontaneous ordering processes. In other words, social movement activity appears to be too constructivist for a liberal to accept as legitimate. However, the reality is that social change does accommodate the possibility that purposive and capable, yet fallible, human beings can, or will attempt to, change institutions, norms, organizations, practices, and values. In other words, "upward causation" processes—whereby individuals and their entities effect broad scale societal changes, including through institutional reform—frequently take place (Hodgson 2000). One of the better expositions of the contribution of human agency toward change is provided by Karen Vaughn, who speaks of intentional activities by individuals as influencing even those gradualist changes customarily identified as evolutionary in their character. Vaughn ([1994] 2018, 231) describes social change as "a tension between human creativity and daring and human reluctance to disturb the known patterns of their lives. Man is part dreamer and part follower of rules."

Great store is placed by Vaughn upon the contribution of ideological entrepreneurs in propounding societal change. These individuals originate visualizations of reform, which are imagined to ease disaffections or tensions felt within society. Furthermore, those same individuals seek to disseminate their reform visions, which are, then, subject to acceptance or refutation by other members of society. The ideological entrepreneur described by Vaughn is necessarily one constrained in their ability to invoke sweeping societal changes all at once. This entrepreneur "has visions of how society should be, of how all the pieces fit together and of how it can be guided or molded to the ideal shape. In having such a vision, he shares some of the characteristics of the constructivist rationalist Hayek decries, but his vision might easily be one of competing spontaneous orders that does not partake of the constructivist fallacy" (Vaughn [1994] 2018, 240).

It is important to appreciate that any given entrepreneur lacks the capacity to impose all-encompassing change upon others. Those seeking change must work for reform at smaller scales, in contestable socio-political environments wherein others seek to advance their change proposals, if their ideas and plans are to have any realistic chance of success. When attempting to convey an agenda for societal change the entrepreneur thus engages in "an *appeal to the other*, a dialogical attempt to arrive at mutual understanding" (Madison 1998, 43). Furthermore, entrepreneurs must also maintain a capacity for critical self-reflection, providing assessments as to how their appeals for change are resonating with others within the broader social environment (Davis 2015).

Another contribution clarifying the place for creative, entrepreneurial intentionality within emergent or spontaneous orders is presented by Scott Beaulier and Peter Boettke. Following the work of institutional economist Warren Samuels, Beaulier and Boettke highlight that a spontaneous order is a process of "working things out," of shaping the performance and outcomes of the order itself. Within this lies an interactive process of deliberation and rational criticism between individuals. This entails "pressing questions concerning whose rights, whose freedom, equality/inequality for whom pervade any spontaneous social order we are interested in" (Beaulier and Boettke 2000, 3). To be sure, it is not clear that the product of multi-person deliberation will, *ex ante*, yield a certain outcome, given the complexities arising from human interaction. Nonetheless, a broad implication of the insights presented here is that deliberative processes do not strictly entail a jettisoning of emergence, or unintentionality, in ordering patterns and structures.

The aforementioned perspectives complement the Bloomington School's priority toward decentralized interaction, and the building of meaningful and productive relationships therein. After all, said Vincent Ostrom (1997, 291), "Great Societies are not organized by some single center of Supreme Authority exercising tutelage over Society. Knowledgeable, skillful, and intelligible persons build great societies by working with one another and mediating conflicts to achieve conflict resolution in forming coherent patterns of relationships with one another." What the Ostroms and Hayek appear to share is resistant posture toward one-sided exaggerations of the use of reason, of an acontextual or ahistorical nature (Sciabarra 2000). As an additional safeguard for decentralism, liberals see polycentric institutions, and hetero-topic civil societal spaces, as necessary to allow social movements—and other collectives—to reveal, and to harness, epistemic and other kinds of diversity (Muldoon 2016; Müller 2019). These conditions also encourage mobilities allowing people to spatially associate with others of like mind, without imposing totalizing ideas or practices which expunge the equal free-doms of others to realize their own objectives.

It should also be said that purposive actions are not necessarily dele-gitimized from the liberal perspective, if they help to maintain esteem for higher-level generic rules. Abstract orders—which maintain politico-insti-tutional rules consistent with the protection of property, an ability to create and affirm contracts, and the rule of law—do not necessarily *guarantee* that specific outcomes conducive to human flourishing will be realized. However, such orders certainly do appear to increase the likelihood of satisfactory outcomes. To some extent, this is because heterotopic spaces of freedom are sufficiently secured for those individuals wishing to engage with specific issues within the social environment (Leach and Haunss 2009; Wandel and Valentinov 2014; Novak 2020). Hayek recognized that people feel resent-ments toward the results of emergent or spontaneous orders, but the freedom to carry out specialized activities, including within spatialized and temporal-ized settings, might help to qualm animosities about the social order in the main. In other words, the workings of certain SMOs and other movement participants could, even if unintentionally, help usher an acceptance of (or reduced *animus* toward) generic rules characterizing emergent or spontane-ous orders.

In their paper outlining the potential to reconcile generality and particularity within societal orders, Wandel and Valentinov largely restricted themselves to the case of nonprofit social-service providers. They contend that such enti-ties "are evidently a part of the spontaneous order just as much as for-profit firms and accordingly contribute to the evolution of civilizational complex-ity" (Wandel and Valentinov 2014, 142). It is our view that this logic could be extended to social movements, including those which take part in mutual aid and work to provide other forms of assistance, sidestepping governmental welfare states which tend to disempower their recipients (R. Wagner [1998] 2019). For example, there are contemporary social movements actively involved in community development initiatives and mutual aid projects (e.g., A. Katz 1981; Green 2008; Spade 2020a). Social movements which work in localized action spaces are often doing so to resolve particularized knowledge problems. To the extent that such movements are succeeding, they are helping to avoid the potential for any scaled-up backlash, conflict, and unintended adverse consequences arising from misplaced efforts to impose solutions on a societal-wide scale. Of course, there is the issue that movement participants may feel the need to devise their own responses because conventional methodologies, or the conduct of powerful entities, within society are deemed to be unsatisfactory in some respect.

There is, yet, another issue concerning order theories for one to grapple with. Descriptions of emergent or spontaneous orders usually do not entail normative evaluations about the outcomes of such phenomena, or, when they do, they tend to focus upon the beneficial results of such orderings (Albrecht 2017; C. Harrison 2018). However, it is plausible that such processes do not entail benefits for minorities—or, in some cases, even for majorities—because emergent rules and standards tend to benefit some people, and not others (Haeffele and Storr 2019a). It is in this context that social movement activities are commonly seen as directed toward resolving problems arising from dysfunctional, or harmful, aspects of emergent and spontaneous orders. An appreciation of this point has profound implications for both the kind, and scale, of societal change which social movement participants seek to advance.

In recent years a small number of studies have considered the possibility of *perverse* emergent or spontaneous orders, or large-scale patterns of social order *with malign effects* arising from "bottom-up," decentralized interactions between individuals. Examples of this have been identified with respect to patriarchy and rape culture (Johnson 2013; Christmas 2016), white supremacy (C. Harrison 2018), and transphobia (Novak 2015; Malamet 2018). Each of these examples relate to situations wherein cultural and social norms threaten (if not normalize) violence and other forms of harm, and limit the personal autonomy and effective liberties (e.g., freedom of expression, or of movement) of those at the receiving end of the threats. In a key paper introducing perverse orders into contemporary scholarship, Nona Martin and Virgil Storr (2008, 79) intriguingly depicted rioting as "a spontaneous coalescence of individual reactions in a distressing situation." Essentially, perverse emergent or spontaneous orders manifest themselves in diverse ways, and social movements can address themselves to resolving problems as they come to the surface.

The examples mentioned in the previous paragraph are said to fit within the realm of the results of human action, but not of human design. They were not the result of conscious, or deliberate, design by any given person in particular. Even so, these orders encompass a range of norms, behaviors, and events of an illiberalizing nature which constrain (or threaten to constrain) agency.

Perverse societal orders have significant connotations regarding the appropriate means to redress their malign outcomes, and how to respond to the underlying causes of harm. It is conceivable that public policies instigated by government may alleviate some of the more serious implications of perverse emergent and spontaneous orders. Examples may include codifying non-discrimination rules regarding access to private- and public-sector services, and ensuring that fiscal, legal, and regulatory policies adhere to generality rules (Buchanan and Congleton [1998] 2003; Holcombe 2014). Public-sector authorities could also adjust internal practices, such as promoting the employment of oppressed group members (e.g., Buchanan 1981).

Beyond the initial suggestions just described, it is unclear how much further governmental actors can, or should, redress perverse societal orders. Many of the problems outlined earlier are of a localized or tacit nature, which may be difficult (though not insurmountable) for actors distanced from the scene to comprehend, let alone resolve (Pennington 2011). There may also be a risk that public policies may be ineffective in changing attitudes, beliefs, and morals. All that policy may succeed in doing is "driving bad ideas underground," such that the malign notions sustaining perverse orders are merely suppressed but not eliminated. Consistent with this, policy that fails to incentivize meaningful and enduring cultural adjustments may perpetuate social climates ripe for "preference falsification" (Kuran 1995), wherein individuals publicly conceal their true (but socially unacceptable) beliefs.

It is not insurmountable for various groups within civil society to counter the harmful manifestations of perverse orders. It may be argued, for instance, that a significant basis for social movement activity in the modern era has been, precisely, in addressing racist, sexist, homophobic, and other harmful aspects of perverse emergent and spontaneous orders. Taking just one example, feminist social movements have long been involved in advocacy work, pushing for the equality of women and men. In his discussion about the characteristics and implications of rape culture, Charles Johnson points to the efforts of:

> women-led social movements to counter the effects of diffuse male violence outside, or beyond, the sphere of government and conventional political lobbying. C.R. groups, speakouts, culture-jamming, building grassroots networks of battered women's shelters, rape crisis centers, and other feminist spaces originally had little if any connection to hierarchical power-politics or the male-dominated state, and all could productively be understood as *voluntarily-coordinated, polycentric*, but *consciously organized* political resistance to a *polycentric, emergent, coercive* order of violent oppression. (Johnson 2013, 25)

Movement projects exposing malign social norms and practices may similarly involve ideological or norm entrepreneurship. The ambition of such entrepreneurial acts is to convince others about the dubiousness of perverse orders, and to seek broader engagement in ushering change. The change considered here need not, necessary, be of a political dimension, as illustrated by the contribution of new social movements in promoting changes to cultural-social beliefs, norms, and practices. It is these acts of "persuasion—not coercion, domination and manipulation—which characterizes the proper relationship of one human life to another" (Palmer 1991, 302).

On a final note, we recognize that numerous social movements aim to adjust societal relationships and structures so as to achieve "social justice" objectives. The relationship between liberal thinking and social justice ideals have been fraught, not least due to Hayek's (1988) brutal criticisms of the social justice concept and its potential as motivation for the expansion of political power. Needless to say, the reckoning that social justice considerations are inadmissible within the liberal system of thought has proven controversial. In his assessment of Hayek's claims about social justice, and counter-claims by his critics, Nick Cowen (2020) concludes that Hayek maintains valuable insights concerning the distributed and partial nature of knowledge, and the consequent human incapability to replan an entire society to achieve a socially just end. However, Hayek's criticisms tend to overlook the human capability to enact marginal improvements to emergent or spontaneous orders without overthrowing them (Rowland 1988). Hayek himself displayed an intellectually adventurous spirit in lending support to a great number of reform causes, including publicly financed welfare systems providing equal minimal income support for all (Hayek [1960] 2011; Bergh 2020; Zwolinski 2020).

We think it is possible to consider a social justice agenda which remains sensitive to liberal commitments. Responding to social justice concerns need not involve overriding organization, or wholesale planning. Indeed, "[m]any individual and collective ends are amenable to attainment through indirect methods" (D. Johnston 1997, 90). Efforts by social movements to shift cultural meanings with regard to identity, recognition, and respect for minorities, and other groups deleteriously affected by relations of domination and subjection, need not demand the involvement of legislators, bureaucrats, or other actors primarily involved within the political domain. As alluded to previously, social movements may play a crucial role in developing non-state alternatives to bureaucratized systems of governmental transfers and services provision. Movement activities along these lines may embrace a prefigurative conception of the social world they ideally wish to see, which may be viewed by participants as socially just, and have that conception put into small-scale practice through standards of decision-making, and representation, within the relevant movement organizations and networks. Pursuit of non-state-centric practices, along the lines described here, were issues which largely appeared to be overlooked by Hayek, and other key twentieth-century liberal figures, during much of their careers (Garnett 2011).

As mentioned, social movements can play an important contribution in identifying and diagnosing actual or potential defects in emergent and spontaneous orders (N. Cowen 2020). This strand of movement activity need not entail political obligation. Even so, there is some (though perhaps limited) prospect for social justice argumentation by social movement participants to translate into a so-called "liberaltarian" policy reform agenda (Lindsey 2006) dually meeting liberal concerns to expand freedom and progressive concerns to reduce discrimination. We have already referred to instances of social movements, past and present, pressing for liberalized policies that practically extended liberty for previously oppressed minorities and, at the same time, suppressed discrimination by promoting free association among diverse peoples and undermining network closures. In short, discourse and actions by social movements, performed in the name of social justice, do not necessarily entail a trip along that "road to serfdom" that liberals fear.

EXTENSIVE (LAVOIEAN) LIBERAL DEMOCRACY: SPEAKING TO, AND CHALLENGING, POWER

Liberalism is a democratic creed. The conception of a *liberal democracy* is the combination of democratic principles (i.e., that individuals have the right to express and register their views about matters of public interest, including aspects of public policy) and liberal principles (i.e., that individuals have freedom and rights of equal standing which are not to be diminished by others, such as political rulers). It is our firm understanding that liberal democracy is anti-authoritarian insofar as "[e]quality before the law leads to the demand that all men should also have the same share in making the law" (Hayek [1960] 2011, 168). In expounding the case for political arrangements that are democratic *and* liberal, we submit that liberal democracy supposes the need for institutions, laws, principles, and rules upholding the freedoms and rights of individual citizens (Little 2020).

Democracy is a much-lauded proposition, even if its basic institutions are occasionally subject to stress tests. In addition to the institutional qualities of liberal democracy, its significance "lies not in its method of selecting those who govern but in the fact that, because a great part of the population takes an active part in the formation of opinion, a correspondingly wide range of persons is available from which to select. . . . It is in its dynamic, rather than in its static, aspects that the value of democracy proves itself" (Hayek [1960] 2011, 174). The opportunity for members of the general public to play their part in opinion formation has motivated generations of activists to engage in struggles for political democratization. Indeed, an impressive variety of individuals and groups, including through social movements, have been implicated in the development of democratic technology. In a previous chapter, we described the efforts of early feminists in nineteenth-century Britain demanding the right to vote, representing a constitutive element of the modern democratic form.

Majority voting is typically assumed as the decision rule *par excellence* for liberal-democratic political systems, determining which electoral choice is to be implied as embodying electoral consent and, therefore, accepted as binding upon citizen-voters. The majoritarian voting procedure is evaluated to balance, albeit in a satisficing manner, the "decision" costs associated with reaching a given collective decision with the "external" costs associated with that same decision being inconsistent with the preferences of given individuals (Buchanan and Tullock [1962] 1999). If a polity adopts the unanimity voting decision (requiring the agreement of *all* voters for a given choice to be assented) instead, the external costs borne by the public are infinitesimal, whereas the decision costs are likely to be high given the prospect that "hold-out" voters threatening to veto the electoral decision-making process. Alternatively, if the polity adopts a dictatorial voting rule in which only one person decides a collective outcome the decision costs are infinitesimal, yet the external costs are likely to be extremely high because of the presumed lack of public consultation by the dictator.

Majority voting is largely viewed as a convention to incorporate a degree of agency in democratic political decision-making. The registry of this agentic element is seen to be achieved, under majority voting, without the undue intransigency associated with obtaining assent from literally every participant in the voting exercise. However, a series of objections have emerged concerning the efficiency and effectiveness of majority voting procedures. One of the main concerns are potentially inconsistent outcomes arising from majority voting mechanisms. The implication of such inconsistencies, at least for some, is the raising of doubts over the adequacy of democratic decisions in registering public opinion, leading to subsequent questions over the legitimacy of political outcomes under democracy.

A commonly held dilemma in social choice relates to the "cycling" problem affecting majority voting among more than two alternatives (be they candidates, issues, or some other matter subject to collective evaluation and decision). Specifically, the problem is that the presence of cycling between alternatives may not provide a consistent aggregation of individual preferences. To use a simple example, assume the voting population is faced with choosing either A, B, or C. The cycling problem arises when A is preferred to B, and B is preferred to C, yet, paradoxically, *C is preferred to A*. In this respect, every alternative loses to at least one other alternative and, accordingly, it is impossible to unambiguously discern the majoritarian preference. As stated by Buchanan (2003, 14), "election results rotate in continuous cycles with no equilibrium or stopping point. The suggestion of this analysis was that majoritarian democracy is inherently unstable."

Twentieth-century welfare economist Kenneth Arrow generalized the majority voting cyclicity proposition, which is originally traced as far back to the eighteenth-century mathematicians Condorcet and Borda. Arrow's "impossibility theorem" states that, under conditions of rational, well-ordered preferences, there is no available voting rule to convert individual preferences into a consistent aggregative decision. According to Arrow (1951, 60), "[i]f consumers' values can be represented by a wide range of individual orderings, the doctrine of voters' sovereignty is incompatible with that of collective rationality." The implication of Arrow's findings is that restricting the range of individual preferences, or imposing dictatorial preferences, may ensure consistent and rational modes of collective choice via voting. In other words, "either collective choices are democratic, but irrational, or they are rational, but dictatorial" (Boettke and Leeson 2002, 15).

Added to Arrow's maudlin account of the efficacy of democratic voting decisions is the influence of "rational ignorance" in electoral decision-making (Downs 1957). The probability of a given individual's casting vote proving decisive, that is, in determining the ultimate outcome of a large-scale electoral contest, is miniscule. Consequently, individuals will be rationally deterred from providing significant amounts of time, labor, and other resources to learn more about the collective issues at stake, or the alternative positions of individual candidates with respect to those issues. This proposition does present an obvious question: Why it is that considerable shares of the voting-eligible population still turn out to vote? One answer to that question has been provided by Brennan and Lomasky (1993), suggesting that voters maintain non-instrumental, or "expressive," reasons to vote, such as the impulse to cast votes to signal esteem and support toward their favored candidates or public issues.

To what extent should students of democracy put store in the key criticisms of voting procedures? An argument could be made that the aforementioned criticisms of majority voting should be contextualized, with an understanding, once more, of the dynamic affordances of democratic political action. Liberal democracy is a rule-guided process facilitating the formation and settlement of opinion about issues in the public interest, the results of which cannot be foreseen *ex ante* (diZerega 1989). For democracy to be at its most effective, voting outcomes should be permitted to fluctuate over time in accordance with the proposition that *public opinions are contestable* and, perhaps more importantly, *subject to change.*

In an important retort to Arrow's social choice strictures about majoritarian voting, James Buchanan argued that apparent instability within social choice ordering is a propitious feature of democracy. Majoritarianism potentially achieves more than just the breaking of stalemates, by minimizing the sum of decision and external costs of collective action via voting. It "serves to insure that competing alternatives may be experimentally and provisionally adopted, tested, and replaced by new compromise alternatives approved by a majority group of ever changing composition" (Buchanan 1954b, 119). The acceptability of majority voting is attributable, then, to the idea that "ordinary majority decision is subject to reversal and change, while individual decision cannot readily be made so. With identical majority orderings, the majority would, of course, always choose the same leaders, and this advantage of majority rule would be lost" (ibid., 120).

Buchanan (2003) later indicated his concern to address Arrow's impossibility theorem was to ensure democracies did not discriminate against minority groups, or those who subscribe to minoritarian views. This concern naturally led Buchanan, and other public choice theorists, to consider the need for safeguard conventions and institutions—such as constitutional limitations of political power. To be clear, in an extensive liberal democracy collective action is not informed solely by majority voting episodes: "it is not necessarily desirable to use the same voting rule for all collective decisions; and that the public's interest can be best protected if exit options are preserved by making collective choices at the lowest feasible level of political authority" (Shughart 2007). Vincent Ostrom (1997) reinforced the perspective that democratic effectiveness is also contingent upon cultural and social norms, including the capacity of citizen-voters to exercise self-governance by working cooperatively with others to resolve public problems.

The contrast between the Arrow and Buchanan-Hayek-Ostrom conceptions of democracy are stark. Arrow is concerned about the *efficiency* of democracy to transform given preferences into a "general will," so to speak, whereas Buchanan, Hayek, and the Ostroms consider the *efficacy* of democracy as a procedure for forming, discovering, and utilizing opinions and conjectural solutions (Wohlgemuth 2002). Embracing the interpretations of the three figureheads of liberal political economy lends itself to an appreciation of robust democratic life, one which extends beyond a so-called "low-intensity" vision of democracy reducible to voting procedures (Sen 2009; Tully 2013).

It should also be added that liberal soundings on democracy are a logical extension of normative individualism. Liberals, such as Humboldt, Mill, and Hayek, extolled the virtues of minorities presenting experiments in living, going against the grain of moralistic and politically majoritarian thinking. Other figures suggest democratic procedures are more likely to account for the interests and perspectives of all those affected by political decision-making—especially minorities—if they are conditioned by institutional rules and practices maintaining liberties and rights. The research agenda of James Buchanan was exemplified by his consideration of constitutional-level rules, to ensure that liberal democracies do not retrogress into a system of political domination and subjection (e.g., Buchanan and Tullock [1962] 1999). On a similar basis, Buchanan and Congleton ([1998] 2003) and Hutt (1966) called for explicit nondiscriminatory provisions to prevent political overriding of minority concerns and interests.

It is possible that minoritarian positions may become acceptable to a political majority sometime in the future. As illustrated by the practical case of social movement activities, the career of pivotal public issues—from an individual, or a small group, to eventual habituation by a population at large—requires strategic engagements transcending mere voting and election campaigning. The nesting of voting procedures within a broader context of institutions, mores, and practices is by no way intended to contain democratic processes, or to deny the realities of conflict and contestation. Extensive liberal democracy, rather, seeks to facilitate revelation of perspectival diversities concerning matters of public interest, as well as accommodating the prospect of political change peacefully.

Drawing upon a rich tradition involving the thought of J. S. Mill, Frank Knight, and James Buchanan, liberals have also extolled the democratic virtues of political discussion. Discussion is seen "as a correction to bias and a means by which society's goals are endogenously determined and constantly checked and revised" (D. Levy and Peart 2016, 30; also, Sen 2011; Emmett 2020). This discussion strain of democratic thought implies that an evolutionary political process is at work. To be precise, discussion between citizen-voters, all free and equal, may be aimed at persuading others, but it should not be presumed the polylogue arrives at an all-encompassing, consensual end-point (Madison 1998). Discussion within liberal democracies is assuredly supported by polycentric political arrangements. Increasingly monocentric systems of political organization, in contrast, tend to be associated with monologue, such as political propaganda, suppressing the diffusion and reception of contestable arguments over matters of public interest.

Arguably the most extensive account of the liberal-democratic model we have in mind was advanced by Don Lavoie. Inspired by Hayekian themes, Lavoie states that "[d]emocracy is not a quality of the conscious will of a representative organization that has been legitimized by the public, but a quality of the discursive process of the distributed wills of the public itself" (Lavoie 1993, 111). The efficacy of democracy in opinion formation is enhanced wherever principles of openness are accepted, which, in turn, generates public discussion and distils distributed political arguments and demands. Illiberal measures, disabling perspectival diversities from revealing themselves peacefully through political argumentation, would narrow, if not destroy, the democratic system itself (Lavoie 1992, 1993). According to a recent account, Lavoiean democracy fits in well with a radical picture of liberalism, the latter casting as an affront to all forms of power:

> democracy is defined less by a nation-state's periodic elections and more by the openness of discussion within a society. In this sense, there may be truth to the common chant "This is what democracy looks like," heard at various leftist street protests. In addition to people entering public spaces to express their views together, democracy from this perspective looks like the operation of a free press. It looks like the often acrimonious and discordant discussions that take place in comment sections. Democracy looks like Chelsea Manning, Edward Snowden, Thomas Drake, John Kiriakou, and other whistleblowers alerting the public to opportunistic acts that the state would keep secret. . . . In this view, a radical commitment to democracy does not mean expanding the scope of state decision-making so that more actions can be controlled through elections. Instead, it means maintaining a culture of openness and preserving freedom of speech, freedom of the press, and freedom to challenge power. (Goodman 2019, 143)

The idea that not all valuable knowledge about how to coordinate in a political sense rests in the majoritarian view, once again, reaffirms our claim that democratic processes should be institutionally contextualized to support, and not suppress, difference. To allow democracies to evolve and to function, minorities should be afforded the liberty to persuade the majority of the merits of different viewpoints, without fear or favor. Of course, in suggesting this, we accept the liberal insight that the concept of the "public," and politically identifiable "majority" and "minority" segments therein, is a conjectural construct that is amenable to change (Buchanan 1954b; Aligica et al. 2019).

We consider it is in the context of extensive liberal democracy that the value(s) of social movements reveal themselves. Social movement organizers, activists, and other participants collaborate in the development and publicization of messages demanding societal change, which often, though not entirely, entail calls upon political actors to instigate (or support) reforms. As is also well known, social movements seek to persuade, or expediently gain concessions from, their compatriots, politically, by engaging in protest and other contentious actions. At the risk of adopting a style of economic parlance, social movement activity serves as a form of "input" into democratic processes. At the micro- and meso-levels of engagement, involvement within social movements adds to the overall impression that "democracy not only gives the people a voice but also it gives them a feeling of contribution, participation, and meaning" (Nell 2016, 160). The democratic engagements by social movements, interest groups, and other associations may, along various margins, help reduce the epistemic inefficacies arising from entry barriers to party-political organization and parliamentary representation (Wohlgemuth 1999).

Another important respect in which social movements add to the informational base of democracy is through their involvement, along with many other actors within society, as *co-producers* of public policies and democratic political norms. The notion of co-production is attributed to the work of the Ostroms, describing involvement by users in the development, and provision, of public goods or localized forms of public governance (E. Ostrom 1993). In their recent contribution, Aligica et al. (2019, 128) consider democracy as a site for the co-production of rules: "In a self-governing democratic system the rules satisfy the preferences of those subjected to those rules, and, for this to happen, citizens need to have some input into the creation of those rules." It is in this regard that citizens may seek input into political rules through collective engagement in social movements, instead of acting on an individual basis.

To be sure, the nature of social movement co-production toward democratic decisions and practices can frequently assume contentious, extra-institutional tones. In this respect, policymakers may accommodate social movement demands for change indirectly, perhaps through the counsel of other interests who have embraced the social movement position, rather than giving activists an "insider," or elitist, role in the constructions of democratic novelty. It is also true that certain social movements wish to bypass the political process as they press for broader cultural, economic, or social change. To some extent, it would appear that extra-institutional labor by social movements aims to reduce the agency costs otherwise associated with delegating responsibilities to political agents. Irrespective of the means of, or parties to, engagement, it is apparent that democratic co-production entails "a process of public conversation, debate, compromise, and consent; innovation and collaboration on projects; and a learning process based upon trial and error" (Nell 2016, 130).

The unfortunate reality is that, in actually existing societies, there remain significant elements of illiberalism woven into our entangled political economies. The problem here is not that formal institutions reflective of liberal values do not exist but that, in the eyes of some, those institutions do not yield outcomes living up to the weighty liberal ideals that inspired their development (Chantal Mouffe, cited in D. Taylor 2017, 107). It is against this background that people participate in democratic forums, and use various mechanisms and means to mobilize democratically. According to Burczak (2006, 81), "real-world democracy may be imperfect and messy, but given the contestable nature of questions concerning justice, . . . democratic politics institutes a forum for multiple, competing views of justice to be heard and debated." Democratic opportunities may prove to be particularly valuable for people with strong expressive political preferences, given the previously mentioned limitations of solely relying upon voting mechanisms to register demands (Chong 1991). Even if movement participants tend to harbor particularly intense feelings about certain issues, their activities can still play a constructive role in helping to correct the epistemic biases and disconnections of political actors and others in powerful positions (Anderson 2014).

Another relevant consideration is that of social movement effectiveness. How effective have social movements been in ushering change within the liberal-democratic order? Addressing this question is certainly an ongoing topic for research, however one might suggest the following hypothesis: political systems respecting the freedoms of assembly, association, expression, and speech for individuals and non-state collectives enhance the ability of social movements to achieve their objectives (Goldstone 2004; Dalton et al. 2010; Welzel 2013). To affirm, or deny, this proposition is ultimately an empirical matter, and any research on this basis must consider the extent to which movements deploy nonviolent, or violent, tactical approaches in an effort to attain their objectives (e.g., Chenoweth and Stephan 2011).

One might disagree with the approaches they adopt, but there seems little doubt that social movements provide significant information value in liberal democracies. In between elections, and even during election campaigns, participants of social movements act on the basis of their (subjective) valuations with respect to their favored causes. By virtue of their involvement, movement participants send signals, and other kinds of information, to nonparticipants—including decision-makers in business and politics—about the intensity, or level, of their valuations concerning proposals for societal change. As part of this, social movements can signal actual or potential harms felt by their participants, supporters, and allies, and they can demand change to ameliorate such harms. It is true that different demands are produced simultaneously by a variety of actors besides social movements, and that what movements actually want are subject to varying interpretations. Nonetheless, it is testament to the capacities of liberal-democratic political arrangements that ordinary people can associate, through social movements, to challenge authority and to vocalize opposition to oppression.

MEETING ILLIBERAL SOCIAL
MOVEMENT CHALLENGES

Liberals have acknowledged pluralism as a central plank of their social thought. The liberal recognition, and affirmation, of pluralism is a reflection of an underlying belief: "that reasonable persons properly pursue a wide variety of lifestyles, goals, projects, and commitments" (Macedo 1990, 207). Key thinkers in the liberal canon, such as Wilhelm von Humboldt and John Stuart Mill, have provided a conceptual account favoring pluralism, resting in the development of idiosyncratic personality and the concomitant realization of individual autonomy. To the extent that pluralism is mapped with diversity, the coexistence of multiple ways of being, doing, and knowing is also seen to promote moral and social progress, via the inter-personal and inter-group elucidation of discoveries and learnings.

Another important defense of pluralism came from twentieth-century British philosopher Isaiah Berlin's (2002) conception of "value pluralism." The diversity of values among the populace was seen by Berlin to find its greatest support in the principle of "negative" liberty, which indicates that a lack of interference allows individuals to live according to their own prerogatives. This perspective finds an added purpose of refuting totalitarian political projects, many of which aim at imposing a singular value, or limited sets of values, for all humankind. There are other positions affirming pluralism, as located in libertarian thought valorizing the freedom of the individual and of association. In recognition of interpersonal differences that are attached to conceptions of the good life, Robert Nozick (1974), for example, explicated a framework for competing utopian experiments enabling people to choose their preferred arrangements.

Despite the clear presentation within liberal thought for the plural life, an ongoing challenge for liberals has been to negotiate the socio-political tensions arising from difference. An important feature of the contractarian political project, most conspicuously prosecuted in recent decades by John Rawls and James Buchanan, has been to identify (constitutional and other relevant) rules which may (hypothetically) garner the support of all people to be governed by them, and to work out the procedures necessary to secure the necessary consensus. Contractarianism outlines mechanisms for the fundamental working arrangements of politics to be renegotiated, should they outlive their usefulness. It is important to appreciate that a motivation for a contractarian, such as Buchanan, is that rules should ensure that minorities, and the diverse manner in which they contribute politically, are not suppressed by the majority. However, within the contractarian model outlined by Buchanan and Tullock ([1962] 1999) there are crucial assumptions appearing to abstract away some resemblances of pluralism which might operate, under some circumstances, to frustrate the ratification of certain rules. Consensus is likely to be unachievable if certain potential parties to constitutional agreement maintain strongly-held political views, labeled "unreasonable," or if there exists sharply diverging views due to heterogeneity. Both of these issues are subject to critical investigation by Haeffele and Storr (2018).

Fairly or otherwise, liberalism has been castigated by critics over the years of deploying contractarian thought experiments to paper over the reality of what we call "framework disagreements." What we are referring to here are not the relatively marginal disagreements about, say, policy appropriateness under given democratic institutions and rules—for example, "what should the corporate tax rate be?" The framework disagreement proposition is more fundamental than that. Political framework disagreements imply plurality in the shape of variegated frameworks, and worldviews, in respect to how a community should be governed *in toto*. As expressed by Matt Sleat (2013, 1), framework disagreements embody "a vision of the political in which disagreement and conflict over all political questions, including the most important and fundamental such as the terms that govern our shared political association, is an essential, inevitable, and ineradicable feature of politics." Framework disagreements expose the reality of socially tectonic clashing about the nature and operationalization of politics itself, reflecting a general insight that political outcomes or processes may entail senses of acquiescence, duress, and force, as felt by members of the public (R. Wagner 2016).

Growing recognition has been afforded to the significant, perhaps endemic, degree of disputation within liberal-democratic politics. Contrasting the universality of Enlightenment liberalism, the philosopher John Gray presented a model of "agonistic liberalism," which arguably extends value pluralism to its logical limit, by contemplating the possibility of endemic *dis*agreement. The centerpiece of agonistic liberalism is the idea "there is an irreducible diversity of ultimate values (goods, excellences, options, reasons for action, and so forth) and that when these values come into conflict or competition with one another there is no overarching standard or principle, no common currency or measure, whereby such conflicts can be arbitrated or resolved" (Gray 1995, 116).

The particularity of perspectives arising through political interaction, says Gray, challenges liberal views that lean toward an (unrealistic) antiseptic view of consensus politics. The ambition to endorse those institutions, practices, and rules which command consensus aims, futilely from the agonistic perspective, to abolish or nullify the deep disagreements that are said to be at the core of political activity. This is a sentiment that appears to be shared by post-structural theorist, Chantal Mouffe, who also suggests that pluralism is politically characterized by conflictual perspectives among individuals and groups. Mouffe considers that conflict cannot be resolved. In this spirit, she refines the "enemy-friend" relational distinction of anti-liberal philosopher Carl Schmitt by positionally categorizing individuals and groups into three political categories: friends; enemies; and adversaries.

The distinction between friends and enemies is troubling. Endorsement of such distinctions may lead certain individuals to suppose the political demands of the other to be illegitimate, and even deserving of elimination. This perspective represents the worst of those "universal adversarialism" tendencies which are, regrettably, identifiable throughout human history (Hartley and Potts 2014). Now, the addition of the adversary category by Mouffe may be read as an attempt to create a subtler "we/they relation where the conflicting parties, although acknowledging that there is no rational solution to their conflict, nevertheless recognize the legitimacy of their opponents" (Mouffe 2005, 20). Whichever way we conceptualize political conflict, framework disagreements do not easily lend themselves to societal-wide resolution—for instance, by having regard to rational principles and consistent operating procedures under a contractarian arrangement (Jones 2014).

The conceptual representations by Gray and Mouffe appear as severe criticisms of the liberal political approach. But how divorced are these views from liberal thinking overall? Madison (1998) harkens back to the philosophy of Immanuel Kant, and in particular the latter's invocation of "unsocial sociability" as a determinant of progress. As a matter of course, human beings seek the betterment of self and, consequently, the realization of one's own priorities. However, such a pursuit could generate disquiet, and opposition, from others, including as one's life plan is juxtaposed with those held by others. The continuous carriage and publicization of individual plans bring to the fore an appreciation of entrepreneurship as nonconventional *dissensus* (Boettke and Coyne 2009), a notion as applicable to questions of public governance as it is to economic exchange. Stephen Macedo (1990, 58) makes the related point that, "[l]iberals need dissenters from liberalism: unless we keep debating and remain open to new and better reasons we could have no confidence in the reasons we now think are good."

In recent years there have been attempts to engage with political incommensurability within a liberal philosophical frame. The "realist" approach to political liberalism, attributable to the works of Sleat (2013) and Sabl (2017), submits that liberal-democratic institutions and outcomes are, by no means, subject to agreement by all those governed by them. An implication of this view, to be addressed in further detail later, is that *liberal* realists perceive "liberalism as a fighting creed in the sense that it is engaged in a perpetual contest with rival visions of the political good but also in that it is a model of co-existence worth fighting for" (Sleat 2013, 139). Democracy is an order in which public opinion is actively shaped and reshaped, reflective of a grand interplay of contestable (indeed, antagonistic) demands, ideas, and proposals.

Within this, liberal perspectives vie with other worldviews for the support, if not the affection, of women and men.

Throughout this book we have placed great store upon the constructive contribution of certain social movements towards the development of liberal institutions and practices. Individuals banding together under social movement banners have proven to be influential collective projectors of liberalizing change to economies, polities, and societies. That all said, it is patently obvious that many social movement causes have been pursued for ends which stridently oppose liberalism. Participants within social movements of an anti-liberal orientation may see themselves as purveyors of an agonistic politics, in that they are seeking changes to ease their sense of disaffection about what they perceive to be a hegemonic liberal order. Similarly, such movement participants see themselves as extra-institutional countervailing forces against what they perceive as the concentration of power in economic and political organizations (Sabl 2017).

As important as the contractarian approach is to liberal theory, liberal democracy does not practically require unanimity and consensus to remain operational. At any given point in time, it will be possible to identify people who disagree not only with electoral political outcomes, or governmental policy decisions, but who substantively find living within a liberal political order to be problematic. According to Sleat (2013, 47), "[d]isagreement in politics is the rule rather than the exception. The persistence of disagreement is one of the fundamental and 'stubborn facts' of political life which ensures that there is rarely any natural harmony or order in human affairs. The most basic political question, what I shall call '*the* political question,' is how we are to live together in the face of such deep and persistent disagreement." Therefore, an important matter to be considered is how a set of political commitments—worthy of the liberal name—can accommodate the existence of "indefinite and multiple values and purposes" (Sabl 2017, 353), including incommensurable ones.

How might liberals respond to social movements conveying *anti-liberal* commitments? Specifically, how could liberals respond to such movements, without stooping to an illiberal expunging of movement participants' basic freedoms to assemble, associate, express, and speak? One of the vital ingredients for living an entangled life consistent with liberal values is to maintain *toleration* in respect of alternative modes of action, expressions of viewpoint, and ways of living. The very idea of toleration obtains epistemic credence in that there is a ready recognition that, in our socio-political world, people maintain diverse, albeit often disagreeable, ideas about how one should live (and, crucially, how others should live). Assuming a stance of living our own lives freely, and equally affording others to do much the same, not only imparts a meaningful degree of civil forbearance. This disposition serves as a precaution against coercive attempts to extinguish the plurality of projects pursued within the political community (Macedo 1990; Leeson and Boettke 2006). The general view is that the more extensive a degree that toleration is exercised politically, the greater the prospect that peace and plurality can coincide as social *praxis*.

Properly understood, toleration need not entail acceptance, or enthusiasm, for everything under the sun. Nonetheless, as described by van de Haar (2015, 9), "[l]iberals feel it is the duty of all people to allow certain behavior or the propagation of certain ideas, even if one does not agree or even when one finds them despicable." Individuals who carry out their lives in the spirit of toleration recognize that other people suitably possess agency to commit to their preferred ways of life, even if that risks an element of contentious bumping and scraping against one another. All of this is in keeping with the sentiment once expressed by Hayek that "peace is not a result of agreement but by toleration of disagreement" (quoted in Horwitz 2012). It is still notable, however, that liberal theorists contend that engagement with diverse others is likely to corrode animosities, and bring people closer together in states of fruitful cooperation (Novak 2018b). Liberal-democratic societies which facilitate participation, as part of a generic process of opinion formation, are seen to yield "an incitement to self-examination and invitation to experiment" (Macedo 1990, 278).

Liberal thinking that embraces a "thick" approach to freedom is one which is concerned about departures from freedom in all contexts, and in every situation. Numerous social movements, even those whose participants do not subscribe to liberal values, nonetheless subscribe to particular ends which are, occasionally, similar to those of liberalism. Liberals, too, care about equality, justice, and liberty. Indeed, and as stated by Fawcett (2014), only a peculiar kind of liberal would not respond to violations of freedom with indignation and outrage. It seems a key difference is that liberals tend to vouch for non-state, polycentric solutions to those problems identified by non-liberal social movements. But to avoid lapses in our commitments to freedom, and the innovations necessary to support it, it might be possible to learn from social movement participants who demand that the proponents of liberalism live up to the letter, if not the spirit, of their principles politically.

Certain critics have chided liberals for being tolerant to a fault, for tolerating the intolerant and for desiring to learn from the seemingly incommensurable. This position may be interpreted to be in line with a perception of liberalism as "the supreme form of generosity; it is the right which the majority concedes to minorities and hence it is the noblest cry that has ever resounded in this planet. It announces the determination to share existence with the enemy" (José Ortega y Gasset, quoted in Munger and Diaz 2019, 341). Contrary to surface appearances, our view should not be taken to imply, by any stretch of the imagination, a reticence or timidity when prosecuting the liberal case. Liberalism needs its defenders, too, much like the conservatives, progressives, and socialists, who lack hesitation in propounding their respectively preferred economic, political, and social configurations. At the risk of belaboring the point, defenses of liberalism do not magically appear as Heavenly endowments; therefore, defenses of liberalism must be devised and publicized by women and men on Earthly ground.

Over the centuries liberal proponents have demonstrated great intellectual skill and dexterity when responding to the opportunities and challenges of their times. Historical precedent and contemporary experience show that "[l]iberalism is not . . . neutral in its consequences: life in a liberal regime will tend to favour certain patterns of human flourishing" (Macedo 1990, 253). Indeed, if liberalism were, somehow, impartial or neutral in its stance toward modes of human existence its proponents would not stand to resist the economic sclerosis, social fragmentation, and political dysfunction that come with illiberal projects of all stripes.

As mentioned, liberalism has its political adversaries and enemies, including among certain social movement organizers, activists, and supporters. Nonetheless, the manner in which self-identified liberals in positions of political power discharge their duties and responsibilities have significant implications with respect to the credibility, if not esteem, attached to the liberal agenda. In addressing the issue as to how to reconcile framework disagreements with (coercive) political authority, Matt Sleat (2013) calls for a sense of "moderate rulership" on the part of liberal governors. To attain a sufficient political legitimacy, liberals in political offices must exercise restraint, chiefly by adhering to the rule of law. In doing so, politicians suppress, and hopefully resist altogether, the temptation to depart from non-discrimination and generality in the treatment of those they govern. A closely related point has been made by Boettke (2018), who says that adherence to the rule of law limits the political temptation to entrench particularized mores in law, which, in turn, defuses an important focal point for conflict.

A similar approach to thinking about political management of framework disagreements is to extend Madison's (1998) idea of "self-limitation" to the political arena itself. Recall the earlier point that self-limitation for social movements translates into the practice of nonviolence, and the observance of a sufficiently minimal degree of respect for others with contrary views. It is clear that moderate rulership in a liberal democracy embodies the same qualities of interaction. Indeed, "one must learn to resist the temptation of sending those with whom one disagrees off to Siberia, since when this attitude is widespread one can be fairly sure that at some point or other one will find oneself exiled to Siberia" (Madison 1998, 114).

Ruling in the manner described here may not necessarily increase the number of liberals in a polity, or numerically reduce its adversaries and enemies. Nonetheless, equanimity and modesty in political rule resonates with the liberal tenet of treating everyone as free and equal. This notion extends to those social movement participants who often disseminate messages, and instigate tactics, for anti-liberal causes, but who do so *peacefully* and, thus, avoiding the destruction of life and property. The underlying principle is that democratic politics is not necessarily an idealized mechanism to obtain agreements or consensual conditions, but is a way to give meaningful structure for the peaceful terms of persistent (framework) disagreements among heterogeneous individuals (Aligica 2019).

A realist political approach suggests that the categorical, groupish distinctions between friend, adversary, and enemy are significant attributes of political existence. However, this proposition does not suggest that some degree turnover across categories is impossible. Friedrich Hayek famously pondered the meaning of the term "catallaxy," and what this term entails for our understanding of the market-oriented economic order. He stated that catallaxy means "not only 'to exchange' but also 'to admit into the community' and 'to change from enemy into friend'" (Hayek [1973–1979] 2015 vol. II, 108). In a Hayekian spirit, is it possible to convert social movement enemies of liberalism into mere adversaries, and, perhaps with extra patience and sound reasoning, render conversions from adversaries to friends?

The answer to this question ultimately rests in observations of practical experiences on the ground, with special regard given to the manner in which disagreements are prosecuted and managed. Within this, it will be crucial to identify whether engagements between movement participants and their varied antagonists are infused with values of moderation (Craiutu 2019) and forgiveness (Boettke and Coyne 2007), adherence to good-faith discursive exchange (Chamlee-Wright 2020), and a commitment to refrain from destructive contestation (Baumol 1990; Vanberg 1994). To be certain, these qualities of human interaction stand in sharp contrast with the "militarized" or "war-like" demeanor in regard to the treatment of those with divergent views, as has been discerned in more recent times (Vallier 2021).

CONCLUSION

Liberalism is a fertile enterprise aimed at upholding freedom for each and all. At its normative core is a commitment to empower heterogeneous individuals with agency to discover, and implement, their preferred pathways of living. Granting the fallibility of individuals, proponents of liberalism, nevertheless, indicate that people are capable of learning from, and responding to, errors and mistakes through trial-and-error economic, political, and social processes. Coercion by individuals or groups that pre-empts individualized visions of the good life—or, otherwise, seeks to expunge experiments in living in accordance to divine, scientific, or some other, criterion—is ruled out under the liberal scheme.

A central feature of liberalism's intellectual fertility is that it is not static. The esteemed figurehead of twentieth-century Austrian economics, Ludwig von Mises ([1927] 2005, xix), rightly noted: "[l]iberalism is not a completed doctrine or a fixed dogma. On the contrary: it is the application of the teachings of science to the social life of man." Liberalism is alive with innovation that, in no small part, responds to current events. One of the issues brought about into sharp relief by liberal innovation is how well emergent social phenomena are explainable using its conceptual and analytical tools. Whereas social movements appear to pose a challenge to liberal modes of explanation, given their characterizations as group-oriented phenomena intentionally aiming at some aspect of societal change, we have attempted to show that these collectives can be understood with the use of liberal theoretical constructs.

This chapter has sought to adopt some of liberalism's core principles to comprehend social movements and their activities. We indicate that intentional acts by social movement participants do not necessarily breach the bounds of liberal conceptualization and analysis, insofar as such they are part of the broader tapestry of human action in which individuals remain free to act. In addition, a "simple and natural system of democracy" suggests we are all free and equal to be involved in the creation of ideas, as well as institutions, and practices, affecting how we shall be governed through political means. Our democratic freedom facilitates extensive forms of participation. This includes the ability to form social movements, allowing us to express our political desires, together with the right to nonviolently express one's dissatisfaction with contemporary institutions, organizations, and practices.

It is true that the demands of any given individual, or group, may be structurally divergent from those made by others. Whereas a realist approach to political philosophy suggests limits upon the realization of consensus, it still illuminates some politically constructive ways of engaging those with divergent opinions. In the final analysis, a liberal interpretation of political realism implies the need to appreciate social movement campaigners for instrumental, and non-instrumental, reasons. In the case of the former, we obtain valuable information from them, and they from us, when we publicly express demands, feelings, needs, opinions, and viewpoints. With regard to the latter, we share a common humanity in which differences ought to be managed, and not liquidated. A liberal slant on political realism would encourage peaceful interactions between social movement proponents and opponents, which refuse to aim at wiping out divergent perspectives. On the contrary, it is better to grasp opportunities to learn alternative outlooks through the prism of openness, as well as reasoning and discovering ways to feasibly negotiate, or otherwise reconcile with, difference.

Chapter 8

Summary of Key Themes and Arguments

In the modern world people have experienced multiple structural transformations of the economies, polities, and societies in which they interact. Social scientists have spent incalculable time and effort in tracing the drivers of large-scale, and constantly transformational, changes to our lives. This book accords social movements as a key contributor to the multi-pronged evolutions that we are experiencing, and to which we continue to adjust. It is correct to suggest that social movement activities are nothing new and, indeed, have posed as a critical feature of our societal landscapes for many years, if not decades and centuries. Putting that fact aside, renewed growth in movement activities—with new networks of participants collaborating over contentious strategies and tactical exercises, in response to a wide range of issues—calls for the need to better understand these phenomena. In this book, we have sought to understand social movements through the perspectives of liberal political economy and, in parts, liberalism more broadly as a moral, political, and philosophical framework.

Social movements have been critically implicated in some major social changes, but it is difficult to describe their nature, range of activity, and impact in a straightforward fashion. Indeed, some researchers have suggested that movements have an unnerving habit of evading definitional, conceptual, and analytical clarity (Kolers 2016). In between the polar extremes of strongly hierarchical organizations and severely segmented network structures, social movements may be construed as somewhat improvisational, yet highly dynamized, efforts by people to achieve certain aims relating to societal change. Those aims may reflect expressive or instrumental concerns, or a mixture of both.

One could be drawn into thinking of social movements as a kind of "relational glue," helping to thread contentious pockets of civil society together.

However, this characterization probably discounts the informality, or, more accurately, the tenuousness, of movement activity. Composed of heterogeneous individuals assuming various roles, and largely sustained by voluntary effort, social movements tend to embody more diffuse, and spontaneous, traits than certain other civil societal entities, such as nonprofit organizations or social enterprises. A number of case studies featured in this book shows it cannot be presumed that social movement participants will maintain a united front, given the potential for factionalism, organizational splintering, disagreements over which issues to prioritize publicly, and tactical disputations.

Social movements are noted for their tendency to dynamically conjoin with actors, within broader networks of supporters and alliance partners. Contrasting this collaborate dimension, movement participants contentiously entangle with identifiable opponents, and targets, situated across multiple domains of human action. Specifically, movements engage with governmental agencies, private corporations, educational institutions, nonprofit entities, and other actors in robust and typically (but not always) contentious ways. Supporters of movements, and of counter-movements, attempt to persuade others to shift their conception of preferred states of the world. These considerations add additional layers of conceptual and analytical complexities.

We have applied liberal political economy principles to comprehend social movements and their activities. One may conceive social movements as improvisational mechanisms of collective action and commitment. As part of this, social movement participants invoke shared efforts of relationality through creative citizenship, operating within diverse institutional environments under conditions of legal, social, and other kinds of uncertainty. It is in this context that social movements have the potential of "enabling us to understand what others do and accomplish as a function of living their lives in association with others" (Sabetti 2014, 25–56). Through social movement activities, it is often found that people can propose and implement solutions to collective action problems and social dilemmas.

Social movements are extremely active in political affairs, and their participants are reputed for their robust use of contentious activity, but it is important to be mindful that movements remain, ultimately, *voluntary* collectives. They require motivation, energy, and tactical novelty on the part of individual participants to organize and mobilize effectively, but also to avoid defection, or reduced commitment, on the part of those who previously chose to get involved. Entrepreneurship is deeply implicated in our story, and understandably so given our use of conceptual and analytical tools drawn from Austrian, Bloomington, and Virginia political economy. Entrepreneurs involved in advancing a social movement cause: receive information about phenomena in the world that potentially causes individual- or group-level discontent, or harm; categorize and shape them in a socially constructivist manner into digestible problems registered by others; and publicize them using captivating frames and narratives.

Another core idea is that social movements significantly contribute to the broader informational set of economic, political, and social processes. For now, consider the political dimension. Social movement challenges are one way in which the purveyors of political power remain answerable to members of the general public, as matters of public interest emerge and take shape. It is difficult to imagine a functionally robust liberal-democratic polity in the absence of social movements, which play a part in revealing problems, the intensity with which those problems are being felt, as well as drawing attention to them (Lavoie 1993; Goodman 2019). The deployment of tactics from previous campaigns, and engagement with fresh tactical innovations, can potentially serve to empower individuals and promote human liberties (Welzel 2013).

In the preceding chapters, we have critically reflected upon the value of social movements in sustaining a liberal order. At first glance, social movements largely appear to pose a challenge to liberal modes of explanation. This perception is derived from characterizing features of movements as group-oriented phenomena intentionally aiming at some aspect of societal change, and deploying often disruptive tactics in an attempt to fulfil objectives. Furthermore, movement participants may conduct themselves violently, or explicitly promote illiberal causes, which can naturally raise great concerns among liberal adherents. Each of these elements of social movement activity and participation may be viewed as obstacles to the realization of liberal commitments.

There are numerous examples of social movement activity contributing toward regressive sliding toward illiberalism on several fronts. These may be legitimately critiqued using liberal theories and analysis. However, it is also possible to fashion a social movement history of liberalism in which certain movements have meaningfully contributed to human liberty, enatailing the shifting of governance, institutional, and organizational boundaries from coercion toward voluntarism. Movements have successfully engaged in struggles against political authorities, for example, with respect to trade, property rights, tax limitation and fiscal nondiscrimination, voting rights, feminism, and racial equality.

Over the past twenty years or so, groups have formed alliances to contest policy-induced degradation of economic opportunities, and resist police abuses and crackdowns on peaceful protest and contentious public assemblies. These alliances have been forged in offline and, increasingly, online spaces of engagement and interaction. A number of contemporary movements are noted to be partaking in efforts to help pursue a range of goals. These include the realization of market orderings for economic exchange, liberal-democratic decision-making within, and across, multiple levels of government, and an open society exemplified by freedom of association and cultural pluralism. In these cases, the argument may be sustained that success depends, at least in part, upon "a well-orchestrated, task-specific strategy, courageous action, and a great deal of discipline" (Popović and Djinovic 2018, 67), although it is also clear that success for pro-liberty movements in the years ahead will be dependent upon strategic innovation and tactical creativity on the part of organizers, activists, and supporters alike.

Recent polarizing trends regrettably reveal that conflicts over framework conditions of public governance, and other key aspects of living, are infusing our interactions. There seem no easy answers to fix such disagreements, especially when discursive and interactional environments have become conducive to the categorization of our fellow human beings as friends, adversaries, or enemies. A living liberalism of open impartiality—in which we engage one another meaningfully, and try to understand divergent positions on public issues—may deliver opportunities for mutual collaborations and exchanges with respect to shared ends. Within this, socio-political catallactic projects that redress individual rights, social justice, and identity politics concerns, and which are attributed to ill-treatment by governmental and other major actors, may yet prove to be effective drivers of popular mobilization and action by social movements in the years, and decades, to come.

It is our view that social movements have played an often unheralded, but nonetheless critical role, in promoting the development of institutions and practices reflecting liberal commitments. To the extent that social movements have contributed to the realization of the liberties we enjoy today, then they surely have acted in a manner consistent with Hayek's plea for a liberal utopia:

> We must make the building of a free society once more an intellectual adventure, a deed of courage. What we lack is a liberal Utopia, a program which seems neither a mere defense of things as they are nor a diluted kind of socialism, but truly liberal radicalism which does not spare the susceptibilities of the mighty (including the trade unions), which is not too severely practical and which does not confine itself to what appears today as politically possible. . . . The main lesson which the true liberal must learn from the success of the socialists is that it was their courage to be Utopian which gained them the support of the intellectuals and therefore an influence on public opinion which is daily making possible what only recently seemed utterly remote. (Hayek 1949, 432–433)

Daring to challenge their compatriots that liberalization along economic, political, and social dimensions is, indeed, feasible, social movements have contributed to transforming the seemingly impossible into the actual possible. Added to this is the temporal dimension of change. As mentioned by Chris

Matthew Sciabarra (2000, 7), in his context of discussion about the advancement of liberal perspectives, "tomorrow's respectable 'mainstream' often derives from yesterday's 'extremists.'" Participants of certain movements not only sought to carry and express their grievances over constructed economic, political, and social problems, but they networked together to consider, publicize, and, on occasion, implement proposals for reform and change in functionally liberalizing directions.

In certain passages of this book, we have referred to a potentially fruitful research agenda that expounds a non-state-centric interpretation of social movement activity. The significance of this approach to social movement studies not only rests in its stark contrast with the state-centric point of view, the latter couching movement activity as primarily political in character. When it is shown that movement participants are striving to figure out their own, non-politicized methods of making decisions, resolving disputes, and engaging with potential allies and adversaries, it is possible to use these examples to reinforce a broader point: it is possible to detect non-state practices of collaboration, governance, and innovation. Not all social movements aim for political objectives, and some movements deliberately avoid political entanglements. When such movements succeed, they undermine the notion that it is impossible to achieve societal change in the absence of political engagement or public-sector involvement. It is true that some movements make demands upon political actors, but it is also the case that others do not.

As noted in this book, the tendency for social movements to engage outside of the realm of the political has become a critical feature of contemporary scholarship. In keeping with this theme, there is every potential for movement participants to become key players in the modification of technologies, institutional forms, and organizational practices into the future—and without reference to governmental approval or direction. This speculative point is more likely to come to fruition if political actors refuse to enact liberalizing changes swiftly, or if upward economic and social opportunities, otherwise, appear to remain out of reach for most people. The potential of social movements to distance themselves from formal politics, combined with their capacity to induce societal changes that cannot necessarily be predicted beforehand, reinforces the need for further research building toward a non-state-centric approach to movement studies.

An additional contribution of social movements and their activities toward liberty is that they, conversely, aid in *transforming the possible into the impossible*. As we have attempted to illustrate in this book, certain social movement organizers, activists, and supporters have collectively played a commendable role in relegating a range of coercive, cruel, and domineering practices of illiberalism to the unenvied past. To be certain, there remains much work to do, and especially so in our contemporary age. In recent years we have borne witness to virulent illiberal challenges, in the shape of economic cronyism, political authoritarianism, and social intolerance, which all need to be urgently tackled. These tasks must be undertaken if the ambition and promise of freedom is to be grasped by present and future generations. Social movements are likely to be crucial partners in this project. After all, have played their part in raising the relative costs of illiberalism in the past, and will need to continue to help do so, both for today and tomorrow.

Bibliography

ACT UP. n.d. "Candidate GORE Zaps." Accessed February 23, 2021. https://actupny .org/actions/gorezaps.html.

Adams, Charles. 2001. *For Good and Evil: The Impact of Taxes on the Course of Civilization.* Second Edition. Lanham: Madison Books.

Ahrne, Göran, and Nils Brunsson. 2011. "Organization Outside Organizations: The Significance of Partial Organization." *Organization* 18, no. 1: 83–104.

Aidt, Toke S., and Raphaël Franck. 2015. "Democratization under the Threat of Revolution: Evidence from the Great Reform Act of 1832." *Econometrica* 83, no. 2: 505–547.

Albrecht, Brian C. 2017. "The Breakdown of Spontaneous Order: Smith and Hayek Diverge." *New York University Journal of Law & Liberty* 11: 346–370.

Albright, Alex, James Feigenbaum, and Nathan Nunn. 2020. "After the Burning: The Economic Effects of the 1921 Tulsa Race Massacre." https://scholar.harvard.edu/ files/nunn/files/tulsa.pdf.

Aligica, Paul Dragos. 2015. "Public Administration, Public Choice and the Ostroms: The Achievements, the Failure, the Promise." *Public Choice* 163, no. 1–2: 111–127.

Aligica, Paul Dragos. 2019. "Public Entrepreneurship, Public Choice and Self-governance." *Review of Austrian Economics.* https://doi.org/10.1007/s11138-019-00458-9.

Aligica, Paul Dragos, and Vlad Tarko. 2012. "Polycentricity: From Polanyi to Ostrom, and Beyond." *Governance: An International Journal of Policy, Administration, and Institutions* 25, no. 2: 237–262.

Aligica, Paul Dragos, Peter J. Boettke and Vlad Tarko. 2019. *Public Governance and the Classical-Liberal Perspective.* Oxford: Oxford University Press.

Al Ismaily, Salem Ben Nasser, Miguel Cervantes, and Fred McMahon. 2019. *Economic Freedom of the Arab World: 2019 Annual Report.* Vancouver, Canada: Fraser Institute.

Allport, Gordon W. 1954. *The Nature of Prejudice.* Cambridge, MA: Addison-Wesley.

Almeida, Paul. 2019. *Social Movements: The Structure of Collective Mobilization.* Oakland: University of California Press.

Almeida, Paul, and Nella Van Dyke. 2014. "Social Movement Partyism and the Tea Party's Rapid Mobilization." In *Understanding the Tea Party Movement*, edited by Nella Van Dyke, 55–71. New York: Routledge.

Almudi, Isabel, Francisco Fatas-Villafranca, Luis Izquierdo, and Jason Potts. 2017. "The Economics of Utopia: A Co-evolutionary Model of Ideas, Citizenship and Socio-political Change." *Journal of Evolutionary Economics* 27, no. 4: 629–662.

Aminzade, Ron, Jack A. Goldstone, and Elizabeth J. Perry. 2001. "Leadership Dynamics and Dynamics of Contention." In *Silence and Voice in the Study of Contentious Politics*, edited by Ronald R. Aminzade, Jack A. Goldstone, Doug McAdam, Elizabeth J. Perry, William H. Sewell, Sidney Tarrow, and Charles Tilly, 126–154. Cambridge, UK: Cambridge University Press.

Ammons, Joshua, and Christopher J. Coyne. 2018. "Gene Sharp: The 'Clausewitz of Nonviolent Warfare.'" *Independent Review* 23, no. 1: 149–156.

Ammons, Joshua, and Christopher J. 2020. "Nonviolent Action." In *Bottom-up Responses to Crisis*, edited by Stefanie Haeffele, and Virgil Henry Storr, 29–55. Cham, Switzerland: Palgrave Macmillan.

Anderson, Elizabeth. 2014. "Social Movements, Experiments in Living, and Moral Progress: Case Studies from Britain's Abolition of Slavery." University of Kansas, Lindley Lecture, February 11. https://kuscholarworks.ku.edu/handle/1808/14787.

Andreas, Joel. 2013. "Charisma." In *The Wiley-Blackwell Encyclopedia of Social and Political Movements*, edited by David A. Snow, Donatella della Porta, Bert Klandermans, and Doug McAdam, 1–3. Malden: John Wiley & Sons.

Andreas, Peter. 2013. *Smuggler Nation: How Illicit Trade Made America.* New York: Oxford University Press.

Archer, John E. 2000. *Social Unrest and Popular Protest in England 1780-1840.* Cambridge, UK: Cambridge University Press.

Arena, Richard. 2010. "Friedrich von Wieser on Institutions and Social Economics." In *Austrian Economics in Transition: From Carl Menger to Friedrich Hayek*, edited by Harald Hageman, Tamotsu Nishizawa, and Yukihiro Ikeda, 109–137. Cham, Switzerland: Palgrave Macmillan.

Arrow, Kenneth J. 1951. *Social Choice and Individual Values.* New York: John Wiley & Sons.

Atak, Kivanc, and Donatella della Porta. 2016. "Popular Uprisings in Turkey: Police Culpability and Constraints on Dialogue-oriented Policing in Gezi Park and Beyond." *European Journal of Criminology* 13, no. 5: 610–625.

Audretsch, David B., and Arthur G. Woolf. 1987. "Regulatory Reform in the 1980s: An Anti Rent-Seeking Movement?" *European Journal of Political Economy* 3, no. 3: 335–349.

Auyero, Javier, and Timothy Patrick Moran. 2007. "The Dynamics of Collective Violence: Dissecting Food Riots in Contemporary Argentina." *Social Forces* 85, no. 3: 1341–1367.

Badhwar, Neera. 2008. "Friendship and Commercial Societies." *Politics, Philosophy & Economics* 7 no. 3: 301–326.

Bahgat, Karim, Halvard Buhaug, and Henrik Urdal. 2018. *Urban Social Disorder: An Update*. Oslo, Norway: Peace Research Institute Oslo.

Baker, David. 2019. "Public Order Policing Approaches to Minimize Crowd Confrontation During Disputes and Protests in Australia." *Policing: A Journal of Policy and Practice*. https://doi.org/10.1093/police/paz071.

Balko, Radley. 2013. *Rise of the Warrior Cop: The Militarization of America's Police Forces*. New York: Public Affairs.

Barker, Colin, Laurence Cox, John Krinsky, and Alf Gunvald. 2013. *Marxism and Social Movements*. Leiden, Netherlands: Brill.

Barnes, Barry. 1990. "Macro-Economics and Infant Behaviour: A Sociological Treatment of the Free-Rider Problem." *Sociological Review* 38, no. 2: 272–292.

Barry, Norman. 1982. "The Tradition of Spontaneous Order." *Literature of Liberty: A Review of Contemporary Liberal Thought* 5, no. 2: 7–58.

Baumol, William E. 1990. "Entrepreneurship: Productive, Unproductive, and Destructive." *Journal of Political Economy* 98, no. 5: 893–921.

Bavetta, Sebastiano, Pietro Navarra, and Dario Maimone. 2014. *Freedom and the Pursuit of Happiness: An Economic and Political Perspective*. New York: Cambridge University Press.

Bearman, C. J. 2005. "An Examination of Suffragette Violence." *English Historical Review* 120, no. 486: 365–397.

Bearman, C. J. 2007. "An Army Without Discipline? Suffragette Militancy and the Budget Crisis of 1909." *Historical Journal* 50, no. 4: 861–889.

Bearman, C. J. 2009. "The Legend of Black Friday." *Historical Research* 83, no. 222: 693–718.

Beaulier, Scott, and Peter Boettke. 2000. "Of Norms, Rules and Markets: A Comment on Samuels." *Journal des Economistes et des Etudes Humaines* 10, no. 4 (Art. 6): 1–6.

Becchio, Giandomenica. 2014. "Carl Menger on States as Orders, not Organizations: Entangled Economy into a Neo-Mengerian Approach." *Advances in Austrian Economics* 18: 55–66.

Becker, Gary S. 1964. *Human Capital: A Theoretical and Empirical Analysis, with Special Reference to Education*. National Bureau of Economic Research. Washington, DC: Columbia University Press.

Becker, Gary S. 1971. *The Economics of Discrimination*. Second Edition. Chicago: University of Chicago Press.

Becker, Markus C., and Thorbjørn Knudsen. 2002. "Schumpeter 1911: Farsighted Visions of Economic Development." *American Journal of Economics and Sociology* 61, no. 2: 387–403.

Becker, Marckus C., and Thorbjørn Knudsen. 2003. "The Entrepreneur at a Crucial Juncture in Schumpeter's Work: Schumpeter's 1928 Handbook Entry Entrepreneur." *Advances in Austrian Economics* 6: 199–233.

Benford, Robert D., and David A. Snow. 2000. "Framing Processes and Social Movements: An Overview and Assessment." *Annual Review of Sociology* 26: 611–639.

Bennett, W. Lance, and Alexandra Segerberg. 2013. *The Logic of Connective Action: Digital Media and the Personalization of Contentious Politics*. Cambridge, UK: Cambridge University Press.

Bennett, W. Lance, and Alexandra Segerberg. 2015. "Communication in Movements." In *The Oxford Handbook of Social Movements*, edited by Donatella della Porta, and Mario Diani, 367–382. Oxford: Oxford University Press.

Berberoglu, Berch. 2019. *The Palgrave Handbook of Social Movements, Revolution, and Social Transformation*. Cham, Switzerland: Palgrave Macmillan.

Bereni, Laure, and Anne Revillard. 2012. "A Paradigmatic Social Movement? Women's Movements and the Definition of Contentious Politics." *Sociétés Contemporaines* 85: 17–41.

Berg, Chris. 2015. *Liberty, Equality, and Democracy*. Ballarat, Australia: Connor Court Publishing.

Berg, Chris. 2016. *The Libertarian Alternative*. Melbourne, Australia: Melbourne University Press.

Berggren, Niclas. 2003. "The Benefits of Economic Freedom: A Survey." *Independent Review* 8, no. 2: 193–211.

Berggren, Niclas. 2014. "The Soft Side of Economic Freedom." In *Annual Proceedings of the Wealth and Well-Being of Nations*, edited by Joshua C. Hall, 43–66. Beloit: Beloit College Press.

Berggren, Niclas, and Jerg Gutmann. 2020. "Securing Personal Freedom through Institutions: The Role of Electoral Democracy and Judicial Independence." *European Journal of Law and Economics* 49, no. 2: 165–186.

Bergh, Andreas. 2020. "Hayekian Welfare States: Explaining the Coexistence of Economic Freedom and Big Government." *Journal of Institutional Economics* 16, no. 1: 1–12.

Berlin, Ira. 1998. *Many Thousands Gone: The First Two Centuries of Slavery in North America*. Cambridge: Belknap Press of Harvard University Press.

Berlin, Isaiah. 1969. "Two Concepts of Liberty." In *Four Essays on Liberty*, edited by Isaiah Berlin, 118–172. Oxford: Oxford University Press.

Berlin, Isaiah. 2002. *Liberty*. edited by Henry Hardy. Oxford: Oxford University Press.

Beyers, Jan, Rainer Eising, and William Maloney. 2008. "Researching Interest Group Politics in Europe and Elsewhere: Much We Study, Little We Know?" *West European Politics* 31, no. 6: 1103–1128.

Blasi, Anthony J. 1988. *Early Christianity as a Social Movement*. New York: Peter Lang.

Blease, Walter Lyon. 1913. *A Short History of English Liberalism*. London: T. F. Unwin.

Blumer, Herbert [1951] 1995. "Social Movements." In *Social Movements: Critiques, Concepts, Case-Studies*, edited by Stanford M. Lyman, 60–83. Washington Square: New York University Press.

Boettke, Peter J. 2012. *Living Economics: Yesterday, Today, and Tomorrow*. Oakland: Independent Institute.

Boettke, Peter J. 2017. "The Reconstruction of the Liberal Project." *Foundation for Economic Education*, November 7, 2017. https://fee.org/articles/the-reconstruction -of-the-liberal-project.

Boettke, Peter J. 2018. *F. A. Hayek: Economics, Political Economy and Social Philosophy*. Cham, Switzerland: Palgrave Macmillan.

Boettke, Peter. 2019. "The Courage to Be Utopian." American Institute for Economic Research. *Daily Economy*, August 22. https://www.aier.org/article/the-courage-to -be-utopian.

Boettke, Peter J., and Rosolino A. Candela. 2021. "The Positive Political Economy of Analytical Anarchism." In *The Routledge Handbook of Anarchy and Anarchist Thought*, edited by Gary Chartier, and Chad Van Schoelandt, 222–234. New York: Routledge.

Boettke, Peter J., and Christopher J. Coyne. 2007. "Political Economy of Forgiveness." *Society* 44, no. 2: 53–59.

Boettke, Peter J., and Christopher J. Coyne. 2008. "The Political Economy of the Philanthropic Enterprise." In *Non-Market Entrepreneurship: Interdisciplinary Approaches*, edited by Gordon E. Shockley, Peter M. Frank, and Roger R. Stough, 71–88. Cheltenham: Edward Elgar.

Boettke, Peter J., and Christopher J. Coyne. 2009. "Context Matters: Institutions and Entrepreneurship." *Foundations and Trends in Entrepreneurship* 5, no. 3: 135–209.

Boettke, Peter J., and Peter T. Leeson. 2002. "Hayek, Arrow, and the Problems of Democratic Decision-Making." *Journal of Public Finance and Public Choice* 20, no. 1: 9–21.

Boettke, Peter J., and Nicholas A. Snow. 2014. "Political Economy and the Science of Association: A Suggested Reconstruction of Public Choice through the Alliance of the Vienna, Virginia, and Bloomington Schools of Political Economy." *Review of Austrian Economics* 27, no. 1: 97–110.

Boettke, Peter J., and Virgil Henry Storr. 2002. "Post-Classical Political Economy: Polity, Society and Economy in Weber, Mises and Hayek." *American Journal of Economics and Sociology* 61, no. 1: 161–191.

Boettke, Peter J., and Henry A. Thompson. 2019. "Identity and Off-diagonals: How Permanent Winning Coalitions Destroy Democratic Governance." *Public Choice*. https://doi.org/10.1007/s11127-019-00683-7.

Boettke, Peter J., Jayme S. Lemke, and Liya Palagashvili. 2016. "Re-evaluating Community Policing in a Polycentric System." *Journal of Institutional Economics* 12, no. 2: 305–325.

Boettke, Peter J., Liya Palagashvili, and Ennio E. Piano. 2017. "Federalism and the Police: An Applied Theory of 'Fiscal Attention.'" *Arizona State Law Journal* 49, no. 3: 907–933.

Bolick, Clint. 2008. "Racism." In *The Encyclopedia of Libertarianism*, edited by Ronald Hamowy, 411–412. Los Angeles: SAGE Publications.

Bosi, Lorenzo, and Stefan Malthaner. 2015. "Political Violence." In *The Oxford Handbook of Social Movements*, edited by Donatella della Porta, and Mario Diani, 439–451. Oxford: Oxford University Press.

Bosi, Lorenzo, Chares Demetriou, and Stefan Malthaner. 2014. *Dynamics of Political Violence: A Process-Oriented Perspective on Radicalization and the Escalation of Political Conflict.* Surrey: Ashgate.

Boudon, Raymond. 1986. *Theories of Social Change: A Critical Appraisal.* Berkeley, CA: University of California Press.

Bouie, Jamelle. 2020. "The Police Are Rioting. We Need to Talk About It." *New York Times*, June 5. https://www.nytimes.com/2020/06/05/opinion/sunday/police-riots.html.

Bourdieu, Pierre. 1977. *Outline of a Theory of Practice.* Cambridge, UK: Cambridge University Press.

Bourdieu, Pierre. 1986. "The Forms of Capital." In *Handbook of Theory and Research for the Sociology of Education*, edited by John G. Richardson, 241–258. New York: Greenwood Press.

Boykoff, Jules. 2006. *The Suppression of Dissent: How the State and Mass Media Squelch USAmerican Social Movements.* New York: Routledge.

Boyte, Harry, Stephen Elkin, Peter Levine, Jane Mansbridge, Elinor Ostrom, Elinor, Karol Soltan, and Rogers Smith. 2014. "The New Civic Politics: Civic Theory and Practice for the Future." *The Good Society* 23, no. 4: 206–211.

Brannen, Samuel J., Christian S. Haig, and Katherine Schmidt. 2020. *The Age of Mass Protests: Understanding an Escalating Global Trend.* Washington, DC: Center for Strategic & International Studies.

Brennan, Geoffrey. 2015. "Olson and Imperceptible Differences: The Tuck Critique." *Public Choice* 164, no. 3–4: 235–250.

Brennan, Geoffrey. 2018. "Liberty: A PPE Approach." In *The Routledge Handbook of Libertarianism*, edited by Jason Brennan, Bas van der Vossen, and David Schmidtz, 184–198. New York: Routledge.

Brennan, Geoffrey, and Buchanan, James M. [1980] 2000. "The Power to Tax: Analytic Foundations of a Fiscal Constitution." In *The Collected Works of James M. Buchanan: Volume 9*, edited by Geoffrey Brennan, Hartmut Kliemt, and Robert D. Tollison. Indianapolis: Liberty Fund.

Brennan, Geoffrey, and Loren Lomasky. 1993. *Democracy and Decision: The Pure Theory of Electoral Preference.* Cambridge, UK: Cambridge University Press.

Brennan, Jason. 2019. *When All Else Fails: The Ethics of Resistance to State Injustice.* Princeton: Princeton University Press.

Brieger, Steven A., Siri A. Terjesen, Diana M. Hechavarría, and Christian Welzel. 2019. "Prosociality in Business: A Human Empowerment Framework." *Journal of Business Ethics* 159, no. 2: 361–380.

Briscoe, Forrest, and Abhinav Gupta. 2016. "Social Activism In and Around Organizations." *Academy of Management Annals* 10, no. 1: 1–57.

Buchanan, James M. 1954a. "Individual Choice in Voting and the Market." *Journal of Political Economy* 62, no. 4: 334–343.

Buchanan, James M. 1954b. "Social Choice, Democracy, and Free Markets." *Journal of Political Economy* 62, no. 2: 114–123.

Buchanan, James M. 1981. "Equal Treatment and Reverse Discrimination." In *Social Justice*, edited by Randolph L. Braham, 79–83. Dordrecht, Netherlands: Springer.

Buchanan, James M. [1975] 2000. *The Limits of Liberty: Between Anarchy and Leviathan.* In *The Collected Works of James M. Buchanan,* Volume 7, edited by Geoffrey Brennan, Hartmut Kliemt, and Robert D. Tollison. Indianapolis: Liberty Fund.

Buchanan, James M. 2003. "Public Choice: Politics Without Romance." *Policy* 19, no. 3: 13–18.

Buchanan, James M. 2005a. "Afraid to Be Free: Dependency as Desideratum." *Public Choice* 124, no. 1–2: 19–31.

Buchanan, James A. 2005b. *Why I, Too, Am Not A Conservative.* Cheltenham: Edward Elgar.

Buchanan, James M., and Roger D. Congleton. [1998] 2003. "Politics by Principle, Not Interest: Toward Nondiscriminatory Democracy." In *The Collected Works of James M. Buchanan: Volume 11,* edited by Geoffrey Brennan, Hartmut Kliemt and Robert D. Tollison. Indianapolis: Liberty Fund.

Buchanan, James M., and Roger L. Faith. 1987. "Secession and the Limits of Taxation: Toward a Theory of Internal Exit." *American Economic Review* 77 (5): 1023–1031.

Buchanan, James M., and Gordon Tullock. [1962] 1999. "The Calculus of Consent: Logical Foundations of Constitutional Democracy." In *The Collected Works of James M. Buchanan: Volume 3,* edited by Geoffrey Brennan, Hartmut Kliemt and Robert D. Tollison, Indianapolis: Liberty Fund.

Buchanan, James M., and Richard E. Wagner. [1977] 2000. "Democracy in Deficit: The Political Legacy of Lord Keynes." In *The Collected Works of James M. Buchanan, Volume 8,* edited by Geoffrey Brennan, Hartmut Kliemt and Robert D. Tollison. Indianapolis: Liberty Fund.

Buechler, Steven M. 2011. *Understanding Social Movements: Theories from the Classical Era to the Present.* New York: Routledge.

Burczak, Theodore A. 1994. "The Postmodern Moments of F. A. Hayek's Economics." *Economics and Philosophy* 10, no. 1: 31–58.

Burczak, Theodore A. 2006. *Socialism After Hayek.* Ann Arbor: University of Michigan Press.

Burke, Edmund [1790] 2006. *Reflections on the Revolution in France.* Mineola: Dover Publications.

Burke, Peter J., and Jan E. Stets. 2009. *Identity Theory.* New York: Oxford University Press.

Burg, David F. 2004. *A World History of Tax Rebellions: An Encyclopedia of Tax Rebels, Revolts, and Riots from Antiquity to the Present.* New York: Routledge.

Burt, Ronald S. 1992. *Structural Holes: The Social Structure of Competition.* Cambridge: Harvard University Press.

Byrne, Paul. 1997. *Social Movements in Britain.* London: Routledge.

Cain, Frank. 1990. "ASIO and the Australian Labour Movement: An Historical Perspective." *Labour History* 58: 1–16.

Calhoun-Brown, Allison. 2000. "Upon This Rock: The Black Church, Nonviolence, and the Civil Rights Movement." *PS: Political Science and Politics* 33, no. 2: 168–174.

Campagnolo, Gilles, and Christel Vivel. 2012. "Before Schumpeter: Forerunners of the Theory of the Entrepreneur in 1900s German Political Economy—Werner Sombart, Friedrich von Wieser." *European Journal of the History of Economic Thought* 19, no. 6: 908–943.

Campbell, Shannon, Phil Chidester, Jamel Bell, and Jason Royer. 2004. "Remote Control: How Mass Media Delegitimize Rioting as Social Protest." *Race, Gender & Class* 11, no. 1: 158–176.

Candela, Rosolino. 2019. "Institutional Analysis, Polycentricity, and Federalism in the Bloomington School: Social Order Through Evolution or Design?" George Mason University, Department of Economics Working Paper No. 19–28. https://papers.ssrn.com/sol3/papers.cfm?abstract_id=3408548.

Caplan, Bryan. 1994. "The Literature of Nonviolent Resistance and Civilian-Based Defense." *Humane Studies Review* 9, no. 1. https://econfaculty.gmu.edu/bcaplan/nonviolent.pdf.

Caplan, Bryan. 2006. "Terrorism: The Relevance of the Rational Choice Model." *Public Choice* 128 no. 1/2: 91–107.

Carden, Art. 2009. "Inputs and Institutions as Conservative Elements." *Review of Austrian Economics* 22, no. 1: 1–19.

Carter, April. 2010. *Direct Action and Liberal Democracy*. London: Routledge.

Carty, Victoria. 2015. *Social Movements and New Technology*. New York: Routledge.

Chamlee-Wright, Emily. 1997. *The Cultural Foundations of Economic Development: Urban Female Entrepreneurship in Ghana*. London: Routledge.

Chamlee-Wright, Emily. 2008. "The Structure of Social Capital: An Austrian Perspective on its Nature and Development." *Review of Political Economy* 20, no. 1: 41–58.

Chamlee-Wright, Emily. 2020. "The Conversations of a Self-Governing People." https://knightfoundation.org/wp-content/uploads/2020/10/KF-Kettering-The-Conversations-of-a-Self-Governing.pdf.

Chamlee-Wright, Emily, and Justus A. Myers. 2008. "Discovery and Social Learning in Non-Priced Environments: An Austrian View of Social Network Theory." *Review of Austrian Economics* 21, no. 2–3: 151–166.

Chamlee-Wright, Emily, and Virgil Henry Storr. 2015. "Social Economy as An Extension of the Austrian Research Program." In *The Oxford Handbook of Austrian Economics*, edited by Peter J. Boettke, and Christopher J. Coyne, 247–271. New York: Oxford University Press.

Chartier, Gary, and Chad Van Schoelandt. 2021. *The Routledge Handbook of Anarchy and Anarchist Thought*. New York: Routledge.

Chaumont-Chancelier, Frédérique. 2003. "Civil Society and the Contemporary Social Order." In *Rational Foundations of Democratic Politics*, edited by Albert Breton, Gianluigi Galeotti, Pierre Salmon, and Ronald Wintrobe, 68–90. Cambridge, UK: Cambridge University Press.

Chenoweth, Erica, and Maria J. Stephan. 2011. *Why Civil Resistance Works: The Strategic Logic of Nonviolent Protest*. New York: Columbia University Press.

Chesters, Graeme, and Ian Welsh. 2006. *Complexity and Social Movements: Multitudes at the edge of chaos*. London: Routledge.

Choi, Seung Ginny, and Virgil Henry Storr. 2019. "A culture of rent seeking." *Public Choice* 181, no. 1: 101–126.

Chohan, Usman W. 2021. "Counter-Hegemonic Finance: The Gamestop Short Squeeze." https://papers.ssrn.com/sol3/papers.cfm?abstract_id=3775127.

Chong, Dennis. 1991. *Collective Action and the Civil Rights Movement.* Chicago: University of Chicago Press.

Christmas, Billy. 2016. "Libertarianism and Privilege." *Molinari Review* 1, no. 1: 25–46.

Cini, Lorenzo, Daniela Chironi, Eliska Drapalova, and Federico Tomasello. 2017. "Towards a Critical Theory of Social Movements: An Introduction." *Anthropological Theory* 17, no. 4: 429–452.

Císař, Ondřej. 2013. "Interest Groups and Social Movements." In *The Wiley-Blackwell Encyclopedia of Social and Political Movements*, edited by David A. Snow, Donatella della Porta, Bert Klandermans, and Doug McAdam, 1–4. Malden: John Wiley & Sons.

Císař, Ondřej. 2015. "Social Movements in Political Science." In *The Oxford Handbook of Social Movements*, edited by Donatella della Porta, and Mario Diani, 50–67. Oxford: Oxford University Press.

Clay, Alexa. 2017. "Utopia Inc." *Aeon.co*, February 28, 2017. https://aeon.co/essays/like-start-ups-most-intentional-communities-fail-why.

Clement, Matt. 2016. *A People's History of Riots, Protest and the Law.* London: Palgrave Macmillan.

Coase, Ronald H. 1937. "The Nature of the Firm." *Economica* 4, no. 16: 386–405.

Cobb, Charles E., Jr. 2014. *This Nonviolent Stuff'll Get You Killed.* New York: Basic Books.

Coglianese, Cary. 2001. "Social Movements, Law, and Society: The Institutionalization of the Environmental Movement." *University of Pennsylvania Law Review* 150, no. 1: 85–118.

Cohen, Jean L. 1985. "Strategy or Identity: New Theoretical Paradigms and Contemporary Social Movements." *Social Research* 52, no. 4: 663–716.

Cohen, Jean L., and Andrew Arato. 1992. *Civil Society and Political Theory.* Cambridge, MA: MIT Press.

Coleman, James S. 1988. "Social Capital in the Creation of Human Capital." *American Journal of Sociology* 94 (Supplement): S95–S120.

Collins, Kristin A. 2012. "Representing Injustice: Justice as an Icon of Woman Suffrage." *Yale Journal of Law and the Humanities* 24: 191–220.

Collins, Randall. 2001. "Social Movements and the Focus of Emotional Attention." In *Passionate Politics: Emotions and Social Movements*, edited by Jeff Goodwin, James M. Jasper and Francesca Polletta, 27–44. Chicago: University of Chicago Press.

Collins, Randall. 2004. *Interaction Ritual Chains.* Princeton: Princeton University Press.

Collins, William J., and Robert A. Margo. 2007. "The Economic Aftermath of the 1960s Riots in American Cities: Evidence from Property Values." *Journal of Economic History* 67, no. 4: 849–883.

Cone, James H. 2001. "Martin and Malcolm on Nonviolence and Violence." *Phylon* 49, no. 3–4: 173–183.

Congleton, Roger D. 2011. *Perfecting Parliament: Constitutional Reform, Liberalism, and the Rise of Western Democracy.* Cambridge, UK: Cambridge University Press.

Conway, Stephen. 2013. *A Short History of the American Revolutionary War.* London: I. B. Taurus.

Copland, Simon. 2019. "Anti-politics and Global Climate Inaction: The Case of the Australian Carbon Tax." *Critical Sociology* 46, no. 4–5: 623–641.

Cornuelle, Richard C. 1992. "The Power and Poverty of Libertarian Thought." *Critical Review* 6, no. 1: 1–10.

Cowen, Nick. 2020. "Hayek's Appreciative Theory and Social Justice." *Cosmos+Taxis* 7, no. 5–6: 10–19.

Cowen, Tyler. 2019. "Protestors Worldwide Are United by Something Other Than Politics." *Bloomberg Opinion*, 21 October. https://www.bloomberg.com/opinion/articles/2019-10-21/protesters-worldwide-are-united-by-something-other-than-politics.

Cowen, Tyler, and Daniel Sutter. 1997. "Politics and the Pursuit of Fame." *Public Choice* 93, no. 1–2: 19–35.

Cox, Laurence. 2018. *Why Social Movements Matter: An Introduction.* Lanham: Rowman & Littlefield.

Cox, Wendell, and Hugh Pavletich. 2020. *16th Annual Demographia International Housing Affordability Survey: 2020.* http://www.demographia.com/dhi.pdf.

Coyne, Christopher J. 2018. "The Protective State: A Grave Threat to Liberty." In *Buchanan's Tensions: Reexamining the Political Economy and Philosophy of James M. Buchanan*, edited by Peter J. Boettke, and Solomon Stein, 147–169. Arlington, VA: Mercatus Center of George Mason University.

Coyne, Christopher J., and Nathan P. Goodman. 2020a. "Polycentric Defense." *Independent Review* 25, no. 2: 279–292.

Coyne, Christopher J., and Nathan P. Goodman. 2020b. "The Political Economy of the Virtual Wall." *Peace Review: A Journal of Social Justice* 32, no. 2: 172–180.

Coyne, Christopher J., and Abigail R. Hall. 2018. *Tyranny Comes Home: The Domestic Fate of U.S. Militarism.* Palo Alto: Stanford University Press.

Coyne, Christopher J., and Abigail R. Hall-Blanco. 2016. "Foreign Intervention, Police Militarization, and Minorities." *Peace Review: A Journal of Social Justice* 28, no. 2: 165–170.

Coyne, Christopher J., Nathan Goodman, and Abigail R. Hall. 2019. "Sounding the Alarm: The Political Economy of Whistleblowing in the US Security State." *Peace Economics, Peace Science and Public Policy* 25, no. 1: 1–11.

Craiutu, Aurelian. 2019. "In Praise of Eclectism." In *Ostrom's Tensions: Reexamining the Political Economy and Public Policy of Elinor C. Ostrom*, edited by Roberta Q. Herzberg, Peter J. Boettke, and Paul Dragos Aligica, 211–246. Arlington, VA: Mercatus Center of George Mason University.

Crawford, Elizabeth. 1999. *The Women's Suffrage Movement: A Reference Guide 1866-1928.* London: Routledge.

Crider, Paul. 2015. "The Capabilities Approach and Libertarianism." Cato Institute. *libertarianism.org*, June 19. https://www.libertarianism.org/columns/capabilities-approach-libertarianism.

Crimp, Douglas. 2011. "Before Occupy: How AIDS Activists Seized Control of the FDA in 1988." *The Atlantic*, December 7. https://www.theatlantic.com/health/archive/2011/12/before-occupy-how-aids-activists-seized-control-of-the-fda-in-1988/249302.

Crossley, Nick. 2002. *Making Sense of Social Movements*. Buckingham: Open University Press.

Crossley, Nick, and John Krinsky. 2015. *Social Networks and Social Movements: Contentious Connections*. London: Routledge.

Cudd, Ann E. 2002. "Analyzing Backlash to Progressive Social Movements." In *Theorizing Backlash: Philosophical Reflections on the Resistance to Feminism*, edited by Anita M. Superson, and Ann E. Cudd, 3–16. Lanham: Rowman & Littlefield.

Cummings, Scott L. 2017. "Law and Social Movements: An Interdisciplinary Analysis." In *Handbook of Social Movements Across Disciplines*, Second Edition, edited by Conny Roggeband, and Bert Klandermans, 233–270. Cham, Switzerland: Springer.

Cunningham, David. 2003. "The Patterning of Repression: FBI Counterintelligence and the New Left." *Social Forces* 82, no. 1: 209–240.

Cunningham, David. 2012. *Klansville, U.S.A.: The Rise and Fall of the Civil Rights-Era Ku Klux Klan*. Oxford: Oxford University Press.

Dalton, Russell, Alix Van Sickle, and Steven Weldon. 2010. "The Individual-Institutional Nexus of Protest Behaviour." *British Journal of Political Science* 40, no. 1: 51–73.

D'Amico, Daniel J. 2015. "Spontaneous Order." In *The Oxford Handbook of Austrian Economics*, edited by Peter J. Boettke, and Christopher J. Coyne, 115–142. New York: Oxford University Press.

D'Amico, Daniel J., and Claudia R. Williamson. 2019. "An Empirical Examination of Institutions and Cross-country Incarceration Rates." *Public Choice* 180, no. 3–4: 217–242.

Davies, Rodrigo. 2015. "Three Provocations for Civic Crowdfunding." *Information, Communication & Society* 18, no. 3: 342–355.

Davies, Stephen. 2015. "Richard Cobden: Ideas and Strategies in Organizing the Free-Trade Movement in Britain." Liberty Fund. *Online Library of Liberty*, January. https://oll.libertyfund.org/pages/lm-cobden.

Davis, Gerald F., and Tracy A. Thompson. 1994. "A Social Movement Perspective on Corporate Control." *Administrative Science Quarterly* 39, no. 1: 141–173.

Davis, Lennard J. 2006. *The Disabilities Studies Reader*. Second Edition. New York: Routledge.

Davis, John B. 2015. "The Conception of the Socially Embedded Individual." In *The Elgar Companion to Social Economics*, Second Edition, edited by John B. Davis, and Wilfred Dolfsma, 116–130. Cheltenham: Edward Elgar.

de Bakker, Frank G. A., Frank den Hond, Brayden King, and Klaus Weber. 2013. "Social Movements, Civil Society and Corporations: Taking Stock and Looking Ahead." *Organization Studies* 34, no. 5–6: 573–593.

Dekker, Erwin, and Pavel Kuchař. 2017. "Emergent Orders of Worth: Must We Agree on More Than a Price?" *Cosmos+Taxis* 4, no. 1: 23–34.

DeJong, Gerben. 1979. "Independent Living: From Social Movement to Analytic Paradigm." *Archives of Physical Medicine and Rehabilitation* 60, no. 10: 435–446.

Dekker, Erwin, and Stefan Kolev. 2019. "A View from Europe: Austrian Economics, Civil Society, and PPE." *Advances in Austrian Economics* 24: 69–79.

della Porta, Donatella, and Mario Diani. 2020. *Social Movements: An Introduction.* Third Edition. Hoboken: Wiley-Blackwell.

della Porta, Donatella, and Herbert Reiter. 1998. *Policing Protest: The Control of Mass Demonstrations in Western Democracies.* Minneapolis: University of Minnesota Press.

Delmas, Candice. 2018. *A Duty to Resist: When Disobedience Should Be Uncivil.* Oxford: Oxford University Press.

den Hond, Frank, G. A. de Bakker, and Nikolai Smith. 2015. "Social Movements and Organizational Analysis." In *The Oxford Handbook of Social Movements*, edited by Donatella della Porta and Mario Diani, 291–305. Oxford: Oxford University Press.

Diani, Mario. 1992. "The Concept of Social Movement." *The Sociological Review* 40, no. 1: 1–25.

Diani, Mario, and Doug McAdam. 2003. *Social Movements and Networks: Relational Approaches to Collective Action.* New York: Oxford University Press.

DiCenzo, Maria, Lucy Delap, and Leila Ryan. 2011. *Feminist Media History: Suffrage, Periodicals and the Public Sphere.* London: Palgrave Macmillan.

Dillard, Maria K. 2013. "Movement/counter-movement Dynamics." In *The Wiley-Blackwell Encyclopedia of Social and Political Movements*, edited by David A. Snow, Donatella della Porta, Bert Klandermans, and Doug McAdam, 1–4. Malden: John Wiley & Sons.

diZerega, Gus. 1989. "Democracy as a Spontaneous Order." *Critical Review* 3, no. 2: 206–240.

Dold, Malte F. 2019. "A Smithian Critique of James M. Buchanan's Constitutional Contractarianism." In *Interdisciplinary Studies of the Political Order: New Applications of Public Choice Theory*, edited by Donald J. Boudreaux, Christopher J. Coyne, and Bobbi Herzberg, 17–39. Lanham: Rowman & Littlefield.

Donovan, Joan. 2021. "The GameStop Chaos Is Coming for Politics, Too." *Politico Magazine*, 4 February. https://www.politico.com/news/magazine/2021/02/04/how-occupy-wall-street-explains-the-gamestop-fiasco-465878.

Dorf, Michael C., and Sidney Tarrow. 2014. "Strange Bedfellows: How an Anticipatory Countermovement Brought Same-Sex Marriage into the Public Arena." *Law & Social Inquiry* 39, no. 2: 449–473.

Dougherty, Conor. 2020. *Golden Gates: Fighting for Housing in America.* New York: Penguin Press.

Douma, Michael J., and Phillip W. Magness. 2017. *What Is Classical Liberal History?* Lanham: Lexington Books.

Downing, John D. H. 2001. *Radical Media: Rebellious Communication and Social Movements*. Thousand Oaks: Sage Publications.

Downs, Anthony. 1957. *An Economic Theory of Democracy*. New York: Harper & Row Publishers.

Durac, Vincent. 2015. "Social Movements, Protest Movements and Cross-ideological Coalitions—The Arab Uprisings Re-appraised." *Democratization* 22, no. 2: 239–258.

Ealy, Lenore. 2017. "Toward a New Paradigm for the Study of Civil Society." Presentation to Public Choice Society Conference, New Orleans, March. Unpublished working draft.

Ealy, Lenore. 2018. "Lost in *Methodenstreit*: Reflections on Theory, History, and the Quest for a Science of Association." In *What is Classical Liberal History*, edited by Michael J. Douma and Phillip W. Magness, 59–94. Lanham: Lexington Books.

Earl, Jennifer, and Katrina Kimport. 2011. *Digitally Enabled Social Change: Activism in the Internet Age*. Cambridge: MIT Press.

Earl, Jennifer, Sarah A. Soule, and John D. McCarthy. 2003. "Protest under Fire? Explaining the Policing of Protest." *American Sociological Review* 68, no. 4: 581–606.

Economist. 2020. "The George Floyd Effect." December 12, 2020. https://www.eco nomist.com/united-states/2020/12/10/six-months-after-mass-protests-began-what -is-the-future-of-blm.

Edwards, Bob, John D. McCarthy, and Dane R. Mataic. 2019. "The Resource Context of Social Movements." In *The Wiley Blackwell Companion to Social Movements*, Second Edition, edited by David A. Snow, Sarah A. Soule, Hanspeter Kriesi, and Holly J. McCammon, 79–97. Hoboken: Wiley Blackwell.

Edwards, Gemma. 2013. *Social Movements and Protest*. New York: Cambridge University Press.

Edwards, Pearce, and Daniel Arnon. 2019. "Violence on Many Sides: Framing Effects on Protest and Support for Repression." *British Journal of Political Science*. https:/ /doi.org/10.1017/S0007123419000413.

Eigo, Jim, Mark Harrington, Margaret McCarthy, Stephen Spinella, and Rick Sugden. 1988. "FDA Action Handbook." https://actupny.org/documents/FDAhandbook1. html.

Ellickson, Robert C. 2001. "The Market for Social Norms." *American Law and Economics Review* 3, no. 1: 1–49.

Emmett, Ross B. 2020. "James M. Buchanan and Frank H. Knight on Democracy as 'Government by Discussion.'" *Public Choice* 183, no. 3–4: 303–314.

Engels, Bettina. 2015. "Social Movement Struggles against the High Cost of Living in Burkina Faso." *Canadian Journal of Development Studies* 36, no. 1: 107–121.

Fawcett, Edmund. 2014. *Liberalism: The Life of an Idea*. Princeton: Princeton University Press.

Fearon, James D. 1999. "What is Identity (As We Now Use the Word)?" Stanford University, Department of Economics. https://web.stanford.edu/group/fearon-research/cgi-bin/wordpress/wp-content/uploads/2013/10/What-is-Identity-as-we-now-use-the-word-.pdf.

Fehr, Ernst, and Klaus M. Schmidt. 1999. "A Theory of Fairness, Competition, and Cooperation." *Quarterly Journal of Economics* 114, no. 3: 817–868.

Feinberg, Matthew, Rob Willer, and Chloe Kovacheff. 2020. "The Activist's Dilemma: Extreme Protest Actions Reduce Popular Support for Social Movements." *Journal of Personality and Social Psychology: Interpersonal Relations and Group Processes* 119, no. 5: 1086–1111.

Fetner, Tina. 2012. "The Tea Party: Manufactured Dissent or Complex Social Movement?" *Contemporary Sociology* 41, no. 6: 762–766.

Fike, Rosemarie. 2018. *Impact of Economic Freedom and Women's Well-Being.* Vancouver: Fraser Institute.

Fine, Gary Alan. 1995. "Public Narration and Group Culture: Discerning Discourse in Social Movements." In *Social Movements and Culture*, edited by Hank Johnston and Bert Klandermans, 127–143. Minneapolis: University of Minnesota Press.

Fine, Gary Alan. 2010. "The Sociology of the Local: Action and its Publics." *Sociological Theory* 28, no. 4: 355–376.

Finkelstein, Avram. 2017. "SILENCE = DEATH: How an Iconic Protest Poster Came Into Being." *Lit Hub*, 1 December. https://lithub.com/silence-death-how-an-iconic -protest-poster-came-into-being.

Fireman, Bruce, and William Gamson. 1979. "Utilitarian Logic in the Resource Mobilization Perspective." In *The Dynamics of Social Movements: Resource Mobilization, Social Control, and Tactics*, edited by Mayer N. Zald, and John D. McCarthy, 8–44. Cambridge: Winthrop.

Flamm, Michael W. 2007. *Law and Order: Street Crime, Civil Unrest, and the Crisis of Liberalism in the 1960s.* New York: Columbia University Press.

Fleischer, Doris Zames, and Frieda Zames. 2001. *The Disability Rights Movement: From Charity to Confrontation.* Philadelphia: Temple University Press.

Fligstein, Neil, and Doug McAdam. 2019. "States, Social Movements and Markets." *Socio-Economic Review* 17, no. 1: 1–16.

Foweraker, Joe. 1995. *Theorizing Social Movements.* Boulder: Pluto Press.

Francis, Megan Ming. 2019. "The Price of Civil Rights: Black Lives, White Funding, and Movement Capture." *Law & Society Review* 53, no. 1: 275–309.

Francisco, Ronald A. 2010. *Collective Action Theory and Empirical Evidence.* Dordrecht, Netherlands: Springer.

Frank, Peter M., and Gordon E. Shockley. 2016. "A Critical Assessment of Social Entrepreneurship: Ostromian Polycentricity and Hayekian Knowledge." *Nonprofit and Voluntary Sector Quarterly* 45, no. 4 (Supplement): 61S–77S.

Freedom House. 2015. *Voices in the Streets: Mass Social Protests and the Right to Peaceful Assembly.* https://freedomhouse.org/sites/default/files/2020-02/0320201 5_updated_Voices_in_the_Street_Freedom_of_Assembly_report.pdf.

Freedom House. 2019. *Freedom on the Net 2019: The Crisis of Social Media.* https ://freedomhouse.org/sites/default/files/2019-11/11042019_Report_FH_FOTN_ 2019_final_Public_Download.pdf.

Frey, Bruno S., and Reto Jegen. 2001. "Motivation Crowding Theory." *Journal of Economic Surveys* 15, no. 5: 589–611.

Frey, R. Scott., Thomas Dietz, and Linda Kalof. 1992. "Characteristics of Successful American Protest Groups: Another Look at Gamson's Strategy of Social Protest." *American Journal of Sociology* 98, no. 2: 368–387.

Friedman, Milton [1970] 1987. "The Social Responsibility of Business." In *The Essence of Friedman*, edited by Kurt R. Leube, 36–42. Stanford: Hoover Institution Press.

Friedman, Milton [1962] 2002. *Capitalism And Freedom*. Fortieth Anniversary Edition. Chicago: University of Chicago Press.

Fuchs, Christian. 2006. "The Self-Organization of Social Movements." *Systemic Practice and Action* 19, no. 1: 101–137.

Fukuyama, Francis. 1989. "The End of History?" *The National Interest* 16: 3–18.

Fuller, Steve. 2016. "What Is the Problem for Which Interdisciplinarity Is the Solution?" https://items.ssrc.org/interdisciplinarity/what-is-the-problem-for-which -interdisciplinarity-is-the-solution.

Galli, Anya M. 2016. "How Glitter Bombing Lost Its Sparkle: The Emergence and Decline of a Novel Social Movement Tactic." *Mobilization: An International Quarterly* 21, no. 3: 259–281.

Gamson, William A. 1975. *The Strategy of Social Protest*. Homewood, IL: Dorsey Press.

Gamson, William A. 1989. "Reflections on *The Strategy of Social Protest*." *Sociological Forum* 4, no. 3: 455–467.

Gamson, William A. 1992. *Talking Politics*. New York: Cambridge University Press.

Gamson, William A. 2013. "Injustice Frames." In *The Wiley-Blackwell Encyclopedia of Social and Political Movements*, edited by David A. Snow, Donatella della Porta, Bert Klandermans, and Doug McAdam, 1–2. Malden: John Wiley & Sons.

Gamson, William A., and Gadi Wolfsfeld. 1993. "Movements and Media as Interacting Systems." *Annals of the American Academy of Political and Social Sciences* 528, no. 1: 114–125.

Gamson, William, Bruce Fireman, and Stephen Rytina. 1982. *Encounters with Unjust Authority*. Homewood: Dorsey Press.

Gans, Herbert. 1979. *Deciding What's News: A Study of CBS Evening News, NBC Nightly News, Newsweek and Time*. New York: Vintage Books.

Gara, Larry. 1961. *The Liberty Line: The Legend of the Underground Railroad*. Lexington: University of Kentucky Press.

Garín, Alberto. 2017. "A Non-Manifesto of Liberal History." In *What is Classical Liberal History?*, edited by Michael J. Douma, and Phillip W. Magness, 209–226. Lanham: Lexington Books.

Garner, Les. 1984. *Stepping Stones to Women's Liberty: Feminist ideas in the women's suffrage movement 1900-1918*. London: Heineman Educational Books.

Garnett, Robert F., Jr. 2011. "Hayek and Philanthropy: A Classical Liberal Road Not (yet) Taken." In *Hayek, Mill, and the Liberal Tradition*, edited by Andrew Farrant, 148–162. New York: Routledge.

Gartzke, Erik. 2007. "The Capitalist Peace." *American Journal of Political Science* 51, no. 1: 166–191.

Gasset, José Ortega y. 1932. *The Revolt of The Masses*. New York: W.W. Norton & Company.

Gastil, John. 2018. "The Lessons and Limitations of Experiments in Democratic Deliberation." *Annual Review of Law and Social Science* 14: 271–291.

Gaus, Gerald F. 2008. "The (Severe) Limits of Deliberative Democracy as the Basis for Political Choice." *Theoria: A Journal of Social and Political Theory* 117: 26–53.

Gaus, Gerald. 2018a. "It Can't Be Rational Choice All The Way Down." In *Buchanan's Tensions: Reexamining the Political Economy and Philosophy of James M. Buchanan*, edited by Peter J. Boettke, and Solomon Stein, 117–146. Arlington: Mercatus Center of George Mason University.

Gaus, Gerald. 2018b. "Liberalism." *Stanford Encyclopedia of Philosophy*. https:// plato.stanford.edu/entries/liberalism.

Geloso, Vincent, and Steven Horwitz. 2017. "Inequality: First, Do No Harm." *Independent Review* 22, no. 1: 121–134.

Geloso, Vincent, and Raymond March. 2020. "Rent-Seeking for Madness: The Political Economy of Mental Asylums in the US, 1870 to 1910." https://papers. ssrn.com/sol3/papers.cfm?abstract_id=3421728.

Georgallis, Panayiotis. 2017. "The Link Between Social Movements and Corporate Social Initiatives: Toward a Multi-level Theory." *Journal of Business Ethics* 142, no. 4: 735–751.

Gitlin, Todd. 1980. *The Whole World is Watching: Mass Media in the Making and Unmaking of the New Left*. Berkeley: University of California Press.

Glaeser, Edward L., and Joseph Gyourko. 2003. "The Impact of Building Restrictions on Housing Affordability." *Economic Policy Review* 9, no. 2: 21–39.

Glaeser, Edward L., Joseph Gyourko, and Raven E. Saks. 2005. "Why Have Housing Prices Gone Up?" *American Economic Review* 95, no. 2: 329–333.

Gloppen, Siri. 2013. "Social Movement Activism and the Courts." *Mobilizing Ideas* blog, February 4. https://mobilizingideas.wordpress.com/2013/02/04/social-movement-activism-and-the-courts.

Goffman, Erving. 1974. *Frame Analysis: An Essay on the Organization of Experience*. Cambridge: Harvard University Press.

Goldstone, Jack A. 1980. "The Weakness of Organization: A New Look at Gamson's *The Strategy of Social Protest*." *American Journal of Sociology* 85, no. 5: 1017–1042.

Goldstone, Jack. 2004. "More Social Movements or Fewer? Beyond Political Opportunity Structures to Relational Fields." *Theory and Society* 33, no. 3–4: 333–365.

Goldstone, Jack A. 2010. "Introduction: Bridging Institutionalized and Noninstitutionalized Politics." In *States, Parties, and Social Movements*, edited by Jack A. Goldstone, 1–24. New York: Cambridge University Press.

Goodman, Nathan P. 2018. "The Coproduction of Justice." In *Rethinking Punishment in the Era of Mass Incarceration*, edited by Chris W. Supranant, 49–68. New York: Routledge.

Goodman, Nathan P. 2019. "Don Lavoie's Dialectical Liberalism." In *The Dialectics of Liberty: Exploring the Context of Human Freedom*, edited by Roger E. Bissell, Chris Matthew Sciabarra, and Edward W. Younkins, 133–148. Lanham: Lexington Books.

Goodwin, Jeff, and James M. Jasper. 1999. "Caught in a Winding, Snarling Vine: The Structural Bias of Political Process Theory." *Sociological Forum* 14, no. 1: 27–54.

Goodwin, Jeff, and René Rohas. 2015. "Revolutions and Regime Change." In *The Oxford Handbook of Social Movements*, edited by Donatella della Porta and Mario Diani, 793–804. Oxford: Oxford University Press.

Goodwin, Jeff, James M. Jasper and Francesca Polletta. 2004. "Emotional Dimensions of Social Movements." In *The Blackwell Companion to Social Movements*, edited by David A. Snow, Sarah A. Soule, and Hanspeter Kriesi, 413–432. Malden: Blackwell Publishing.

Gopnik, Adam. 2019. *A Thousand Small Sanities: The Moral Adventure of Liberalism*. New York: Basic Books.

Gould, Roger V. 1991. "Multiple Networks and Mobilization in the Paris Commune, 1871." *American Sociological Review* 56, no. 6: 716–729.

Granovetter, Mark. 1985. "Economic Action and Social Structure: The Problem of Embeddedness." *American Journal of Sociology* 91, no. 3: 481–510.

Grasso, Maria T., and Marco Guigni. 2016. "Protest Participation and Economic Crisis: The Conditioning Role of Political Opportunities." *European Journal of Political Research* 55, no. 4: 663–680.

Gray, John. 1995. "Agonistic Liberalism." *Social Philosophy and Policy* 12, no. 1: 111–135.

Green, John J. 2008. "Community Development as Social Movement: A Contribution to Models of Practice." *Community Development* 39, no. 1: 50–62.

Greenfield, Liah. 2018. "Revolutions." In *The SAGE Handbook of Political Sociology*, Volume Two, edited by William Outhwaite and Stephen P. Turner, 685–698. Los Angeles: SAGE Publishing.

Greenland, Andrew, Damon Proulx, and David A. Savage. 2020. "Dying for the Cause: The Rationality of Martyrs, Suicide Bombers and Self-immolators." *Rationality and Society* 32, no. 1: 93–115.

Gregory, Anthony. 2017. "The Historicity of Civil Liberties, a Challenge for Liberals." In *What is Classical Liberal History?*, edited by Michael J. Douma, and Phillip W. Magness, 17–38. Lanham: Lexington Books.

Grynaviski, Jeffrey D., and Michael C. Munger. 2017. "Reconstructing Racism: Transforming Racial Hierarchy from 'Necessary Evil' into 'Positive Good.'" *Social Philosophy and Policy* 34, no. 1: 144–163.

Guigni, Marco. 2009. "Political Opportunities: From Tilly to Tilly." *Swiss Political Science Review* 15, no. 2: 361–368.

Gurri, Adam. 2020. "The Ordinary Made Revolutionary: The Life and Deaths of Mohamed Bouazizi." *Liberal Currents* blog, March 29. https://www.liberalc urrents.com/the-ordinary-made-revolutionary-the-life-and-deaths-of-mohamed -bouazizi.

Gurri, Martin. 2018. *The Revolt of the Public and The Crisis of Authority in The New Millennium*. San Francisco: Stripe Press.

Habermas, Jürgen. 1981. "New Social Movements." *Telos* 49: 33–37.

Haeffele, Stefanie, and Virgil Henry Storr. 2018. "Unreasonableness and Heterogeneity in Buchanan's Constitutional Project." In *Buchanan's Tensions: Reexamining the Political Economy and Philosophy of James M. Buchanan*, edited by Peter J. Boettke, and Solomon Stein, 99–116. Arlington, VA: Mercatus Center of George Mason University.

Haeffele, Stefanie, and Virgil Henry Storr. 2019a. "Is Social Justice a Mirage?" *Independent Review* 24, no. 1: 145–154.

Haeffele, Stefanie, and Virgil Henry Storr. 2019b. "Understanding Nonprofit Social Enterprises: Lessons from Austrian Economics." *Review of Austrian Economics* 32, no. 3: 229–249.

Hafez, Mohammed M. 2006. "Rationality, Culture, and Structure in the Making of Suicide Bombers: A Preliminary Theoretical Synthesis and Illustrative Case Study." *Studies in Conflict & Terrorism* 29, no. 2: 165–185.

Haines, Herbert H. 1984. "Black Radicalization and the Funding of Civil Rights: 1957-1970." *Social Problems* 32 no. 1: 31–43.

Haines, Herbert H. 1988. *Black Radicals and the Civil Rights Mainstream, 1954-1970*. Knoxville: University of Tennessee Press.

Hall, Joshua C., and Robert A. Lawson. 2014. "Economic Freedom of the World: An Accounting of the Literature." *Contemporary Economic Policy* 32, no. 1: 1–19.

Halliday, Daniel, and John Thrasher. 2020. *The Ethics of Capitalism: An Introduction*. New York: Oxford University Press.

Hammond, Samuel. 2017. "Sorry, Pepsi Haters, But Social Justice Needs Capitalism." *Liberal Currents* blog, April 10. https://www.liberalcurrents.com/pepsi-justice.

Handler, Joel F. 1992. "Postmodernism, Protest, and the New Social Movements." *Law & Society Review* 26, no. 4: 697–732.

Hanley, Ryan Patrick. 2017. "Practicing PPE: The Case of Adam Smith." *Social Philosophy and Policy* 34, no. 1: 277–295.

Hannigan, John A. 1991. "Social Movement Theory and the Sociology of Religion: Toward a New Synthesis." *Sociological Analysis* 52, no. 4: 311–331.

Hargittai, Eszter, Jason Gallo, and Matthew Kane. 2008. "Cross-ideological Discussions among Conservative and Liberal Bloggers." *Public Choice* 134, no. 1: 67–86.

Harris, Lasana T., and Susan T. Fiske. 2006. "Dehumanizing the Lowest of the Low: Neuroimaging Responses to Extreme Out-Groups." *Psychological Science* 17, no. 10: 847–853.

Harrison, Brian. 1978. *Separate Spheres: The Opposition to Women's Suffrage in Britain*. London: Croom Helm.

Harrison, Caleb. 2018. "Bad Spontaneous Orders: Trust, Ignorance, and White Supremacy." In *Exploring the Political Economy and Social Philosophy of F. A. Hayek*, edited by Peter J. Boettke, Jayme S. Lemke, and Virgil Henry Storr, 233–258. Lanham: Rowman & Littlefield.

Hart, David M. 2015. "Broken Windows and House-Owning Dogs: The French Connection and the Popularization of Economics from Bastiat to Jasay." *Independent Review* 20, no. 1: 61–84.

Hart, David M., Gary Chartier, Ross Miller Kenyon, and Roderick T. Long. 2018. *Social Class and State Power: Exploring an Alternative Radical Tradition*. Cham, Switzerland: Palgrave Macmillan.

Hart, Oliver, and Liugi Zingales. 2017. "Companies Should Maximize Shareholder Value Not Market Value." *Journal of Law, Finance, and Accounting* 2, no. 2: 247–274.

Hartley, John, and Jason Potts. 2014. *Cultural Science: A Natural History of Stories, Demes, Knowledge and Innovation*. London: Bloomsbury Academic.

Hartz, Louis. 1955. *The Liberal Tradition in America*. New York: Harcourt Brace.

Hasenfeld, Yeheskel, and Benjamin Gidron. 2005. "Understanding Multi-purpose Hybrid Voluntary Organizations: The Contributions of Theories on Civil Society, Social Movements and Non-profit Organizations." *Journal of Civil Society* 1, no. 2: 97–112.

Haslam, Nick. 2006. "Dehumanization: An Integrative Review." *Personality and Social Psychology Review* 10, no. 3: 252–264.

Hawley, George. 2017. *Making Sense of the Alt-Right*. New York: Columbia University Press.

Haydu, Jeffrey. 2020. "Adding Time to Social Movement Diffusion." *Social Movement Studies* 19, no. 5–6: 625–639.

Hayek, Friedrich A. 1945. "The Use of Knowledge in Society." *American Economic Review* 35, no. 4: 519–530.

Hayek, Friedrich A. 1948. "Individualism: True and False." In *Individualism and Economic Order*, edited by Friedrich A. Hayek, 1–32. Chicago: University of Chicago Press.

Hayek, Friedrich A. 1949. "The Intellectuals and Socialism." *University of Chicago Law Review* 16, no. 3: 417–433.

Hayek, Friedrich A. 1967. "The Corporation in a Democratic Society: In Whose Interest Ought It To and Will It Be Run?" In *Studies in Philosophy, Politics, and Economics*, edited by Friedrich A. Hayek, 300–312. New York: Simon & Schuster.

Hayek, Friedrich A. 1988. *The Fatal Conceit: The Errors of Socialism*. In *The Collected Works of F. A. Hayek: Volume 1*, edited by W. W. Bartley. Chicago: University of Chicago Press.

Hayek, Friedrich A. [1944] 2006. *The Road to Serfdom*. Routledge Classics Edition. New York: Routledge.

Hayek, Friedrich A. [1960] 2011. "The Constitution of Liberty." In *The Collected Works of F. A. Hayek: Volume 17*, edited by Ronald Hamowy. Chicago: University of Chicago Press.

Hayek, Friedrich A. [1973–1979] 2013. *Law, Legislation and Liberty: A New Statement of the Liberal Principles of Justice and Political Economy*. Routledge Classics Edition. Abingdon: Routledge.

Heaney, Michael T., and Fabio Rojas. 2015. *Party in the Street: The Antiwar Movement and the Democratic Party after 9/11*. New York: Cambridge University Press.

Hebert, David J. 2019. "The Spontaneous Order of Politics." *Advances in Austrian Economics* 19: 131–144.

Heller, Charles, and Lorenzo Pezzani. 2019. "Contentious Crossings: Struggles and Alliances for Freedom of Movement across the Mediterranean Sea." *South Atlantic Quarterly* 118, no. 3: 644–653.

Heller, Charles, Lorenzo Pezzani, and Maurice Stierl. 2017. "Disobedient Sensing and Border Struggles at the Maritime Border of EUrope." *Spheres* 4: 1–15.

Henderson, David. 2001. *Misguided Virtue: False Notions of Corporate Social Responsibility*. London: Institute of Economic Affairs.

Hendy, Peter. 2008. *Captains of Industry: Biographies of the Presidents of the Australian Chamber of Commerce and Industry*. Melbourne, Australia: Melbourne University Publishing.

Higgs, Robert. 1987. *Crisis and Leviathan: Critical Episodes in the Growth of Government*. Oxford: Oxford University Press.

Hilgartner, Stephen, and Charles L. Bosk. 1988. "The Rise and Fall of Social Problems: A Public Arenas Model." *American Journal of Sociology* 94, no. 1: 53–78.

Hilhorst, Thea. 1997. "Discourse Formation in Social Movements. Issues of Collective Action." In *Images and Realities of Rural Life: Wageningen Perspectives on Rural Transformations*, edited by Henk de Haan and Norman Long, 121–149. Wageningen, Netherlands: Van Gorcum.

Hirshleifer, Jack. 1994. "The Dark Side of the Force: Western Economic Association International 1993 Presidential Address." *Economic Inquiry* 32, no. 1: 1–10.

Hirschman, Albert O. 1970. *Exit, Voice, and Loyalty: Responses to Decline in Firms, Organizations, and States*. Cambridge: Harvard University Press.

Hirschman, Albert O. 1993. "Exit, Voice, and the Fate of the German Democratic Republic: An Essay in Conceptual History." *World Politics* 45, no. 2: 173–202.

Hodgson, Geoffrey M. 2000. "What Is the Essence of Institutional Economics?" *Journal of Economic Issues* 34, no. 2: 317–329.

Hodgson, Geoffrey M. 2019. *Is Socialism Feasible? Towards an Alternative Future*. Cheltenham: Edward Elgar Publishing.

Holcombe, Randall G. 2014. "Improving Spontaneous Orders." In *Austrian Theory and Economic Organization*, edited by Guinevere Liberty Nell, 9–28. New York: Palgrave Macmillan.

Holdo, Markus. 2019. "Cooptation and Non-cooptation: Elite Strategies in Response to Social Protest." *Social Movement Studies* 18, no. 4: 444–462.

Holleran, Max. 2020. "Millennial 'YIMBYs' and Boomer 'NIMBYs': Generational Views on Housing Affordability in the United States." *Sociological Review*. https://doi.org/10.1177/0038026120916121.

Holton, Sandra Stanley. 1994. "'To Educate Women into Rebellion': Elizabeth Cady Stanton and the Creation of a Transatlantic Network of Radical Suffragists." *American Historical Review* 99, no. 4: 1112–1136.

Holton, Sandra Stanley. 1995. "Women and the Vote." In *Women's History: Britain, 1850-1945: An Introduction*, edited by June Purvis, 277–305. New York: St. Martin's Press.

Holton, Sandra Stanley. 2019. "The Language of Suffrage History." *Women's History Review* 28, no. 7: 1227–1234.

Horwitz, Steven. 2001. "From Smith to Menger to Hayek: Liberalism in the Spontaneous-Order Tradition." *Independent Review* 6, no. 1: 81–97.

Horwitz, Steven. 2012. "Hayek's Tolerant and Pluralistic Liberal Vision." *Foundation of Economic Education*, May 10. https://fee.org/articles/hayeks-tolerant-and-pluralistic-liberal-vision.

Hsieh, Chang-Tai, and Enrico Moretti. 2019. "Housing Constraints and Spatial Misallocation." *American Economic Journal: Macroeconomics* 11, no. 2: 1–19.

Hsieh, Hui-Cheng, Ying-Che Hsieh, and Thi Huyen Chi Vu. 2019. "How Social Movements Influence Crowdfunding Success." *Pacific-Basin Finance Journal* 53: 308–320.

Huemer, Michael. 2012. *The Problem of Political Authority: An Examination of the Right to Coerce and the Duty to Obey*. Basingstoke: Palgrave Macmillan.

Huemer, Michael. 2017. "Is Taxation Theft?" Cato Institute. *libertarianism.org*, March, 16. https://www.libertarianism.org/columns/is-taxation-theft.

Hume, Leslie Parker. 1982. *The National Union of Women's Suffrage Societies, 1897-1914*. New York: Garland Publishing.

Hutt, W. H. 1966. "Unanimity versus Non-Discrimination (as Criteria for Constitutional Validity)." *South African Journal of Economics* 34, no. 2: 133–147.

Iannaccone, Laurence R. 1992. "Sacrifice and Stigma: Reducing Free-riding in Cults, Communes, and Other Collectives." *Journal of Political Economy* 100, no. 2: 271–291.

Ikeda, Sanford. 2008. "The Meaning of "Social Capital" as It Relates to the Market Process." *Review of Austrian Economics* 21, no. 2: 167–182.

Ikeda, Sanford. 2012. "Entrepreneurship in Action Space." *Advances in Austrian Economics* 16: 105–139.

Ikeda, Sanford. 2018. "The Nature and Limits of Gary Becker's Theory of Racial Discrimination." *Review of Austrian Economics* 31, no. 4: 403–417.

Inglehart, Ronald F. 2018. *Cultural Evolution: People's Motivations Are Changing, and Reshaping the World*. Cambridge: Cambridge University Press.

International Network of Civil Liberties Organizations (INCLO). 2013. "Take Back the Streets: Repression and Criminalization of Protest Around the World." https://www.aclu.org/report/take-back-streets-repression-and-criminalization-protest-around-world.

Irwin, Douglas A. 1989. "Political Economy and Peel's Repeal of the Corn Laws." *Economics and Politics* 1, no. 1: 41–59.

Irwin, Douglas A., and Maksym G. Chepeliev. 2020. "The Economic Consequences of Sir Robert Peel: A Quantitative Assessment of the Repeal of the Corn Laws." https://www.nber.org/system/files/working_papers/w28142/w28142.pdf.

Isaac, Larry W. 2019. "Performative Power in Nonviolent Tactical Adaptation to Violence: Evidence from US Civil Rights Movement Campaigns." In *Social

Movements, Nonviolent Resistance, and the State, edited by Hank Johnston, 27–53. New York: Routledge.

Jasper, James. 2004. "A Strategic Approach to Collective Action: Looking for Agency in Social-Movement Choices." *Mobilization: An International Quarterly* 9, no. 1: 1–16.

Jasper, James M. 2011. "Emotions and Social Movements: Twenty Years of Theory and Research." *Annual Review of Sociology* 37: 285–303.

Jasper, James M. 2014. "Constructing Indignation: Anger Dynamics in Protest Movements." *Emotion Review* 6, no. 3: 208–213.

Jasper, James M., Kevin Moran, and Marisa Tramontano. 2015. "Strategy." In *The Oxford Handbook of Social Movements*, edited by Donatella della Porta and Mario Diani, 399–409. Oxford: Oxford University Press.

Jayadev, Arjun, and Samuel Bowles. 2006. "Guard Labor." *Journal of Development Economics* 79, no. 2: 328–348.

Jeffries, Fiona. 2011. "Saying Something: The Location of Social Movements in the Surveillance Society." *Social Movement Studies* 10, no. 2: 175–190.

Jenkins, J. Craig. 1983. "Resource Mobilization Theory and the Study of Social Movements." *Annual Review of Sociology* 9: 527–553.

Jenkins, J. Craig, and Bert Klandermans. 1995. "The Politics of Social Protest." In *The Politics of Social Protest: Comparative Perspectives on States and Social Movements*, edited by J. Craig Jenkins and Bert Klandermans, 3–13. Minneapolis: University of Minneapolis Press.

Jenkins, J. Craig, Michael Wallace, and Andrew S. Fullerton. 2008. "A Social Movement Society? A Cross-National Analysis of Protest Potential." *International Journal of Sociology* 38, no. 3: 12–35.

Johnson, Charles W. 2011. "We Are Market Forces." In *Markets Not Capitalism: Individualist Anarchism against Bosses, Inequality, Corporate Power, and Structural Poverty*, edited by Gary Chartier, and Charles W. Johnson, 391–394. Brooklyn: Autonomedia.

Johnson, Charles W. 2013. "Women and the Invisible Fist: How Violence Against Women Enforces the Unwritten Law of Patriarchy." http://charleswjohnson.name/essays/women-and-the-invisible-fist.

Johnston, David. 1997. "Hayek's Attack on Social Justice." *Critical Review* 11, no. 1: 81–100.

Johnston, Hank. 2011. *States and Social Movements*. Malden: Polity Press.

Johnston, Hank. 2014. *What Is A Social Movement?* Cambridge, UK: Polity Press.

Johnston, Hank, and Shoon Lio. 1998. "Collective Behavior and Social Movements in the Postmodern Age: Looking Backward to Look Forward." *Sociological Perspectives* 41, no. 3: 453–472.

Jones, Matthew. 2014. "Chantal Mouffe's Agonistic Project: Passions and Participation." *Parallax* 20, no. 2: 14–30.

Joseph, George, and Murtaza Hussain. 2018. "FBI Tracked an Activist Involved with Black Lives Matter as They Travelled across the U.S., Documents Show." *The Intercept*, March 20. https://theintercept.com/2018/03/19/black-lives-matter-fbi-surveillance.

Jumet, Kira D. 2018. *Contesting the Repressive State: Why Ordinary Egyptians Protested During the Arab Spring*. New York: Oxford University Press.

Kapstein, Ethan B., and Joshua W. Busby. 2013. *AIDS Drugs for All: Social Movements and Market Transformations*. Cambridge, UK: Cambridge University Press.

Karpf, David. 2016. *Analytic Activism: Digital Listening and the New Political Strategy*. New York: Oxford University Press.

Kasper, Wolfgang, Manfred E. Streit, and Peter J. Boettke. 2012. *Institutional Economics: Property, Competition, Policies*. Cheltenham: Edward Elgar.

Katz, Alfred H. 1981. "Self-Help and Mutual Aid: An Emerging Social Movement?" *Annual Review of Sociology* 7: 129–155.

Katz, Elihu. 2006. "Rediscovering Gabriel Tarde." *Political Communication* 23, no. 3: 263–270.

Kelly, William R., and David Snyder. 1980. "Racial Violence and Socioeconomic Changes Among Blacks in the United States." *Social Forces* 58, no. 3: 739–760.

King, Brayden G., and Mary-Hunter McDonnell. 2015. "Good Firms, Good Targets: The Relationship among Corporate Social Responsibility, Reputation, and Activist Targeting." In *Corporate Social Responsibility in a Globalizing World*, edited by Kiyoteru Tsutsi, and Alwyn Lim, 430–454. Cambridge, UK: Cambridge University Press.

King, Brayden G., and Sarah A. Soule. 2007. "Social Movements as Extra-Institutional Entrepreneurs: The Effect of Protests on Stock Price Returns." *Administrative Science Quarterly* 52, no. 3: 413–442.

King, Hanna. 2010. "U.S. AIDS Coalition to Unleash Power (ACT-UP) Demands access to Drugs, 1987-89." *Global Nonviolent Action Database*. https://nvdatab ase.swarthmore.edu/content/us-aids-coalition-unleash-power-act-demands-access -drugs-1987-89.

King, Martin Luther, Jr. 1960. "Pilgrimage to Nonviolence." http://okra.stanford .edu/transcription/document_images/Vol05Scans/13Apr1960_Pilgrimageto Nonviolence.pdf.

Kinna, Ruth, Alex Prichard, and Thomas Swann. 2019. "Occupy and the Constitution of Anarchy." *Global Constitutionalism* 8, no. 2: 357–390.

Kirzner, Israel M. 1973. *Competition and Entrepreneurship*. Chicago: University of Chicago Press.

Kirzner, Israel M. 2009. "The Alert and Creative Entrepreneur: A Clarification." *Small Business Economics* 32, no. 2: 145–152.

Klandermans, Bert, and Jacquelien van Stekelenburg. 2013. "Social Movements and the Dynamics of Collective Action." In *The Oxford Handbook of Political Psychology*, Second Edition, edited by Leonie Huddy, David O. Sears, and Jack S. Levy, 774–811. Oxford: Oxford University Press.

Klandermans, Bert, Jacquelien van Stekelenburg, and Marie-Louise Damen. 2015. "Beneficiary and Conscience Constituents: Of Interests and Solidarity." In *Austerity and Protest: Popular Contention in Times of Economic Crisis*, edited by Marco Guigni, and Maria T. Grasso, 155–170. Farnham: Ashgate.

Klein, Daniel B., Xiaofei Pan, Daniel Houser, and Gonzalo Schwarz. 2015. "A Demand for Encompassment: A Hayekian Experimental Parable about Political Psychology." *Rationality and Society* 27, no. 1: 70–95.

Klein, Steven, and Cheol-Sung Lee. 2019. "Toward a Dynamic Theory of Civil Society: The Politics of Forward and Backward Infiltration." *Sociological Theory* 37, no. 1: 62–88.

Kligo, Danielle K., and Summer Harlow. 2019. "Protests, Media Coverage, and a Hierarchy of Social Struggle." *The International Journal of Press/Politics* 24, no. 4: 508–530.

Knight, Frank H. 1960. *Intelligence and Democratic Action*. Cambridge: Harvard University Press.

Knollenberg, Bernhard [1975] 2003. *Growth of the American Revolution: 1766-1775*. Liberty Fund Edition. Indianapolis: Liberty Fund.

Kolers, Avery. 2016. "Social Movements." *Philosophy Compass* 11, no. 10: 580–590.

Kolev, Stefan. 2019a. "Smith and Marx Walk into a Bar: A History of Economics Podcast." Interview by Scott Scheall, November 15, 2019. Audio, 59:11. http://het podcast.libsyn.com/episode-twenty-six.

Kolev, Stefan. 2019b. "The Puzzles of a Triumvir: Friedrich von Wieser as Political Economist and Sociologist." *European Journal of the History of Economic Thought* 26, no. 5: 942–972.

Koopmans, Ruud. 1999. "Political. Opportunity. Structure. Some Splitting to Balance the Lumping." *Sociological Forum* 14, no. 1: 93–105.

Koopmans, Ruud. 2004a. "Movements and Media: Selection Processes and Evolutionary Dynamics in the Public Sphere." *Theory & Society* 33, no. 3–4: 367–391.

Koopmans, Ruud. 2004b. "Protest in Time and Space: The Evolution of Waves of Contention." In *The Blackwell Companion to Social Movements*, edited by David A. Snow, Sarah A. Soule, and Hanspeter Kriesi, 19–46. Malden: Blackwell Publishing.

Koppl, Roger. 2002. *Big Players and the Economic Theory of Expectations*. London: Palgrave Macmillan.

Koppl, Roger. 2006. "Entrepreneurial Behavior as a Human Universal." In *Entrepreneurship: The Engine of Growth—Volume 1: People*, edited by Maria Minniti, 1–20. Westport: Greenwood Publishing.

Kretschmer, Kelsy, and David S. Meyer. 2007. "Platform Leadership: Cultivating Support for a Public Profile." *American Behavioral Scientist* 50, no. 10: 1395–1412.

Kuran, Timur. 1995. *Private Truths, Public Lies: The Social Consequences of Preference Falsification*. Cambridge: Harvard University Press.

Kurer, Thomas, Silja Häusermann, Bruno Wüest, and Matthias Enggist. 2019. "Economic Grievances and Political Protest." *European Journal of Political Research* 58, no. 3: 866–892.

Kurzman, Charles. 2008. "Introduction: Meaning-Making in Social Movements." *Anthropological Quarterly* 81, no. 1: 5–15.

Kymlicka, Will. 2007. *Multicultural Odysseys: Navigating the New International Politics of Diversity*. Oxford: Oxford University Press.

Lafi, Nora. 2017. "The 'Arab Spring' in Global Perspective: Social Movements, Changing Contexts and Political Transitions in the Arab World (2010-2014)." In *The History of Social Movements in Global Perspective: A Survey*, edited by Stefan Berger, and Holger Nehring, 677–702. Cham, Switzerland: Palgrave Macmillan.

Lal, Deepak. 2006. *Reviving the Invisible Hand: The Case for Classical Liberalism in the Twenty-First Century*. Princeton: Princeton University Press.

Lance, Keith Curry. 1979. "Strategy Choices of the British Women's Social and Political Union, 1903-18." *Social Science Quarterly* 60, no. 1: 51–61.

Lavoie, Don. 1992. "Glasnost and the Knowledge Problem: Rethinking Economic Democracy." *Cato Journal* 11, no. 3: 435–455.

Lavoie, Don. 1993. "Democracy, Markets, and the Legal Order: Notes on the Nature of Politics in a Radically Liberal Society." *Social Philosophy and Policy* 10, no. 2: 103–120.

Lavoie, Don. 1994. "Cultural Studies and the Conditions for Entrepreneurship." In *The Cultural Context of Economics and Politics*, edited by T. William Boxx, and Gary M. Quinlivan, 51–69. Lanham: University Press of America.

Lawrence, Adria K. 2017. "Repression and Activism among the Arab Spring's First Movers: Evidence from Morocco's February 20th Movement." *British Journal of Political Science* 47, no. 3: 699–718.

Leach, Darcy K., and Sebastian Haunss. 2009. "Scenes and Social Movements." In *Culture, Social Movements, and Protest*, edited by Hank Johnston, 255–276. Burlington, VT: Ashgate.

Leenders, Reinoud. 2013. "Social Movement Theory and the Onset of Popular Uprising in Syria." *Arab Studies Quarterly* 35, no. 3: 273–289.

Leeson, Peter T. 2014. *Anarchy Unbound: Why Self-Governance Works Better than You Think*. Cambridge, UK: Cambridge University Press.

Leeson, Peter T., and Peter J. Boettke. 2006. "Liberal Tolerance as Robust Political Economy." In *Tolerance in the Twenty-First Century: Prospects and Challenges*, edited by Gerson Moreno-Riaño, 201–212. Lanham: Lexington Books.

Leicht, Kevin T. 2020. "Social Change." *Oxford Bibliographies*. https://www.oxfordbibliographies.com/view/document/obo-9780199756384/obo-9780199756384-0047.xml.

Lemke, Jayme S. 2015. "An Austrian Approach to Class Structure." *Advances in Austrian Economics* 19: 167–192.

Levi, Margaret. 1988. *Of Rule and Revenue*. Berkeley: University of California Press.

Levin, Sam. 2016. "ACLU Finds Social Media Sites Gave Data to Company Tracking Black Protestors." *The Guardian*, October 12. https://www.theguardian.com/technology/2016/oct/11/aclu-geofeedia-facebook-twitter-instagram-black-lives-matter.

Levine, Peter. 2011. "Seeing Like a Citizen: The Contributions of Elinor Ostrom to 'Civic Studies.'" *The Good Society* 20, no. 1: 3–14.

Levine, Peter. 2016. "Why Don't Social Movements Have Great Leaders Any More?" https://peterlevine.ws/?p=16616.

Levine, Peter. 2018. "Gandhi on the Primacy of Means over Ends." https://peterlevine.ws/?p=19931.

Levine, Peter. 2019. "'What Should We Do?' The Bloomington School and the Citizen's Core Question." In *Ostrom's Tensions: Reexamining the Political Economy and Public Policy of Elinor C. Ostrom*, edited by Roberta Q. Herzberg, Peter J. Boettke, and Paul Dragos Aligica, 105–125. Arlington: Mercatus Center of George Mason University.

Levine, Peter, and Karol Edward Soltan. 2014. *Civic Studies: Bringing Theory to Practice*. Washington, DC: Bringing Theory to Practice.

Levine, Philippa. 1987. *Victorian Feminism: 1850-1900*. London: Hutchinson.

Levy, David M., and Sandra J. Peart. 2016. *Escape from Democracy: The Role of Experts and the Public in Economic Policy*. New York: Cambridge University Press.

Levy, Jacob T. 2018. "Who's Afraid of Judith Shklar?" *Foreign Policy* 229: 79–81.

Lewis, Paul. 2011. "Varieties of Emergence: Minds, Markets and Novelty." *Studies in Emergent Order* 4: 170–192.

Lichbach, Mark I. 1995. *The Rebel's Dilemma*. Ann Arbor: University of Michigan Press.

Lind, JoEllen. 1994. "Dominance and Democracy: The Legacy of Woman Suffrage for the Voting Right." *UCLA Women's Law Journal* 5, no. 1: 103–216.

Lindsey, Brink. 2006. "Liberaltarians." *New Republic*, December 11. https://newrepublic.com/article/64443/liberaltarians.

Lindsey, Brink, and Steven M. Teles. 2017. *The Captured Economy: How the Powerful Enrich Themselves, Slow Down Growth, and Increase Inequality*. New York: Oxford University Press.

Lips, Brad. 2020. *The Freedom Movement: Its Past, Present, and Future*. Arlington: Atlas Network.

Little, Daniel. 2020. "Mounk on the Crisis of Democracy." *Understanding Society*, July 20. https://understandingsociety.blogspot.com/2020/07/mounk-on-crisis-of-democracy.html.

Lo, Clarence Y. H. 1982. "Countermovements and Conservative Movements in the Contemporary U.S." *Annual Review of Sociology* 8: 107–134.

Locke, John. [1689] 1988. *Two Treatises of Government*. Cambridge Texts in the History of Political Thought, edited by Peter Laslett. Cambridge, UK: Cambridge University Press.

Lohmann, Susanne. 1993. "A Signaling Model of Informative and Manipulative Political Action." *American Political Science Review* 87, no. 2: 319–333.

Lomasky, Loren. 1998. "Libertarianism As If (The Other 99 Percent of) People Mattered." *Social Philosophy and Policy* 15, no. 2: 350–371.

Lomasky, Loren. 2002. "Classical Liberalism and Civil Society." In *Alternative Conceptions of Civil Society*, edited by Simone Chambers, and Will Kymlicka, 50–70. Princeton: Princeton University Press.

Loury, Glenn C. 1998. "Discrimination in the Post-Civil Rights Era: Beyond Market Interactions." *Journal of Economic Perspectives* 12, no. 2: 117–126.

Luders, Joseph. 2006. "The Economics of Movement Success: Business Responses to Civil Rights Mobilization." *American Journal of Sociology* 111, no. 4: 963–998.

Lynd, Staughton. 2013. *Accompanying: Pathways to Social Change*. Oakland: PM Press.

Maccatory, Bénédicte, Makama Bawa Oumarou, and Marc Poncelet. 2010. "West African Social Movements 'Against the High Cost of Living': From the Economic to the Political, from the Global to the National." *Review of African Political Economy* 37, no. 125: 345–359.

MacDonald, Trent J. 2019. *The Political Economy of Non-Territorial Exit: Cryptosecession*. Cheltenham: Edward Elgar.

Macedo, Stephen. 1990. *Liberal Virtues: Citizenship, Virtue, and Community in Liberal Constitutionalism*. New York: Oxford University Press.

Machovec, Martin. 2009. "The Types and Functions of Samizdat Publications in Czechoslovakia, 1948-1989." *Poetics Today* 30, no. 1: 1–26.

Macmillan, Rob. 2013. "Decoupling the State and the Third Sector? The 'Big Society' as a Spontaneous Order." *Voluntary Sector Review* 4, no. 2: 185–203.

Madison, Gary Brent. 1998. *The Political Economy of Civil Society and Human Rights*. New York: Routledge.

Maeckelbergh Marianne E. 2014. "Social Movements and Global Governance." In *The Routledge Companion to Alternative Organization*, edited by Martin Parker, George Cheney, Valérie Fournier, and Chris Land, 345–358. London: Routledge.

Magness, Phillip W. 2020. "The Anti-discriminatory Tradition in Virginia school Public Choice Theory." *Public Choice* 183, no. 3–4: 417–441.

Main, Thomas J. 2018. *The Rise of the Alt-Right*. Washington, DC: Brookings Institution Press.

Malamet, Akiva. (2018). "Spontaneous Order as Social Construction: A Social Analysis of Emergent Institutions." https://www.dropbox.com/s/1jtvmdar1qngb8b/R_1l4B6vJWu2vhDdU_Spontaneous%20Order%20as%20Social%20Construction%20%28Menger%20Essay%20Contest%29.pdf?dl=0.

Mantena, Karuna. 2012. "Gandhi and the Means-Ends Question in Politics." https://www.sss.ias.edu/files/papers/paper46.pdf.

Markey-Towler, Brendan. 2019a. "The Competition and Evolution of Ideas in the Public Sphere: A New Foundation for Institutional Theory." *Journal of Institutional Economics* 15, no. 1: 27–48.

Markey-Towler, Brendan. 2019b. "The New Microeconomics: A Psychological, Institutional, and Evolutionary Paradigm with Neoclassical Economics as a Special Case." *American Journal of Economics and Sociology* 78, no. 1: 95–135.

Markoff, John. 2015. "Historical Analysis and Social Movements Research." In *The Oxford Handbook of Social Movements*, edited by Donatella della Porta and Mario Diani, 68–85. Oxford: Oxford University Press.

Marshall, Anna-Maria, and Daniel Crocker Hale. 2014. "Cause Lawyering." *Annual Review of Law and Social Science* 10: 301–320.

Martin, Adam. 2010. "Emergent Politics and the Power of Ideas." *Studies in Emergent Order* 3: 212–245.

Martin, Adam. 2015a. "Austrian Methodology: A Review and Synthesis." In *The Oxford Handbook of Austrian Economics*, edited by Peter J. Boettke, and Christopher J. Coyne, 13–42. New York: Oxford University Press.

Martin, Adam. 2015b. "Degenerate Cosmopolitanism." *Social Philosophy and Policy* 32, no. 1: 74–100.

Martin, Adam. 2019. "The Limits of Liberalism: Good Boundaries Must Be Discovered." In *Economic Freedom and Prosperity: The Origins and Maintenance of Liberalization*, edited by Benjamin Powell, 48–60. New York: Routledge.

Martin, Adam, and Matias Petersen. 2019. "Poverty Alleviation as an Economic Problem." *Cambridge Journal of Economics* 43, no. 1: 205–221.

Martin, Isaac William. 2008. *The Permanent Tax Revolt: How the Property Tax Transformed American Politics.* Stanford: Stanford University Press.

Martin, Isaac William. 2009. "Proposition 13 Fever: How California's Tax Limitation Spread." *California Journal of Politics & Policy* 1, no. 1: 1–17.

Martin, Isaac William. 2013. *Rich People's Movements: Grassroots Campaigns to Untax the One Percent.* New York: Oxford University Press.

Martin, Daniel D. 2013. "The Drama of Dissent: Police, Protestors, and Political Impression Management." In *The Drama of Social Life: A Dramaturgical Handbook*, edited by Charles Edgley, 157–180. London, Routledge.

Martin, Nicola. 2012. "Disability Identity—Disability Pride." *Perspectives: Policy and Practice in Higher Education* 16, no. 1: 14–18.

Martin, Nona P. and Virgil Henry Storr. 2008. "On Perverse Emergent Orders." *Studies in Emergent Order* 1: 73–91.

Marwell, Gerald, and Pamela Oliver. 1993. *The Critical Mass in Collective Action: A Micro-Social Theory.* New York: Cambridge University Press.

Marx, Gary T. 1979. "External Efforts to Damage or Facilitate Social Movements: Some Patterns, Explanations, Outcomes, and Complications." In *The Dynamics of Social Movements*, edited by John D. McCarthy, and Mayer N. Zald, 94–125. Cambridge: Winthrop.

Marx, Gary T. 2012. "Looking at Smelser's Theory of Collective Behavior After Almost 50 Years: A Review and Appreciation." *The American Sociologist* 43, no. 2: 135–152.

Maxwell, Angie and Wayne T. Parent. 2012. "The Obama Trigger: Presidential Approval and Tea Party Membership." *Social Science Quarterly* 93, no. 5: 1384–1401.

Mayer, Frederic W. 2014. *Narrative Politics: Stories and Collective Action.* New York: Oxford University Press.

Mayhall, Laura E. Nym. 2000. "Defining Militancy: Radical Protest, the Constitutional Idiom, and Women's Suffrage in Britain, 1908-1909." *Journal of British Studies* 39, no. 3: 340–371.

McAdam, Doug. 1982. *Political Process and the Development of Black Insurgency, 1930-1970.* Chicago: University of Chicago Press.

McAdam, Doug. 1983. "Tactical Innovation and the Pace of Insurgency." *American Sociological Review* 48, no. 6: 735–754.

McAdam, Doug. 1986. "Recruitment to High Risk Activism: The Case of Freedom Summer." *American Journal of Sociology* 92, no. 1: 64–90.

McAdam, Doug. 1988. *Freedom Summer.* New York: Oxford University Press.

McAdam, Doug. 2003. "Beyond Structural Analysis: Toward a More Dynamic Understanding of Social Movements." In *Social Movements and Networks: Relational Approaches to Collective Action*, edited by Mario Diani, and Doug McAdam, 281–298. Oxford: Oxford University Press.

McAdam, Doug. 2014. "The Civil Rights Movement." In *The Oxford Handbook of Racial and Ethnic Politics in the United States*, edited by David L. Leal, Teaku Lee and Mark Sawyer. New York: Oxford University Press. https://www.oxfordha ndbooks.com/view/10.1093/oxfordhb/9780199566631.001.0001/oxfordhb-9780 199566631-e-10.

McAdam, Doug, Sidney Tarrow, and Charles Tilly. 2001. *Dynamics of contention.* Cambridge, UK: Cambridge University Press.

McCallum, Gerald C., Jr. 1967. "Negative and Positive Freedom." *Philosophical Review* 76, no. 3: 312–334.

McCammon, Holly J., Lyndi Hewitt, and Sandy Smith. 2004. "'No Weapon Save Argument': Strategic Frame Amplification in the U.S. Woman Suffrage Movements." *Sociological Quarterly* 45, no. 3: 529–556.

McCann, Michael. 2004. "Law and Social Movements." In *The Blackwell Companion to Law and Society*, edited by Austin Sarat, 506–522. Malden: Blackwell Publishing.

McCarthy, John D., and Clark McPhail. 1998. "The Institutionalization of Protest in the United States." In *The Social Movement Society: Contentious Political for a New Century*, edited by David S. Meyer, and Sidney Tarrow, 83–110. Boulder: Rowman and Littlefield.

McCarthy, John D., and Mayer N. Zald. 1977. "Resource Mobilization and Social Movements: A Partial Theory." *American Journal of Sociology* 82, no. 6: 1212–1241.

McCloskey, Deirdre. 2006. *The Bourgeois Virtues: Ethics for an Age of Commerce.* Chicago: University of Chicago Press.

McCloskey, Deirdre N. 2010. *Bourgeois Dignity: Why Economics Can't Explain the Modern World.* Chicago: University of Chicago Press.

McCloskey, Deirdre Nansen. 2019. "Fukuyama Was Correct: Liberalism *Is* the Telos of History." *Journal of Contextual Economics* 139, no. 2–4: 285–304.

McCormick, Erin. 2017. "Rise of the Yimbys: The Angry Millennials with a Radical Housing Solution." *The Guardian*, October 2. https://www.theguardian.com/cities/ 2017/oct/02/rise-of-the-yimbys-angry-millennials-radical-housing-solution.

McGee, Michael Calvin. 1980. "'Social Movement': Phenomenon or Meaning." *Central States Speech Journal* 31, no. 4: 233–244.

McWhorter, Diane. 2001. *Carry Me Home: Birmingham, Alabama: The Climactic Battle of the Civil Rights Revolution.* New York: Simon & Schuster.

Mead, Rebecca J. 2013. "Suffrage Movement, International." In *The Wiley-Blackwell Encyclopedia of Social and Political Movements*, edited by David A. Snow, Donatella della Porta, Bert Klandermans, and Doug McAdam, 1–9. Malden: John Wiley & Sons.

Meadowcroft, John, and Elizabeth A. Morrow. 2017. "Violence, Self-Worth, Solidarity and Stigma: How a Dissident, Far-Right Group Solves the Collective Action Problem." *Political Studies* 65, no. 2: 373–390.

Meadowcroft, John, and Mark Pennington. 2008. "Bonding and Bridging: Social Capital and the Communitarian Critique of Liberal Markets." *Review of Austrian Economics* 21, no. 2: 119–133.

Melucci, Alberto. 1985. "The Symbolic Challenge of Contemporary Movements." *Social Research* 52, no. 4: 789–816.

Melucci, Alberto. 1989. *Nomads of the Present: Social Movements and Individual Needs in Contemporary Society*. Philadelphia: Temple University Press.

Merquior, J. G. 1991. *Liberalism, Old and New*. Boston: Twayne Publishers.

Merton, Robert K. 1936. "The Unanticipated Consequences of Purposive Social Action." *American Sociological Review* 1, no. 6: 894–904.

Meyer, David S., and Kelsy Kretschmer. 2007. "Social Movements." In *21st Century Sociology: A Reference Handbook*, edited by Clifton D. Bryant, and Dennis L. Peck, 540–548. Thousand Oaks: SAGE Publications.

Meyer, David S., and Sidney Tarrow. 1998. *The Social Movement Society: Contentious Politics for a New Century*. Lanham: Rowman & Littlefield.

Micheletti, Michele, and Dietlind Stolle. 2015. "Consumer Strategies in Social Movements." In *The Oxford Handbook of Social Movements*, edited by Donatella della Porta and Mario Diani, 478–493. Oxford: Oxford University Press.

Michelon, Giovanna, Michelle Rodrigue, and Elisabetta Trevisan. 2020. "The Marketization of a Social Movement: Activists, Shareholders and CSR Disclosure." *Accounting, Organizations and Society* 80. https://doi.org/10.1016/j.aos.2019.101074.

Mill, John Stuart. [1859] 1985. *On Liberty*. Penguin Classics Edition. London: Penguin Books.

Miller, Henry. 2012. "Popular Petitioning and the Corn Laws, 1833-46." *English Historical Review* 127, no. 527: 882–919.

Miller, Henry, and Ciara Stewart. 2018. "How 17,000 Petitions Helped Deliver Votes for Women." *The Conversation*, February 5. https://theconversation.com/how-17-000-petitions-helped-deliver-votes-for-women-91093.

Mische, Ann. 2003. "Cross-Talk in Movements: Reconceiving the Culture-Network Link." In *Social Movements and Networks: Relational Approaches to Collective Action*, edited by Mario Diani, and Doug McAdam, 258–280. Oxford: Oxford University Press.

Mises, Ludwig von. [1920] 1988. *Socialism: An Economic and Sociological Analysis*. Liberty Fund Edition. Indianapolis: Liberty Fund.

Mises, Ludwig von. [1927] 2005. *Liberalism: The Classical Tradition*. Liberty Fund Edition. Indianapolis: Liberty Fund.

Mises, Ludwig von [1949] 2007. *Human Action: A Treatise on Economics*. Liberty Fund Edition. Indianapolis: Liberty Fund.

Molotsky, Irvin. 1987. "U.S. Approves Drug to Prolong Lives of AIDS Patients." *New York Times*, March 21. https://www.nytimes.com/1987/03/21/us/us-approves-drug-to-prolong-lives-of-aids-patients.html.

Monaghan, Jake. 2017. "The Special Moral Obligations of Law Enforcement." *Journal of Political Philosophy* 25, no. 2: 218–237.

Montesquieu, Charles de Secondat. [1748] 2008. *The Spirit of the Laws*. Cambridge Texts in the History of Political Thought, edited by Anne M. Cohler, Basia C. Miller, and Harold S. Stone. Cambridge, UK: Cambridge University Press.

Moraro, Piero. 2019. *Civil Disobedience: A Philosophical Overview*. Lanham: Rowman & Littlefield.

Morley, John. 1914. *The Life of Richard Cobden*. Fourteenth Edition. London: Unwin.

Morrow, Elizabeth A., and John Meadowcroft. 2019. "The Rise and Fall of the English Defence League: Self-Governance, Marginal Members and the Far-Right." *Political Studies* 67, no. 3: 539–556.

Morris, Aldon. 1981. "Black Southern Student Sit-in movement: An Analysis of Internal Organization." *American Sociological Review* 26, no. 6: 744–767.

Morris, Aldon D. 1984. *The Origins of the Civil Rights Movement: Black Communities Organizing for Change*. New York: Free Press.

Morris, Aldon. 2019. "Social Movement Theory: Lessons from the Sociology of W. E. B. Du Bois." *Mobilization: An International Quarterly* 24, no. 2: 125–136.

Morris, Aldon D., and Suzanne Staggenborg. 2004. "Leadership in Social Movements." In *The Blackwell Companion to Social Movements*, edited by David A. Snow, Sarah A. Soule, and Hanspeter Kriesi, 171–196. Malden: Blackwell Publishing.

Mottl, Tahi L. 1980. "The Analysis of Countermovements." *Social Problems* 27, no. 5: 620–635.

Mouffe, Chantal. 2005. *On The Political*. New York: Routledge.

Muldoon, Ryan. 2016. *Social Contract Theory for a Diverse World: Beyond Tolerance*. New York: Routledge.

Muller, Edward N., and Karl-Dieter Opp. 1986. "Rational Choice and Rebellious Collective Action." *American Political Science Review* 80, no. 2: 471–488.

Müller, Julian F. 2019. *Political Pluralism, Disagreement and Justice: The Case for Polycentric Democracy*. New York: Routledge.

Mullins, Daniel R., and Bruce A. Wallin. 2004. "Tax and Expenditure Limitations: Introduction and Overview." *Public Budgeting & Finance* 24, no. 4: 2–15.

Munger, Michael. 2011. "Euvoluntary or Not, Exchange is Just." *Social Philosophy and Policy* 28, no. 2: 192–211.

Munger, Michael C., and Mario Villarreal-Diaz. 2019. "The Road to Crony Capitalism." *Independent Review* 23, no. 5: 331–344.

Muukkonen, Martti. 2008. "Continuing Validity of the Collective Behavior Approach." *Sociology Compass* 2, no. 5: 1553–1564.

Myers, John. 2017. *Yes In My Back Yard: How To End The Housing Crisis, Boost The Economy And Win More Votes*. London: Adam Smith Institute.

Nell, Guinevere Liberty. 2016. *The Driving Force of the Collective: Post-Austrian Theory in Response to Israel Kirzner*. New York: Palgrave Macmillan.

Ness, Immanuel. 2004. *Encyclopedia of American Social Movements*. New York: Routledge.

Nicholls, Walter J. 2007. "The Geographies of Social Movements." *Geography Compass* 1, no. 3: 607–622.

Nicoara, Olga. 2018. "Cultural Leadership and Entrepreneurship as Antecedents of Estonia's Singing Revolution and Post-Communist Success." *Baltic Journal of European Studies* 8, no. 2: 65–91.

Nielsen, Kristian Roed, and Julia Katharina Binder. 2020. "I Am What I Pledge: The Importance of Value Alignment for Mobilizing Backers in Reward-Based Crowdfunding." *Entrepreneurship Theory and Practice*. https://doi.org/10.1177/1042258720929888.

Nimtz, August H. 2016. "Violence and/or Nonviolence in the Success of the Civil Rights Movement: The Malcolm X-Martin Luther King, Jr. Nexus." *New Political Science* 38, no. 1: 1–22.

Novak, Mikayla. 2015. "Gender Identity and Libertarianism." Centre for a Stateless Society. Working Paper. https://c4ss.org/content/38269.

Novak, Mikayla. 2016. "Deirdre McCloskey, Kirznerian Growth and The Role of Social Networks: Comment." *Economic Affairs* 36, no. 2: 217–220.

Novak, Mikayla. 2018a. "Civil Society as a Complex Adaptive Phenomenon." *Cosmos+Taxis* 5, no. 3–4: 3–13.

Novak, Mikayla. 2018b. *Inequality: An Entangled Political Economy Perspective*. Cham, Switzerland: Palgrave Macmillan.

Novak, Mikayla. 2018c. "Review of Ben Cobley's *The Tribe: The Liberal-Left and the System of Diversity*." *Cosmos+Taxis* 6, no. 1/2: 88–96.

Novak, Mikayla. 2020. "Social Innovation and Austrian Economics: Exploring the Gains from Intellectual Trade." *Review of Austrian Economics* 34, no. 1: 129–147.

Nozick, Robert. 1974. *Anarchy, State, and Utopia*. New York: Basic Books.

Nussbaum, Martha. 2006. *Frontiers of Justice: Disability, Nationality, Species Membership*. Cambridge, MA: Belknap Press of Harvard University Press.

Oberschall, Anthony. 1973. *Social Conflict and Social Movements*. Englewood Cliffs: Prentice-Hall.

O'Brien, Patrick K., and Roland Quinault. 1993. *The Industrial Revolution and British Society*. Cambridge, UK: Cambridge University Press.

Okun, Gabrielle. 2020. "Print-Capitalism Created Modern Europe." Cato Institute. *libertarianism.org*, April 8. https://www.libertarianism.org/columns/print-capitalism-created-modern-europe.

Oliver, Pamela E. 1993. "Formal Models of Collective Action." *Annual Review of Sociology* 19: 271–300.

Oliver, Pamela E. 2015. "Rational Action." In *The Oxford Handbook of Social Movements*, edited by Donatella della Porta, and Mario Diani, 246–263. Oxford: Oxford University Press.

Olson, Mancur. 1965. *The Logic of Collective Action: Public Goods and the Theory of Groups*. Cambridge: Harvard University Press.

Olson, Mancur. 1993. "Dictatorship, Democracy, and Development." *American Political Science Review* 87, no. 3: 567–576.

Olzak, Susan, and Emily Ryo. 2007. "Organizational Diversity, Vitality and Outcomes in the Civil Rights Movement." *Social Forces* 85, no. 4: 1561–1591.

O'Neill, Daniel I. 2007. *The Burke-Wollstonecraft Debate: Savagery, Civilization, and Democracy*. University Park: Pennsylvania State University Press.

O'Neill, William L. 1969. *The Woman Movement: Feminism in the United States and England*. London: George Allen & Unwin.

Opp, Karl-Dieter. 1998. "Explaining Revolutions from Below: East Germany in 1989." *Independent Review* 3, no. 1: 91–102.

Opp, Karl-Dieter. 2009. *Theories of Political Protest and Social Movements: A Multidisciplinary Introduction, Critique, and Synthesis*. New York: Routledge.

Osterweil, Vicky. 2020. *In Defense of Looting: A Riotous History of Uncivil Action*. New York: Bold Type Books.

Ostrom, Elinor. 1967. "Strategy and the Structure of Interdependent Decision-Making Mechanisms." Indiana University, Workshop in Political Theory and Policy Analysis Paper No. 67-3. http://dlc.dlib.indiana.edu/dlc/bitstream/handle/10535/3643/eostr004.pdf?sequence=1&isAllowed=y.

Ostrom, Elinor. 1990. *Governing the Commons: The Evolution of Institutions for Collective Action*. Cambridge, UK: Cambridge University Press.

Ostrom, Elinor. 1993. "Covenating, Co-Producing, and the Good Society." *The Newsletter of PEGS (Committee on the Political Economy of the Good Society)* 3, no. 2: 7–9.

Ostrom, Elinor. 2000. "Collective Action and the Evolution of Social Norms." *Journal of Economic Perspectives* 14, no. 3: 137–158.

Ostrom, Elinor. 2005. *Understanding Institutional Diversity*. Princeton: Princeton University Press.

Ostrom, Elinor. 2010. "Beyond Markets and States: Polycentric Governance of Complex Economic Systems." *American Economic Review* 100, no. 3: 641–672.

Ostrom, Vincent. 1980. "Artisanship and Artifact." *Public Administration Review* 40, no. 4: 309–317.

Ostrom, Vincent. 1993. "Epistemic Choice and Public Choice." *Public Choice* 77, no. 1: 163–176.

Ostrom, Vincent. 1997. *The Meaning of Democracy and The Vulnerability of Democracies: A Response to Tocqueville's Challenge*. Ann Arbor: University of Michigan Press.

Ostrom, Vincent, Charles M. Tiebout, and Robert Warren. 1961. "The Organization of Government in Metropolitan Areas: A Theoretical Inquiry." *American Political Science Review* 55, no. 4: 831–842.

Pager, Devah. 2016. "Are Firms That Discriminate More Likely to Go Out of Business?" *Sociological Science* 3, no. 36: 849–859.

Palmer, Tom G. 1991. "The Hermeneutical View of Freedom: Implications of Gademerian Understanding for Economic Policy." In *Economics and Hermeneutics*, edited by Don Lavoie, 299–318. New York: Routledge.

Pankhurst, Emmeline. [1914] 1971. *My Own Story*. New York: Kraus.

Passy, Frédéric [1909] 1972. *Pour la paix: Notes et documents*. New York: Garland.

Peart, Sandra J., and David M. Levy. 2005. *The "Vanity of The Philosopher": From Equality to Hierarchy in Post-Classical Economics*. Ann Arbor: University of Michigan Press.

Peart, Sandra J. and David M. Levy. 2009. "Adam Smith and Place of Faction." In *The Elgar Companion to Adam Smith*, edited by Jeffrey T. Young, 335–345. Cheltenham: Edward Elgar.

Pennington, Mark. 2003. "Hayekian Political Economy and the Limits of Deliberative Democracy." *Political Studies* 51, no. 4: 722–739.

Pennington, Mark. 2011. *Robust Political Economy: Classical Liberalism and the Future of Public Policy*. Cheltenham: Edward Elgar.

Pettit, Philip. 2001. *A Theory of Freedom: From the Psychology to the Politics of Agency*. New York: Oxford University Press.

Pickering, Paul A., and Alex Tyrell. 2000. *The People's Bread: A History of the Anti-Corn Law League*. London: Leicester University Press.

Pierskalla, Jan Henryk. 2010. "Protest, Deterrence, and Escalation: The Strategic Calculus of Government Repression." *Journal of Conflict Resolution* 54, no. 1: 117–145.

Pipes, Sally C. 2015. *The Way Out of Obamacare*. New York: Encounter Books.

Piven, Frances Fox, and Richard A. Cloward. 1979. *Poor People's Movements: Why They Succeed, How They Fail*. New York: Vintage Books.

Peoples, Clayton D. 2019. "Classical and Contemporary Conventional Theories of Social Movements." In *The Palgrave Handbook of Social Movements, Revolution, and Social Transformation*, edited by Berch Berberoglu, 17–34. Cham, Switzerland: Palgrave Macmillan.

Plauche, Geoffrey Allan. 2009. "Aristotelian Liberalism: An Inquiry into the Foundations of a Free and Flourishing Society." PhD diss., Louisiana State University.

Podemska-Mikluch, Marta, and Richard E. Wagner. 2013. "Dyads, Triads, and the Theory of Exchange: Between Liberty and Coercion." *Review of Austrian Economics* 26, no. 2: 171–182.

Politi, Daniel. 2020. "Activists Create Public Online Spreadsheet of Police Violence Videos." *Slate*, June 6. https://slate.com/news-and-politics/2020/06/george-floyd-public-spreadsheet-police-violence-videos.html.

Polletta, Francesca. 1998. "Contending Stories: Narrative in Social Movements." *Qualitative Sociology* 21, no. 4: 419–446.

Polletta, Francesca. 2002. *Freedom Is An Endless Meeting: Democracy in American Social Movements*. Chicago: University of Chicago Press.

Polletta, Francesca and Chen, Pang Ching Bobby. 2012. "Narrative and Social Movements." In *The Oxford Handbook of Cultural Sociology*, edited by Jeffrey C. Alexander, Ron Jacobs, and Philip Smith, 487–506. New York: Oxford University Press.

Polletta, Francecsa, and James M. Jasper. 2001. "Collective Identity and Social Movements." *Annual Review of Sociology* 27: 283–305.

Popović, Srdja, and Matthew Miller. 2015. *Blueprint for Revolution: How to Use Rice Pudding, Lego Men, and other Non-Violent Techniques to Galvanize Communities, Overthrow Dictators, or Simply Change the World*. London: Scribe.

Popović, Srdja, and Slobodan Djinovic. 2018. "How Can Social Movements Help Defend Democracy?" *Contention* 6, no. 2: 65–74.

Popper, Karl. 1944. "The Poverty of Historicism, I." *Economica* 11, no. 42: 86–103.

Powell, Benjamin. 2002. "Private Property Rights, Economic Freedom, and Well-Being." American Institute for Economic Research. *Economic Education Bulletin* 42, no. 11: 1–7.

Powell, Benjamin. 2014. *Out of Poverty: Sweatshops in the Global Economy.* Cambridge, UK: Cambridge University Press.

Powell, Jim. 2000. *The Triumph of Liberty: A 2,000-Year History, Told Through the Lives of Freedom's Greatest Champions.* New York: Free Press.

Pozen, David E. 2008. "We Are All Entrepreneurs Now." *Wake Forest Law Review* 43: 283–340.

Prentice, Archibald. [1853] 1968. *History of the Anti-Corn-Law League.* Two volumes. London: Cass.

Presley, Sharon. 2016. "Black Women Abolitionists and the Fight for Freedom in the 19th Century." Cato Institute. *libertarianism.org*, February 10. https://www.libertarianism.org/columns/black-women-abolitionists-fight-freedom-19th-century.

Price, Charles, Donald Nonini, and Erich Fox Tree. 2008. "Grounded Utopian Movements: Subjects of Neglect." *Anthropological Quarterly* 81, no. 1: 127–159.

Purbrick, Martin. 2019. "A Report of the 2019 Hong Kong Protests." *Asian Affairs* 50, no. 4: 465–487.

Purvis, June. 2019. "Did Militancy Help or Hinder the Granting of Women's Suffrage in Britain?" *Women's History Review* 28, no. 7: 1200–1234.

Purvis, June, and Sandra Stanley Holton. 1998. *Votes for Women.* London: Routledge.

Putnam, Robert D. 2000. *Bowling Alone: The Collapse and Revival of American Community.* New York: Simon & Schuster.

Quarantelli, E. L., and Russell R. Dynes. 1970. "Property Norms and Looting: Their Patterns in Community Crises." *Phylon* 31, no. 2: 168–182.

Radzik, Linda. 2017. "Boycotts and the Social Enforcement of Justice." *Social Philosophy and Policy* 34, no. 1: 102–122.

Rajagopal, Balakrishnan. 2003. *International Law from Below: Development, Social Movements, and Third World Resistance.* Cambridge, UK: Cambridge University Press.

Ramsay, David. [1789] 1990. *History of the American Revolution.* Two volumes. Liberty Fund Edition. Indianapolis: Liberty Fund.

Rao, Hayagreeva, and Simona Giorgi. 2006. "Code Breaking: How Entrepreneurs Exploit Cultural Logics to Generate Institutional Change." *Research in Organizational Behavior* 27: 269–304.

Ratnapala, Suri. 2013. *Jurisprudence.* Fourth Edition. Cambridge, UK: Cambridge University Press.

Reilly, Philip R. 1991. *The Surgical Solution: A History of Involuntary Sterilization in the United States.* Baltimore: John Hopkins University Press.

Rhodes, Jane. 2007. *Framing the Black Panthers: The Spectacular Rise of a Black Power Icon.* New York: New Press.

Roback, Jennifer. 1986. "The Political Economy of Segregation: The Case of Segregated Streetcars." *Journal of Economic History* 46, no. 4: 893–917.

Roberts, Dan. 2018. "Tea Party: A Social Movement Analysis." *Medium*, October 22. https://medium.com/@dan_roberts96/essay-tea-party-a-social-movement-analysis -2312ea32fcbf.

Roggeband, Conny, and Bert Klandermans. 2017. *Handbook of Social Movements Across Disciplines*, Second Edition. Cham, Switzerland: Springer.

Rojas, Fabio. 2006. "Social Movement Tactics, Organizational Change and the Spread of African-American Studies." *Social Forces* 84 no. 4: 2147–2166.

Rojas, Fabio. 2007. *From Black Power to Black Studies: How a Radical Social Movement Became an Academic Discipline*. Baltimore: John Hopkins University Press.

Rojas, Fabio, and Brayden G. King. 2019. "How Social Movements Interact with Organizations and Fields: Protest, Institutions, and Beyond." In *The Wiley Blackwell Companion to Social Movements*, Second Edition, edited by David A. Snow, Sarah A. Soule, Hanspeter Kriesi, and Holly J. McCammon, 203–219. Hoboken: John Wiley & Sons.

Rolley, Katrina. 1990. "Fashion, Femininity and the Fight for the Vote." *Art History* 13, no. 1: 47–71.

Rosen, Andrew. 1974. *Rise Up, Women! The Militant Campaign of the Women's Social and Political Union 1903-1914*. London: Routledge.

Rowland, Barbara M. 1988. "Beyond Hayek's Pessimism: Reason, Tradition and Bounded Constructivist Rationalism." *British Journal of Political Science* 18, no. 2: 221–241.

Rubin, Paul H. 2014. "Emporiophobia (Fear of Markets): Cooperation or Competition?" *Southern Economic Journal* 80, no. 4: 875–889.

Rubinson, Paul. 2009. "Charismatic Leadership and Revolution." In *The International Encyclopedia of Revolution and Protest: 1500 to the Present*, edited by Immanuel Ness, 1–10. Malden: Wiley-Blackwell.

Rubio-Marín, Ruth. 2014. "The Achievement of Female Suffrage in Europe: On Women's Citizenship." *International Journal of Constitutional Law* 12, no. 1: 4–34.

Rucht, Dieter. 2004. "The Quadruple 'A': Media Strategies of Protest Movements since the 1960s." In *Cyberprotest: New Media, Citizens and Social Movements*, edited by Wim Van De Donk, Brian D. Loader, Paul G. Nixon, and Dieter Rucht, 25–48. London: Routledge.

Rucht, Dieter. 2010. "Social Movements." In *International Encyclopedia of Civil Society*, edited by Helmut K. Anheier, Stefan Toepler, and Regina List, 1441–1445. New York: Springer.

Russell, Thaddeus. 2010. *A Renegade History of the United States*. New York: Free Press.

Rüstow, Alexander. 1980. *Freedom and Domination: A Historical Critique of Civilization*. Princeton: Princeton University Press.

Ryan, Charlotte. 1991. *Prime Time Activism: Media Strategies for Grassroots Organizing*. Boston: South End Press.

Sabetti, Filippo. 2014. "Artisans of the Common Life: Building a Public Science of Civics." In *Civic Studies: Approaches to the Emerging Field*, edited by Peter

Levine, and Karol Edward Sohan, 23–32. Washington, DC: American Association of Colleges & Universities.

Sabl, Andrew. 2015. "Review of *Liberal Realism: A Realist Theory of Liberal Politics* by Matt Sleat." *Perspectives on Politics* 13, no. 4: 1141–1143.

Sabl, Andrew. 2017. "Realist Liberalism: An Agenda." *Critical Review of International Social and Political Philosophy* 20, no. 3: 366–384.

Salisbury, Robert H. 1969. "An Exchange Theory of Interest Groups." *Midwest Journal of Political Science* 13, no. 1: 1–32.

Salmon, Pierre. 1987. "The Logic of Pressure Groups and the Structure of the Public Sector." *European Journal of Political Economy* 3, no. 1–2: 55–86.

Salper, Roberta. 2008. "U.S. Government Surveillance and the Women's Liberation Movement, 1968-1973: A Case Study." *Feminist Studies* 34, no. 3: 431–455.

Salsman, Richard M. 2017. *The Political Economy of Public Debt: Three Centuries of Theory and Evidence*. Cheltenham: Edward Elgar.

Sandefur, Timothy. 2018. *Frederick Douglass: Self-Made Man*. Washington, DC: Cato Institute.

Sandell, Rickard, and Charlotta Stern. 1998. "Group Size and the Logic of Collective Action: A Network Analysis of a Swedish Temperance Movement 1896-1937." *Rationality and Society* 10, no. 3: 327–345.

Sarat, Austin, and Stuart A. Sheingold. 2006. *Cause Lawyers and Social Movements*. Stanford: Stanford University Press.

Saunders, Clare. 2007. "Using Social Network Analysis to Explore Social Movements: A Relational Approach." *Social Movement Studies* 6, no. 3: 227–243.

Sawer, Marian, and Sarah Maddison. 2018. "Understanding the Evolution of Social Movements." https://politicsir.cass.anu.edu.au/research/projects/gender-research/mapping-australian-womens-movement/understanding-evolution-social-movements.

Schoeck, Helmut. [1966] 1987. *Envy: A Theory of Social Behavior*. Indianapolis: Liberty Fund.

Schumpeter, Joseph Allois. [1918] 1954. "The Crisis of the Tax State." In *International Economic Papers*, edited by Alan T. Peacock, Wolfgang F. Stolper, Ralph Turvey, and Elizabeth Henderson, 5–38. London: Macmillan.

Schumpeter, Joseph Allois. [1934] 1961. *The Theory of Economic Development: An Inquiry into Profits, Capital, Credit, Interest, and the Business Cycle*, translated by Redvers Opie. Cambridge: Harvard University Press.

Schumpeter, Joseph Allois [1928] 2003. "Entrepreneur." Translated by Markus C. Becker and Thorbjørn Knudsen. *Advances in Austrian Economics* 6: 235–265.

Sciabarra, Chris Matthew. 2000. *Total Freedom: Toward a Dialectical Libertarianism*. University Park: Pennsylvania State University Press.

Scott, James C. 1990. *Domination and the Arts of Resistance*. New Haven: Yale University Press.

Scott, James C. 1998. *Seeing Like A State: How Certain Schemes to Improve the Human Condition Have Failed*. New Haven: Yale University Press.

Scott, John. 2014. *Oxford Dictionary of Sociology*. Oxford: Oxford University Press.

Scott, John C. 2018. *Lobbying and Society: A Political Sociology of Interest Groups.* Cambridge, UK: Polity Press.

Selby, Gary S. 2008. *Martin Luther King and the Rhetoric of Freedom: The Exodus Narrative in America's Struggle for Civil Rights.* Waco: Baylor University Press.

Sen, Amartya. 1981. *Poverty and Famines: An Essay on Entitlement and Deprivation.* Oxford: Oxford University Press.

Sen, Amartya. 2009. *The Idea of Justice.* Cambridge: Belknap Press of Harvard University Press.

Sen, Amartya. 2011. "On James Buchanan." *Journal of Economic Behavior & Organization* 80, no. 2: 367–369.

Sen, Maya, and Omar Wasow. 2016. "Race as a Bundle of Sticks: Designs that Estimate Effects of Seemingly Immutable Characteristics." *Annual Review of Political Science* 19: 499–522.

Serhan, Yasmeen. 2019. "The Common Element Uniting Worldwide pProtests." *The Atlantic*, November 19. https://www.theatlantic.com/international/archive/2019/11/leaderless-protests-around-world/602194.

Shaffer, Butler D. 1975. "Violence as a Product of Imposed Order." *University of Miami Law Review* 29: 732–763.

Shantz, Jeff. 2020. *Organizing Anarchy: Anarchism in Action.* Boston, MA: Brill.

Sharp, Gene. 1973. *The Politics of Nonviolent Action. Part 2: The Methods of Nonviolent Action.* Boston: Porter Sargent.

Sharp, Gene. 1980. *Social Power and Political Freedom.* Boston: Sargent Publishers.

Sharp, Gene. 2010. *From Dictatorship to Democracy: A Conceptual Framework for Liberation.* Fourth Edition. East Boston: Albert Einstein Institution.

Shey, Thomas H. 1977. "Why Communes Fail: A Comparative Analysis of the Viability of Danish and American Communes." *Journal of Marriage and Family* 39, no. 3: 605–613.

Shils, Edward. 1991. "The Virtue of Civil Society." *Government and Opposition* 26, no. 1: 3–20.

Shklar, Judith. 1991. *American Citizenship: The Quest for Inclusion.* Cambridge, MA: Harvard University Press.

Shockley, Gordon E., Peter M. Frank, and Roger R. Stough. 2008. *Non-Market Entrepreneurship: Interdisciplinary Approaches.* Cheltenham: Edward Elgar.

Shughart, William F., II. 2007. "Public Choice." Liberty Fund. *Concise Encyclopedia of Economics.* https://www.econlib.org/library/Enc/PublicChoice.html.

Silver, Morris. 1974. "Political Revolution and Repression: An Economic Approach." *Public Choice* 17, no. 1: 63–71.

Silver, Nate. 2009. "Tea Party Nonpartisan Attendance Estimates: Now 300,000+." *FiveThirtyEight*, April 16. https://web.archive.org/web/20100414104830/https://www.fivethirtyeight.com/2009/04/tea-party-nonpartisan-attendance.html.

Singer, Peter. 2011. *The Expanding Circle: Ethics, Evolution, and Moral Progress.* Princeton: Princeton University Press.

Skocpol, Theda, and Vanessa Williamson. 2012. *The Tea Party and the Remaking of American Conservatism.* New York: Oxford University Press.

Skrentny, John D. 2002. *The Minority Rights Revolution*. Cambridge: Belknap Press of Harvard University Press.

Sleat, Matt (2013). *Liberal Realism: A Realist Theory of Liberal Politics*. Manchester: Manchester University Press.

Smelser, Neil J. 1962. *Theory of Collective Behavior*. London: Routledge and Kegan Paul.

Smith, Adam. [1776] 1999. *An Inquiry into the Nature and Causes of The Wealth of Nations*, edited by Andrew Skinner. Penguin Classics Edition. London: Penguin.

Smith, Adam [1759] 2002. *The Theory of Moral Sentiments*. Cambridge Texts in the History of Philosophy, edited by Knud Haakonssen. Cambridge, UK: Cambridge University Press.

Smith, George H. 2013. *The System of Liberty: Themes in the History of Classical Liberalism*. Cambridge, UK: Cambridge University Press.

Smith, George H. 2017. *The American Revolution and the Declaration of Independence*. Washington, DC: Cato Institute.

Smith, Harold L. 2010. *The British Women's Suffrage Campaign, 1866-1928*. Second Edition. London: Routledge.

Smith, Jackie, John D. McCarthy, Clark McPhail, and Boguslaw Augustyn. 2001. "From Protest to Agenda Building: Description Bias in Media Coverage of Protest Events in Washington, D. C." *Social Forces* 79, no. 4: 1397–1423.

Smith, Laura G. E., Andrew G. Livingstone, and Emma F. Thomas. 2019. "Advancing the Social Psychology of Rapid Societal Change." *British Journal of Social Psychology* 58, no. 1: 33–44.

Smithey, Lee A. 2009. "Social Movement Strategy, Tactics, and Collective Identity." *Sociology Compass* 3, no. 4: 658–671.

Snow, David A. and Robert D. Benford. 1988. "Ideology, Frame Resonance, and Participant Mobilization." *International Social Movement Research* 1: 197–218.

Snow, David A., and Robert D. Benford. 1992. "Master Frames and Cycles of Protest." In *Frontiers in Social Movement Theory*, edited by Aldon D. Morris, and Carol McClurg Mueller, 133–155. New Haven: Yale University Press.

Snow, David A., E. Burke Rochford, Jr., Steven K. Worden, and Robert D. Benford. 1986. "Frame Alignment Processes, Micromobilization, and Movement Participation." *American Sociological Review* 51, no. 4: 464–481.

Snow, David A., Louis A. Zurcher, and Sheldon Ekland-Olson. 1980. "Social Networks and Social Movements: A Microstructural Approach to Differential Recruitment." *American Sociological Review* 45, no. 5: 787–801.

Snow, Nathaneal. 2020. "The Political Economy of the Informal Social Group, and the Origins of Legitimacy." Paper presented at 2020 Research Conference on Voluntary Governance. Arizona State University, Center for the Study of Economic Liberty. 6 November.

Somers, Margaret R. 1994. "The Narrative Constitution of Identity: A Relational and Network Approach." *Theory and Society* 23, no. 5: 605–649.

Soule, Sarah A. 2009. *Contention and Corporate Social Responsibility*. New York: Cambridge University Press.

Soule, Sarah A. 2012. "Social Movements and Markets, Industries, and Firms." *Organization Studies* 33, no. 2: 1715–1733.

Soule, Sarah A. 2018. "Social Movements and Their Impact on Business and Management." *Oxford Research Encyclopedias: Business and Management.* https://doi.org/10.1093/acrefore/9780190224851.013.143.

Soule, Sarah A., and Brayden G. King. 2015. "Markets, Business, and Social Movements." In *The Oxford Handbook of Social Movements*, edited by Donatella della Porta and Mario Diani, 696–708. Oxford: Oxford University Press.

Soule, Sarah A., and Conny Roggeband. 2018. "Diffusion Processes Within and Across Movements." In *The Wiley Blackwell Companion to Social Movements*, edited by David A. Snow, Sarah A. Soule, Hanspeter Kriesi, and Holly J. McCammon, 236–251. Newark: John Wiley & Sons.

Spade, Dean. 2020a. *Mutual Aid: Building Solidarity During This Crisis (and the Next).* New York: Verso Books.

Spade, Dean. 2020b. "Solidarity Not Charity: Mutual Aid for Mobilization and Survival." *Social Text* 38, no. 1: 131–151.

Staggenborg, Suzanne. 2002. "The "Meso" in Social Movement Research." In *Social Movements: Identity, Culture and the State*, edited by David S. Meyer, Nancy Whittier, and Belinda Robnett, 124–139. New York: Oxford University Press.

Staggenborg, Suzanne. 2013. "Entrepreneurs, Movement." In *The Wiley-Blackwell Encyclopedia of Social and Political Movements*, edited by David A. Snow, Donatella della Porta, Bert Klandermans, and Doug McAdam, 1–3. Malden: John Wiley & Sons.

Stark, Jill. 2015. "'Pink Washing': Marketing Stunt or Corporate Revolution?" *Sydney Morning Herald*, June 6. https://www.smh.com.au/national/pink-washing-marketing-stunt-or-corporate-revolution-20150605-ghhthh.html.

Steedly, Homer R., and John W. Foley. 1979. "The Success of Protest Groups: Multivariate Analyses." *Social Science Research* 8, no. 1: 1–15.

Steinberg, Robin, Lillian Kalish, and Ezra Ritchin. 2018. "Freedom Should Be Free: A Brief History of Bail Funds in the United States." *UCLA Criminal Justice Law Review* 2, no. 1: 79–95.

Stenner, Karen. 2005. *The Authoritarian Dynamic.* Cambridge, UK: Cambridge University Press.

Stern, Charlotta. 1999. "The Evolution of Social-Movement Organizations: Niche Competition in Social Space." *European Sociological Review* 15, no. 1: 91–105.

Stierl, Maurice. 2016. "A Sea of Struggle—Activist Border Interventions in the Mediterranean Sea." *Citizenship Studies* 20, no. 5: 561–578.

Stigler, George J. 1974. "Free Riders and Collective Action: An Appendix to Theories of Economic Regulation." *Bell Journal of Economics and Management Science* 5, no. 2: 359–365.

Stockemer, Daniel. 2012. "When do People Protest?—Using a Game Theoretic Framework to Shed Light on the Relationship Between Repression and Protest in Hybrid and Autocratic Regimes." In *Social Sciences and Cultural Studies: Issues of Language, Public Opinion, Education and Welfare*, edited by Ascunción López-Verala, 205–218. Rijeka, Croatia: InTech.

Storr, Virgil Henry. 2008. "The Market as a Social Space: On the Meaningful Extraeconomic Conversations That Can Occur in Markets." *Review of Austrian Economics* 21, no. 2: 135–150.

Storr, Virgil Henry. 2013. *Understanding the Culture of Markets*. New York: Routledge.

Storr, Virgil Henry, Stefanie Haeffele-Balch, and Laura E. Grube. 2015. *Community Revival in the Wake of Disaster: Lessons in Local Entrepreneurship*. New York: Palgrave Macmillan.

Stringham, Edward Peter. 2015. *Private Governance: Creating Order in Economic and Social Life*. Oxford: Oxford University Press.

Sunstein, Cass R. 1997. *Free Markets and Social Justice*. New York: Oxford University Press.

Sunstein, Cass R. 2008. "Neither Hayek nor Habermas." *Public Choice* 134, no. 1: 87–95.

Surprenant, Chris W., and Jason Brennan. 2020. *Injustice for All: How Financial Incentives Corrupted and Can Fix the US Criminal Justice System*. New York: Routledge.

Sutherland, Neil, Christopher Land, and Steffen Böhm. 2014. "Anti-leaders(hip) in Social Movement Organizations: The Case of Autonomous Grassroots Groups." *Organization* 21, no. 6: 759–781.

Sztompka, Piotr. 1993. *The Sociology of Social Change*. Oxford: Blackwell.

Tabarrok, Alex. 2019. "Anarchy is Worse than Socialism." *Marginal Revolution*, May 19. https://marginalrevolution.com/marginalrevolution/2019/05/anarchy-is-worse-than-socialism.html.

Tarko, Vlad. 2017. *Elinor Ostrom: An Intellectual Biography*. New York: Rowman & Littlefield.

Tarko, Vlad, and Kyle O'Donnell. 2019. "Escape from Europe: A Calculus of Consent Model of the Origins of Liberal Institutions in the North American Colonies." *Constitutional Political Economy* 30, no. 1: 70–95.

Tarrow, Sidney. 1998. *Power in Movement: Social Movements, Collective Action, and Politics*. Second Edition. Cambridge, UK: Cambridge University Press.

Tarrow, Sidney. 2012. "Dynamics of Diffusion: Mechanisms, Institutions, and Scale Shift." In *The Diffusion of Social Movements: Actors, Mechanisms, and Political Effects*, edited by Rebecca Kollins Givan, Kenneth M. Roberts, and Sarah A. Soule, 204–220. New York: Oxford University Press.

Tarrow, Sidney. 2015. "Contentious Politics." In *The Oxford Handbook of Social Movements*, edited by Donatella della Porta and Mario Diani, 86–107. Oxford: Oxford University Press.

Tate, Chuck, and Diego Audette. 2001. "Theory and Research on 'Race' as a Natural Kind Variable in Psychology." *Theory and Psychology* 11, no. 4: 495–520.

Taylor, Charles. [1979] 1985. "What's Wrong with Negative Liberty." In *Philosophy and the Human Sciences*, edited by Charles Taylor, 211–229. Cambridge, UK: Cambridge University Press.

Taylor, Dylan. 2017. *Social Movements and Democracy in the 21st Century*. Cham, Switzerland: Palgrave Macmillan.

Taylor, Verta, and Nella Van Dyke. 2008. "'Get up, Stand up': Tactical Repertoires of Social Movements." In *The Blackwell Companion to Social Movements*, edited by David A. Snow, Sarah A. Soule, and Hanspeter Kriesi, 262–293. Chichester: Wiley.

Tharoor, Shashi. 2017. *Inglorious Empire: What the British Did to India*. London: Penguin.

Thierer, Adam. 2020. *Evasive Entrepreneurs and the Future of Governance: How Innovation Improves Economics and Governments*. Washington, DC: Cato Institute.

Thoreau, David Henry. [1849] 2014. *Civil Disobedience*. Salt Lake City: Libertas Institute.

Tickner, Lisa. 1987. *The Spectacle of Women: Imagery of the Suffrage Campaign 1907-14*. Chicago: University of Chicago Press.

Tilly, Charles. 1978. *From Mobilization to Revolution*. Reading: Addison-Wesley.

Tilly, Charles. 1979. "Repertoires of Contention in America and Britain, 1750-1830." In *The Dynamics of Social Movements: Resource Mobilization, Social Control, and Tactics*, edited by Mayer N. Zald and John D. McCarthy, 126–155. Cambridge, MA: Winthrop.

Tilly, Charles. 1981. "Britain Creates the Social Movement." University of Michigan. Center for Research on Social Organization Working Paper No. 232. https://deepblue.lib.umich.edu/bitstream/handle/2027.42/51006/232.pdf.

Tilly, Charles. 1994. "Social Movements as Historically Specific Clusters of Political Performances." *Berkeley Journal of Sociology* 38: 1–30.

Tilly, Charles. 1998. "Social Movements and (All Sorts of) Other Political Interactions—Local, National, and International – Including Identities." *Theory and Society* 27, no. 4: 453–480.

Tilly, Charles. 2006. *Regimes and Repertoires*. Chicago: University of Chicago Press.

Tilly, Charles. 2008. *Contentious Performances*. New York: Cambridge University Press.

Tilly, Charles, and Sidney Tarrow. 2006. *Contentious Politics*. Boulder: Paradigm Press.

Tilly, Charles, and Lesley J. Wood. 2013. *Social Movements, 1768-2012*. Third Edition. Boulder: Paradigm Publishing.

Tindall, D. B., Jeffrey Cormier, and Mario Diani. 2012. "Network Social Capital as an Outcome of Social Movement Mobilization: Using the Position Generator as an Indicator of Social Network Diversity." *Social Networks* 34, no. 4: 387–395.

Ting, Tin-yuet. 2020. "From 'Be Water' to 'Be Fire': Nascent Smart Mob and Networked Protests in Hong Kong." *Social Movement Studies* 19, no. 3: 362–368.

Tiratelli, Matteo. 2018. "Rioting and time: Collective violence in Manchester, Liverpool and Glascow, 1800-1939." PhD diss., University of Manchester.

Tocqueville, Alexis de. [1835] 1998. *Democracy in America*. Wordsworth Classics Edition. Hertfordshire: Wordsworth Editions.

Topak, Özgün E. 2019. "Humanitarian and Human Rights Surveillance: The Challenge to Border Surveillance and Invisibility?" *Surveillance & Society* 17, no. 3/4: 382–404.

Tomaskovic-Devey, Donald, and Dustin Robert Avent-Holt. 2018. *Relational Inequalities: An Organizational Approach*. New York: Oxford University Press.

Touraine, Alain. 1985. "An Introduction to the Study of Social Movements." *Social Research* 52, no. 4: 749–787.

Tresch, Anke, and Manuel Fischer. 2015. "In Search of Political Influence: Outside Lobbying Behaviour and Media Coverage of Social Movements, Interest Groups and Political Parties in six Western European Countries." *International Political Science Review* 36, no. 4: 355–372.

Tuck, Richard. 2008. *Free Riding*. Cambridge: Harvard University Press.

Tufecki, Zeynep. 2017. *Twitter and Tear Gas: The Power and Fragility of Networked Protest*. New Haven: Yale University Press.

Tullock, Gordon. 1967. "The Welfare Costs of Tariffs, Monopolies, and Theft." *Western Economic Journal* 5, no. 3: 224–232.

Tullock, Gordon. 1971. "The Paradox of Revolution." *Public Choice* 11, no. 1: 89–99.

Tullock, Gordon. 1998. *On Voting: A Public Choice Approach*. Cheltenham: Edward Elgar.

Tully, James. 2013. "Two Ways of Realizing Justice and Democracy: Linking Amartya Sen and Elinor Ostrom." *Critical Review of International Social and Political Philosophy* 16, no. 2: 220–232.

Turner, Ralph H. 1981. "Collective Behavior and Resource Mobilization as Approaches to Social Movements: Issues and Continuities." *Research in Social Movements, Conflict and Change* 4: 1–24.

Udehn, Lars. 1993. "Twenty-Five Years with The Logic of Collective Action." *Acta Sociologica* 36, no. 3: 239–261.

Udehn, Lars. 1996. *The Limits of Public Choice: A Sociological Critique of the Economic Theory of Politics*. London: Routledge.

Uhlaner, Carole Jean. 1989. "'Relational Goods' and Participation: Incorporating Sociability into a Theory of Rational Action." *Public Choice* 62, no. 3: 253–285.

Valentine, Gill. 1997. "Making Space: Lesbian Separatist Communities in the United States." In *Contested Countryside Cultures: Otherness, Marginalisation and Rurality*, edited by Paul Cloke, and Jo Little, 109–122. London: Routledge.

Vallier, Kevin. 2021. "Classical Liberals in a Polarized Age: A Warlike Politics Is the Greatest Threat to Liberty." Cato Institute, Cato Unbound, February 12. https://www.cato-unbound.org/2021/02/12/kevin-vallier/classical-liberals-polarized-age-war-politics-greatest-threat-liberty.

Vanberg, Viktor. 1994. "Hayek's Legacy and the Future of Liberal Thought: Rational Liberalism vs. Evolutionary Agnosticism." *Journal des Économistes et des Études Humaines* 5, no. 4: 451–481.

van de Haar, Edwin. 2015. *Degrees of Freedom: Liberal Political Philosophy and Ideology*. London: Taylor and Francis.

Vanhala, Lisa. 2012. "Legal Opportunity Structures and the Paradox of Legal Mobilization by the Environmental Movement in the UK." *Law & Society Review* 46, no. 3: 523–556.

Vann, Burrel Jr. 2018. "Movement-Countermovement Dynamics and Mobilizing the Electorate." *Mobilization: An International Quarterly* 23, no. 3: 285–305.

van Winden, Frans. 1993. "Some Reflections on the Next Twenty-five Years of Public Choice." *Public Choice* 77, no. 1: 213–223.

van Winden, Frans. 2007. "Affective Public Choice." In *Public Choice and the Challenges of Democracy*, edited by José Casas Pedro, and Pedro Schwartz, 45–61. Cheltenham: Edward Elgar.

van Wingerden, Sophia A. 1999. *The Women's Suffrage Movement in Britain, 1866-1928*. Basingstoke: Palgrave Macmillan.

Vaughn, Karen. [1994] 2018. "Can Democratic Society Reform Itself? The Limits of Constructive Change." In *The Market Process: Essays in Contemporary Austrian Economics*, edited by Peter J. Boettke, and David L. Prychitko, 229–243. Arlington: Mercatus Center of George Mason University.

Vessey, David. 2020. "Words as Well as Deeds: The Popular Press and Suffragette Hunger Strikes in Edwardian Britain." *Twentieth Century British History*. https://doi.org/10.1093/tcbh/hwaa031.

Vicari, Stefania. 2010. "Measuring Collective Action Frames: A Linguistic Approach to Frame Analysis." *Poetics* 38, no. 5: 504–525.

Voigt, Stefan. 2020. *Institutional Economics: An Introduction*. Cambridge, UK: Cambridge University Press.

Von Hippel, Eric. 1986. "Lead Users: A Source of Novel Product Concepts." *Management Science* 32, no. 7: 791–805.

Von Hippel, Eric. 2005. *Democratizing Innovation*. Cambridge, MA: MIT Press.

Wagner, Adolph. 1890. *Finanzwissenschaft*. Leipzig, Germany: Puttkammer & Mühlbrecht.

Wagner, Richard E. 1966. "Pressure Groups and Political Entrepreneurs: A Review Article." *Papers on Non-Market Decision Making* 1: 161–170.

Wagner, Richard E. 2005. "Self-governance, Polycentrism, and Federalism: Recurring Themes in Vincent Ostrom's Scholarly Oeuvre." *Journal of Economic Behavior & Organization* 57, no. 2: 173–188.

Wagner, Richard E. 2010. *Mind, Society, and Human Action: Time and Knowledge in a Theory of Social Economy*. London: Routledge.

Wagner, Richard E. 2014. "Entangled Political Economy: A Keynote Address." *Advances in Austrian Economics* 18: 15–36.

Wagner, Richard E. 2015. "The Tax State as a Source of Perpetual Crisis." In *The Oxford Handbook of Austrian Economics*, edited by Peter J. Boettke, and Christopher J. Coyne, 445–463. New York: Oxford University Press.

Wagner, Richard E. 2016. *Politics as a Peculiar Business: Insights from a Theory of Entangled Political Economy*. Cheltenham: Edward Elgar.

Wagner, Richard E. 2017. *James M. Buchanan and Liberal Political Economy: A Rational Reconstruction*. Lanham: Lexington Books.

Wagner, Richard E. [1998] 2019. *To Promote the General Welfare: Market Processes vs. Political Transfers*. Arlington: Mercatus Center of George Mason University.

Walker, Edward T. 2010. "Industry-Driven Activism." *Contexts* 9, no. 2: 44–49.

Walker, Edward T. 2014. *Grassroots for Hire: Public Affairs Consultants in American Democracy*. New York: Cambridge University Press.

Wallmeier, Philip. 2017. "Exit as Critique: Communes and Intentional Communities in the 1960s and Today." *Historical Social Research* 42, no. 3: 147–171.

Walsh-Russo, Cecelia. 2014. "Diffusion of Protest." *Sociology Compass* 8, no. 1: 31–42.

Walton, John, and David Seddon. 1994. *Free Markets and Food Riots: The Politics of Global Adjustment*. Cambridge: Blackwell Publishers.

Wandel, Jürgen, and Vladislav Valentinov. 2014. "The Nonprofit Catallaxy: An Austrian Economics Perspective on the Nonprofit Sector." *Voluntas: International Journal of Voluntary and Nonprofit Organizations* 25, no. 1: 138–149.

Warburg, Jennifer. 2017. "The Rise of the YIMBY Movement." *The Urbanist*, January 11. https://www.spur.org/publications/urbanist-article/2017-01-11/rise-yimby-movement.

Ward, Colin. 1973. *Anarchy in Action*. London: George Allen & Unwin.

Wasow, Omar. 2020. "Agenda Seeding: How 1960s Black Protests Moved Elites, Public Opinion and Voting." *American Political Science Review* 114, no. 3: 638–659.

Weber, Max [1919] 1946. "Politics as a Vocation." In *From Max Weber: Essays in Sociology*, edited by H. H. Gerth, and C. Wright Mills, 77–128. New York: Oxford University Press.

Weber, Max. [1947] 1964. *The Theory of Social and Economic Organization*, translated by A. M. Henderson, and Talcott Parsons. New York: Free Press.

Weber, Max. [1922] 1978. *Economy and Society: An Outline of Interpretive Sociology*, edited by Guenther Roth, and Claus Wittich. Berkeley: University of California Press.

Welzel, Christian. 2013. *Freedom Rising: Human Empowerment and the Quest for Emancipation*. Cambridge, UK: Cambridge University Press.

Wells, Charlie, and Misyrlena Egkolfopoulou. 2021. "GameStop's Reddit Revolution Echoes Occupy Wall Street Crusade." *Bloomberg*, 29 January. https://www.bloomberg.com/news/articles/2021-01-28/why-are-reddit-wall-street-bets-traders-buying-gamestop-and-fighting-hedge-funds.

Whittier, Nancy. 2002. "Meaning and Structure in Social Movements." In *Social Movements: Identity, Culture, and the State*, edited by David S. Meyer, Nancy Whittier, and Belinda Robnett, 289–307. New York: Oxford University Press.

Whittier, Nancy. 2004. "The Consequences of Social Movements for Each Other." In *The Blackwell Companion to Social Movements*, edited by David A. Snow, Sarah A. Soule, and Hanspeter Kriesi, 531–551. Malden: Blackwell Publishing.

Williams, Dana M. 2017. *Black Flags and Social Movements: A Sociological Analysis of Movement Anarchism*. Manchester: Manchester University Press.

Williams, Dana M. 2019. "Tactics: Conceptions of Social Change, Revolution, and Anarchist Organization." In *The Palgrave Handbook of Anarchism*, edited by Carl Levy, and Matthew S. Adams, 107–124. Cham, Switzerland: Palgrave Macmillan.

Williams, Rhys H. 1995. "Constructing the Public Good: Social Movements and Cultural Resources." *Social Problems* 42, no. 1: 124–144.

Willner, Ann Ruth. 1984. *The Spellbinders: Charismatic Political Leadership*. New Haven: Yale University Press.

Wilson, Bart J. 2020. *The Property Species: Mine, Yours, and the Human Mind.* New York: Oxford University Press.

Wittman, Donald. 1995. *The Myth of Democratic Failure: Why Political Institutions Are Efficient.* Chicago: University of Chicago Press.

Wohlgemuth, Michael. 1999. "Entry Barriers in Politics, or: Why Politics, Like Natural Monopoly, Is Not Organised as an Ongoing Market Process." *Review of Austrian Economics* 12, no. 2: 175–200.

Wohlgemuth, Michael. 2002. "Democracy and Opinion Falsification: Towards a New Austrian Political Economy." *Constitutional Political Economy* 13, no. 3: 223–246.

Wolf, Brianne. 2018. "The Silent Role of Emotions in Hayekian Political Economy." In *Exploring the Political Economy and Social Philosophy of F.A. Hayek*, edited by Peter J. Boettke, Jayme S. Lemke, and Virgil Henry Storr, 55–78. Lanham: Roman & Littlefield.

Wollstonecraft, Mary. [1790] 1996. *A Vindication of the Rights of Men.* Amherst: Prometheus Books.

Woodward, Ernest Llewellyn. 1962. *The Age of Reform: 1815-1870.* Oxford: Clarendon Press.

Yoder, Steven. 2017. "Where Did the Tea Party Go?" *Vice*, March 3. https://www.vice.com/en_us/article/vvjm5a/where-did-the-tea-party-go.

Zald, Mayer N. 1996. "Culture, Ideology, and Strategic Framing." In *Comparative Perspectives on Social Movements: Political Opportunities, Mobilizing Structures, and Cultural Framings*, edited by Doug McAdam, John D. McCarthy, and Mayer N. Zald, 261–274. Cambridge, UK: Cambridge University Press.

Zald, Mayer N., and Bert Useem. 1987. "Movement and Countermovement Interaction: Mobilization, Tactics, and State Involvement." In *Social Movements in an Organizational Society: Collected Essays*, edited by Mayer N. Zald, and John D. McCarthy, 247–272. New Brunswick: Transaction Books.

Zelko, Frank. 2017. "Scaling Greenpeace: From Local Activism to Global Governance." *Historical Social Research* 42, no. 2: 318–342.

Zuboff, Shoshana. 2019. *The Age of Surveillance Capitalism: The Fight for a Human Future at the New Frontier of Power.* New York: Public Affairs.

Zwolinski, Matt. 2007. "Sweatshops, Choice, and Exploitation." *Business Ethics Quarterly* 17, no. 4: 689–727.

Zwolinski, Matt. 2020. "A Hayekian Case for Free Markets and a Basic Income." In *The Future of Work, Technology, and Basic Income*, edited by Michael Cholbi, and Michael Weber, 7–26. New York: Routledge.

Index

Note: Page locators in italic refer to tables.

About the Author

Mikayla Novak is a researcher and educator in the School of Sociology, The Australian National University. Her current research interests include classical sociology, economic and fiscal sociology, inequality and social stratification, network theory and analysis, rational choice sociology, social movement studies, and social philosophy and theory.

With an academic and professional background in economics, her publications have appeared in outlets such as *Research Policy, Constitutional Political Economy, Review of Austrian Economics, Journal of Contextual Economics, Journal of Entrepreneurship and Public Policy*, and *Cosmos + Taxis*. Mikayla Novak is the author of *Inequality: An Entangled Political Economy Perspective* (Palgrave Macmillan).

Mikayla Novak is an Associate Director of the Entangled Political Economy Research Network, and is a member of the NOUS Network. She is also a consulting editor for the *Cosmos + Taxis* journal. With an involvement in classical liberal policy advocacy for over two decades, Mikayla has contributed to outlets such as the Cato Institute's libertarianism.org, and the Foundation of Economic Education. Her outreach extends to the production of newspaper opinion articles and blog posts about contemporary economic, political, and social issues within a liberal framework.

Lightning Source UK Ltd.
Milton Keynes UK
UKHW010311100123
415095UK00004B/25